बाबार चिठि

REALIZE THY SELF

YOGODA SAT-SANGA

FORTNIGHTLY INSTRUCTIONS

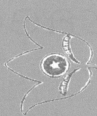

Your Praecepta
Step I

PUBLISHED BY

Yogoda Sat-Sanga

(Self-Realization Fellowship & Shyamacharan Mission)

Founder: PARAMHANSA YOGANANDA

Yogoda Math, Dakshineswar, P.O. Ariadah,

DIST. 24, PARGANAS, WEST-BENGAL INDIA.

YOGODA SAT-SANGA PRESS

Your Praecepta

Step I

TABLE OF CONTENTS

Praecepta Headers

Your Praecepta — Step I

YOGODA SAT-SANGA
FORTNIGHTLY INSTRUCTIONS

PARAMHANSA YOGANANDA

(To be Confidentially Reserved for MEMBER'S USE ONLY)

THE LORD'S PRAYER

An Interpretation

by

Paramhansa Yogananda

"0 Heavenly Father, may the Halo of Thy Presence spread over all minds, all lands. May matter-worship be changed into Thy worship. Since we cannot love anything without Thee, may we learn to love Thee first and most, above all things else. May Thy Heavenly Kingdom of Bliss, which is in Thy Spirit, be manifest in all its Divine qualities on earth, and make this earth free from limitations, imperfections, and miseries.

Father, leave us not in the pit of temptations, wherein we fell through our own misuse of Thy given reason, and when we are free and stronger, if it is Thy wish to test us to see if we love Thee more than temptation, then Father, make Thyself more tempting than temptation itself. Father, if it is Thy will to test us, develop our powers to stand and conquer Thy tests.

Give us our daily bread: food, health, and prosperity for the body, efficiency for the mind, and above all, wisdom and Thy love for our Souls. Teach us to deliver ourselves, with Thy help, from the meshes of ignorance, woven by our own carelessness.

Let Thy Kingdom which is within manifest itself without."

PAX VOBISCUM

ESTEEMED MEMBER:

You have no[w] become a Portal Novitiate Member of the Yogoda Sat-Sanga (Self-Realization Fellowship). Remember, we do not want to burden your mind with untested, impracticable, unfruitful theological beliefs and assertions. Our humble desire is to build and expand the Temple of your Consciousness until it can envelop and glorify all Truths on the Altar of your own, ever present Self- Realization.

Yogoda Sat-Sanga (Self-Realization Fellowship) has formed an association of the Master Minds of India and of the West, in order to offer a solution of the present intricate and perplexing religious and social problems.

Every day science is inventing or discovering some new method of mechanism for increasing the material comforts of man, as evidenced by the scientific magazines. If scientists had journeyed to a temple, locked the doors, and prayed to God for the inventions of radio, flying machines, television, and so forth, they would not have found them.

Scientists only discover the hidden Truths by using concentration, systematic objectivity and experimentation within the laws of Nature, emanating from God. So must religious followers do in order to get anywhere.

Most religious denominations are founded on speculation and are often based upon individual opinions of Truth. That probably explains the apparent stagnation in Religion. Furthermore, if scientists cannot find material Truths by merely praying, how can anyone find Spiritual Truths by mere blind prayers.

The Yogoda Sat-Sanga is formed with the distinct purpose of presenting to you those practical Truths which have already been scientifically tested as universally beneficial in thousands of lives. We have taken only the best and most usable Truths of all Religions, omitting the unproved, dogmatic theologies. Our instructions foster goodwill and fellowship among all true Religions, and invite them to cooperate in God's Name to find those Spiritual Truths which develop man in the Super-Way, no matter whether he is a Christian, Hindu, Jew, or Mohammedan.

Through fellowship and deep experimentation of the moral and esoteric Truths of all Scriptures, especially of the highly developed, usable techniques of the Masters of India, we shall show you the Super-Way of ever-blessed living.

As American and some other Western countries have specialized in material efficiency, so India has specialized in Spiritual efficiency. Therefore, the Yogoda Sat-Sanga Headquarters is a veritable psychophysical and Spiritual Laboratory.

When the Supreme Teacher and his intimate disciples apply and experience these Truths in their own lives, and teach them to others through the world, that Essence of Truth which they think will be beneficial in the highest degree to you, will be sent to you in the Fortnightly Praecepta. We do not teach any hypnotism or mysticism, but concentrate upon Universally-tested Eastern Truths.

To actually realize these truths in your own consciousness, you must devote yourself to regular continued effort. Most people consume their time in nonproductive reading, and lack real creative ability. That is why they suffer from limitations. For your most important benefit you must give time to the finding and analyzing of Truth.

If you want to be different and reap the richest harvest of complete Truth in this short span of Life, you must faithfully make the practical Instructions a part of your Life. Do not put off studying Truths until tomorrow. That "tomorrow" will be ever-receding, while your bad habits will swallow your precious, opportune days of Immortal Achievement. By adapting these Truths to your life, you will more clearly understand the Religion you have embraced. In brief, kindly bear in mind that procrastination and subsequent postponement of effort will only lead to stagnation and retardation in the Climb up the Seven Steps to Self-Realization.

The Fortnightly Praecepta of elaborate, progressive studies consist of many vital parts, including the Scientific Theory to a Technique, the concise Technique itself, invigorating health recipes, a highly enlightening Apologue for you and your family, a vibrant affirmation, and an inspirational poem. Each Fortnightly Praeceptum is complete with a thread of advancing Spiritual continuity running through all Instructions.

Any time, during the day or night, but regularly, you should conscientiously devote a half hour to the study of these essentials for Self-Realization. Analyze these Truths and rearrange the routine of your life accordingly, for therein lies the key to the Infinite.

We graciously welcome your correspondence, if we can be of further assistance in enlightening your understanding and in clarifying and detailing any particular point or problem in the practice of the Instructions.

PRAECEPTUM PRAYER

O Spirit, Sri Krishna, Sri Christ, Saints of All Religions, Supreme Master Babaji , Great Master Lahiri Mahasaya, Master Swami Sriyukteswarji, Guru-Preceptor Paramhansaji, I bow to you all. Free my life from all obstacles and give me material, mental, and Spiritual development.

TUNNEL TO ETERNITY
TELESCOPIC Tunnel Out of the Shell of the Sky,
through which Your Consciousness Must Travel to
Reach Eternity.

CONFINED CONSCIOUSNESS If you were born and grew up within the confines of a large, well ventilated room, but with all the doors and windows sealed so that you would never see the sky, that room would appear to be your only world, and it would be the

biggest space you could comprehend. But if someone told you, after twenty years of your confined residence in that room, that there was a vast space beyond the walls of the room, you would not believe it and would laugh at him. However, if suddenly a little window in your room were opened and you saw the vastness of the sky and the ocean, you would certainly be extremely surprised.

EVEN THE CHICK   The chick lives in the yolk beneath the eggshell, **EXPANDS HIS WORLD**   considering the space within the shell as all the space there is. But when it breaks through the shell, it comes to a large world, appearing before it tier upon tier. In the same way, you are a human chick living on the yolk of the world and surrounded by the star studded blue shell of the sky. You think that this world with its confining sky is the biggest place there is. But suppose you could pierce the shell of the sky with your consciousness and peep into the territory of your own Heavenly Father, then you would be able to see myriads of solar and stellar systems with their worlds floating like dust particles in the eternal void of space.

BE A HUMAN CHICK   The idea is, that as often as you fasten your eyes on your little body, you cannot help thinking that you are confined in a few feet of form, and that you weigh a few pounds of flesh. This idea is what binds you to the body, its tribulations, and limitations, limitations of poverty, sickness, and ignorance. Spirit is the endless chamber of wall-less space, which is decorated with the flickering stars and myriad lamps of planetary lights. If you are made in the image of God, you must forget your limitations and make yourself one with the bigness of God, and thus end all your sorrow and suffering.

FORGET   The little cage enclosing your omnipresent **LIMITATIONS**   consciousness is your body. When you love your family, neighbors, and the world your consciousness flies beyond the edge of your own limiting body, and when you watch the sky and feel yourself spread all over that vast space, your consciousness grows bigger still.

SEEK NOT THE BEGGAR'S PITTANCE The more you worry about the little things which your body needs, the smaller and more limited you become, until eventually you will die of unfulfilled hopes. It is the Law that a beggar gets only the beggar's pittance which he asks for and which is given through chance bounty, but a Divine Son gets his birthright, which consists of acquiring the entire omnipresent Kingdom of God with all created things in it.

EXPANSION OF CONSCIOUSNESS AS SEEN IN THE BIBLE Jesus said: "My Kingdom is not of this world." He was the most prosperous of all the rich men of the world and because he could perform other miracles which no one else could perform. He had material riches, and yet, He had God also, and having Him, He had everything. He said : "The foxes have holes, and the birds of the air have nests, but the Son of Man hath nowhere to lay his head." Jesus did not lament, because he had no place to live but he was speaking of his Omnipresent Soul, which could not be caged in a nest or a house. He lived everywhere on the tract of eternity as well as in every little speck of space. Living everywhere, He could not confine His head of eternal wisdom and consciousness into a small space. We find somewhat similar statements in the Bhagavad Gita.

YOUR DIVINE BIRTHRIGHT You must change your status from a mortal beggar to a Divine Son, and instead of supplicating, you must demand what belongs to you by right, as the Divine Child who is born in the image of God. You must seek the lost Kingdom of God first, and then all the material and Spiritual things which you need and want will be added unto you as your Divine birthright. As a mortal being and beggar, you have been seeking bread and money first, and therefore, you have had great difficulty in securing even these. God and all created things do not come to you with the attainment of material gain, but they come only by seeking and knowing God first.

Bread, and all other things, automatically become your slaves when you have found God. This is the truest and surest way by which you can fulfill your desires. Hence, the following Technique will strike at the roots of your mortal limitations and will make your consciousness the King of the Eternal Kingdom of God, who is your own Father.

POSITION Sit upright, on a woolen blanket, which has been placed on the floor, or over a straight, armless chair. The blanket must run down under your feet, if you sit on a chair, to insulate your body from distracting currents. Place your hands with palms upward at the junction between your thighs and abdomen.

INNER PICTURIZATION Close your eyes and peer down millions of miles below you. Mentally fly upwards millions of miles. Mentally fly behind you and in front of you trillions of miles. Mentally see yourself as the chamber of Eternity, in which all things, including stellar and solar systems, the world and your body, are floating. Fill this chamber of Eternity with Bliss. Remember that you are this ever-happy, ever-living chamber of Eternity.

COSMIC   Picture to yourself and become aware of the inside
PHYSIOLOGY of the flesh walls of your small body. See that in the top of it is the brain, on the back are the vertebrae, and inside the torso are the lungs, heart, liver, pancreas, intestines, and so forth. Now feel the vast chamber of space to be your Cosmic body, and feel that within that Cosmic body are closely situated the convolutions of your brain in the Milky Way.

See the sun and moon as your eyes, and perceive the love of all creatures of all worlds as your heart. See all life as your circulation, with the nebulae as your intestines. See star rivers as your Cosmic body cells, the sky as your skin and the mountains as your bones.

COSMIC   Meditate on the idea that your mind is the accumulated minds of
EXPANSION   all human beings, that your heart is the added hearts of all, your life is the added lives of all creatures, your love is the added loves of all living things.

SPECIAL TECHNIQUE OF MEDITATION
"TUNNEL TO ETERNITY"

PATH TO   With your eyes closed think of yourself as a Soul
ETERNAL LIGHT   chick sitting on the yolk of the earth trying to burst through the shell of the sky into the Kingdom of your Infinite Father.

Visualize in front of you a portion of the white shell of the sky. Then behold in it a big golden tunnel with a fifty foot mouth. Mentally enter this tunnel feeling the presence of Cosmic Vitality. After mentally traveling about one hundred miles in an instant through the golden tunnel, you will see at the end of it an opening twenty five feet wide into a blue tunnel. Then mentally travel a thousand miles instantaneously through this blue tunnel, feeling yourself surrounded by Cosmic Intelligence. At the end of the blue tunnel see a five pointed silver star, which is a five foot gate to Infinitude. Your feeling passes through this silver gate, saturated with Cosmic Ever-new Bliss. You travel instantaneously along a million miles of silver path. (Your mind can travel from America to Jupiter in a second, faster than electricity or light).

As you come out of the gold and blue tunnels, past the silver gate, feeling Power, Intelligence, and Ever-new Joy, you leave the shell of the sky and enter the vastness of Eternal Light.

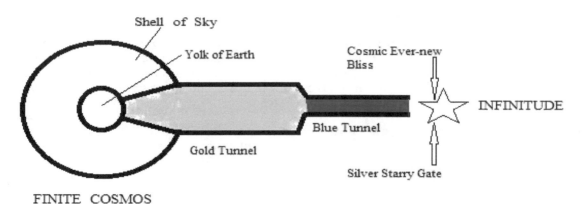

FINITE COSMOS

1.   Finite Creation of Cosmos is ruled by the Immanent Cosmic Consciousness.
2.   Infinitude, Radiating Eternal Light, is Pervaded by Transcendental God.

BE ONE WITH THE ETERNAL LIGHT Behold in front of you the vastness of living, joyous ever-expanding silver light. Merge yourself, body, mind, and Soul, into the light and melt them into the consistency of this solid vastness of ever happy, intelligent silver light. Go on expanding above, beneath, in front, and behind, on all sides equally with it limitlessly until you feel that you and that light are one.

THE TWO CHAMBERS Behold in this visualization of Eternity two chambers, one space less eternal void of the Transcendental God the Father, as ever-existing, ever-conscious, ever-new Bliss, and see the other chamber of the Cosmos, which contains all created things, with the solar and stellar systems, star rivers, United States of the Cosmos, your little earth, your little homestead, and your little body peacefully residing in it.

SON OF SPIRIT Your name, henceforth, will be "Son of Spirit." Your country is Infinity. You live in the United States of all planets, and your home is in the love of all races and of all living creatures. Your color is purity. Your possessions, 0 thou Son of the Cosmic King, include the entire Cosmos.

THE APOLOGUE
"SAINT WHO CHOSE A KING FOR HIS SPIRITUAL MASTER"

Long ago there lived a great Sage named Vyasa. He was the writer of the greatest Hindu Scripture, the Bhagavad Gita. By his power he invoked a saintly Soul to occupy the little body of the baby his wife carried, and taught the unborn child the secrets of the Scriptures through the subconscious mind of the mother. This baby, when born, was named Suka Deva, and, through the training he received while still in his mother's body, he proved to be a most unusual child. At the age of seven he was already versed in all the difficult Hindu Scriptures and was ready to renunciate (sic) the world in search of a true Master.

In India it is customary to seek teachers until one finds the real God-chosen Master. The novitiate, through fitful urgings receives lessons from various sources, but when his Spiritual ardor becomes very great, God sends him a Master (Guru). This Divine-Soul-Vehicle God uses through one life, or through several incarnations, as His messenger to bring the novitiate back to His Spiritual mansion.

When Suka Deva decided to go in search of his Spiritual teacher or Guru, his father, Sage Vyasa, advised him to go to King Janaka, the ruler of that province. As Suka Deva entered the palace grounds his eyes caught sight of the King sitting on an emerald and diamond studded, golden throne, surrounded by flatterers and scantily clad ladies fanning him with big palm leaves, as was the custom in India during the hot season.

King Janaka was smoking a big oriental pipe. This sight was enough for Suka Deva, and, shocked, he returned back and started walking briskly out of the palace gates inwardly ridiculing and muttering: "Shame on my father for sending me to that matter soaked king. How could that object be my teacher."

But King Janaka was both a King and a Saint. He was in the

world but not of the world. He was highly advanced spiritually, and could telepathically sense the thoughts of the fleeing Suka Deva, son of Vyasa. So, the Saint-King sent a messenger after Suka Deva, commanding him to come back.

Thus, the Saint-King Janaka and Suka Deva, son of Sage Vyasa met. The King sent all his courtiers away and entered into an absorbing discourse on the all-protecting God, with Suka Deva. Four hours passed and Suka Deva was getting restless and hungry, but nobody dared to disturb the God-intoxicated King.

Another hour passed when two messengers came running to the King and exclaimed: "Your Highness, your kingdom is on fire and the flames threaten to spread toward your palace. Won't you come and supervise the efforts to extinguish the flames? "To that the King replied: "I am too busy discussing the all-protecting God with my friend Suka Deva. I have no time. Go and put out the flames yourselves."

Another hour passed and the same two messengers came running to the King and cried: "Your Royal Excellency, please flee for the flames have caught the palace and are fast approaching your chamber." To this the King indifferently said: "Never mind. Don't disturb me, for I am drinking God with my friend. Go, do the best you can."

Suka Deva was rather puzzled at the King's action. Still another hour passed and the scorched messengers leaped in front of the King and shouted: "Mighty King, behold the flames approaching your throne. Run, before you both are burnt to death." To that the King replied: "You both run, and save yourselves. I am too busy resting in the arms of the all-protecting God to fear the audacity of the destructive flames."

The messengers fled and the flames leaped toward the pile of books which Suka Deva had by his side, but the King sat motionless, indifferent, talking about God.

At last Suka Deva lost his poise and slapped at the flames and tried to prevent them from burning his precious books. The King, satisfied, smilingly waved his hands at the flames and they disappeared at his miraculous touch. Then, as Suka Deva, in great awe, regained his composure and settled down on his seat, the King finally and wisely spoke:

"0, Young Saint Suka Deva, you thought of me as a matter-drenched King, but look at yourself. You forsook the all-protecting thought of God to protect a pile of books, while I paid no attention to my burning kingdom and palace. God worked this miracle to show you that you, though a man of renunciation, are more attached to your books than to God, or than I am to my Kingdom, even though I live in the world instead of in a monastery or hermitage."

Thus humbled, the young Saint Suka Deva then took this Saint-King Janaka as his Guru Preceptor, or Spiritual Teacher.

The King began to put Suka Deva through a process of discipline, and taught him the art of living in the world without misery-making-attachment to it. All of us should remember this lesson in order to live happily in the material world without allowing it to make us miserable through ignorance.

The King Janaka gave his new disciple two cup shaped oil lamps, filled to the brim, and commanded: "Hold a lamp on the palm of each hand, and go about visiting all the gorgeously furnished rooms of my palace. Then come back to me after you have seen everything, but remember, I will send you back home and refuse to train you if you dare to spill a drop of oil on my carpets."

The King instructed two messengers to accompany Suka Deva and keep the two lamps full of oil as they burned down. This was a hard test. However, after two hours Suka Deva returned triumphantly without dropping any oil from the oil cups he held.

Then the king said: "Young Suka Deva, tell me in detail what you saw in each chamber of my palace". To this Suka Deva replied; "Royal Preceptor, all I accomplished was, that I did not spill any oil on your carpets. My mind was so concentrated upon the thought of not drooping oil that I could not possibly see anything that was in the rooms.

The King cried out; "I am disappointed, you have not completely passed my test. My injunction was that you should see everything that was in all the chambers of my palace and, at the same time, you should not drop any oil from the oil lamps. Go back with the lamps, and remember, no spilling of the oil while you look carefully at everything about the palace."

Suka Deva calmly returned at the end of ten hours, and behold, he had not dropped any oil, nor was he sweating with excitement as before, and he could now answer all the King's questions about the most minute contents of all the palace chambers.

Then, the King gently whispered: "My son, attachment to possessions and not possession, is the source of misery in this world we do not own anything; we are only given the use of things. Some have more to use than others, but remember, the millionaire and the poor man alike have to leave everything, all possessions, when death comes. People must not live one sided lives, thinking only of God, like your concentrating on the oil lamp and not seeing my palace, but, as on the second trip, you kept your attention principally on the oil lamps without spilling oil, and, at the same time, thoroughly and minutely saw everything in the palace, so must you keep your major attention on God without letting a drop of your desire slip away from the lamp of God-revealing wisdom. And then, also, you must keep part of your attention on thoroughly performing the God given duties of maintaining yourself and others given in your charge."

This instructive story distinctly shows you what could be the basis of our modern depression, which is caused by indifference to Spiritual matters, leading to industrial selfishness and unequal prosperity amidst plenty. Hence, if you want the unlimited, unfailing Divine Power to work for you in your business and family affairs, then be as earnest about meditation as you are about earning money. If you make it a business to actually contact God first, then you in find imperishable happiness as well as the material comforts you need. So, remember, you must not be too busy to try to contact God. If God stops your heart beating, you will not have any chance for business success. Since all your success depends upon the powers borrowed from God, you must give enough time for God contact. Our purpose is not to make a theological Victrola out of you, parroting beautiful phrases. We want you to actually get hold of the Cosmic power, which you can use in everything, by making you work for it by the quickest method. Remember, one hour's deep meditation will give you more power and peace than one month's reading of holy books six hours a day. Try it.

HEALTH CULTURE
TO BEAUTIFY THE FACE: Primarily, and above all else, keep a genuine

smile in which your heart smilingly glows through your eyes, constantly playing on your face. Some Masters of India advise their disciples to thoroughly mix two tablespoonful of the milk (water) of a fresh coconut with 2 tablespoonful of thick cream, and then massage a teaspoonful or more of this preparation all over the face until the mixture dries up. (Very effective for beautifying and glorifying the features of men and women; in place of cream the thick layer that sets on the boiled milk when it is cooled may be used.)

HEALTH HINTS 1. Eat one raw carrot every day.

2.   Fast one day a week on orange juice and fruits or 2 tablespoonful of ground nuts; fast on fruits only, cleansing your system with a suitable laxative.

3.   Avoid eating meat.

4.   A very satisfactory meat substitute may be found in Chhana (prepared from milk).

5.   Eat only 100% whole wheat blend.

6.   If you are susceptible to cold or catarrh, do not drink much milk.

7.   The usual menu should consist mostly of slightly cooked or raw vegetables and of fresh fruits.

8.   [10. (sic)] Eat spinach for vitality and strength.

A VITALIZING SPINACH SALAD   Thoroughly wash sixteen leaves or so of spinach and dry with a cloth. Chop them fine and mix with buttermilk (obtained by churning 'dahi') or curd (dahi) to suit the taste. This salad is not only delicious but is very vitalizing and body-building.

PRAYER VIBRATIONS
(From Headquarters)

Reinforce your demand to God by tuning in with devoted faith any time between the hours of six and eleven in the morning (your standard time), or, if prohibitive, any time during the day and night, with the prayers of Yogoda Sat-Sanga (Self-Realization Fellowship) Healers, under the inspirational leadership of Paramhansa Yogananda, whose vibrations are emanating in the ether to you. The Prayer Vibrations emanate day and night, so that whenever you tune in the radio of your mind by conscientious concentration, you will get our help. If you require any special healing, or immediate help, write to the Gurudev Paramhansa Yoganandaji to that effect.

FORTNIGHTLY AFFIRMATIONS

"Heavenly Father, I will reason, I will will, I will act, but guide thou my reason, will and activity, to the right thing which I should do ."

"Father, Thou art in me. I am well." "Father, manifest Thy ever-new Joy and Wisdom through me.
NEW PEACE! NEW BLISS! NEW BLISS!

YOGODA SAT-SANGA FORTNIGHTLY INSTRUCTION
BY
PARAMHANSA YOGANANDA.
(To be confidentially Reserved FOR MEMBER'S USE ONLY)
"Thy Self-Realization Will Blossom Forth From Thy Soulful Study"

INSPIRATIONAL RESOLUTION

Father Divine, this is my prayer: I care not what I may permanently possess, but give to me the power to acquire at will whatever I may daily need. 0 Father, Mother, Friend, Beloved God, I will reason, I will will, I will act; but lead Thou my reason, will, and activity to the right thing that I should do.

I am the Captain of the ship of my judgment, will, and activity. I will guide my ship of life, ever beholding the Pole Star of His Peace shining in the firmament of my deep meditation. I am the lark of Life flitting in the skies of Thy Cosmic Presence, thirstily looking for the raindrops of Thy manifestations. Filter through the cruel clouds of silence Thy showering Omnipresence. Make me Thy Lark, looking for no other water but the waters of Thy Solace, flowing through the heavens of Thy Being everywhere.

"I will my life to charge.
With godly will I will it
charge. Through my nerves and
muscles all, My tissues, limbs,
and all,
With vibrant tingling fire,
With burning joyous power.
In blood and glands,
By sov'ran command,
I bid you flow.
By my command
I bid you glow."

AWAKENING "Heavenly Father, Jesus Christ, Lord Krishna, Supreme Master
PRAYER Babaji, Great Master Lahiri Mahasaya, Master Swami Sriyukteswarji, Saints of all Religions, and Swami-Preceptor-Guru Paramhansaji, I bow to you all. I bow to the Spirit in the body Temple. I bow to Thee in front and behind, on the left, and on the right, above and beneath. I bow to Thee everywhere, for Thou art everywhere.

Every sound that I make, let it have the vibration of Thy Voice. Every thought that I think, let it be saturated with the consciousness of Thy Presence.

Let every feeling that I have glow with Thy Love. Let every will I will be impregnated with Thy Divine Vitality. Let every thought, every expression, every ambition, be ornamented by Thee."

"0 Divine Sculptor, chisel Thou my life according to Thy Design.

HISTORICAL The Self-Realization Fellowship Instruction is made up of two
BACKGROUND distinct parts, one part, the basic principle of which is the discovery by Paramhansa Yoga-

nanda, and the other part, the contribution of the ancient Sages of India, adapted by Swami Yogananda for the use of Western peoples.

Paramhansa Swami Yogananda received his title of "Swami" and "Paramhansa" from his Great Master, Swami Sree-Yukteswar Giriji Maharaja of Bengal, who gave up his mortal body while in *Samadhi* in his hermitage at Purl in Orissa, India. "Swami" meaning "Master," or one who aims to master himself, can only be bestowed on a qualified disciple by one who is himself a Swami, tracing his title through the line of successive Swamis back to the Seventh century, A.D., when the great sage and saint, Lord Shankaracharyya, reorganized the ancient Order of Swamis in India.

Paramhansa Yogananda belongs to the "Sat-Sanga Order" in India. "Sat-Sanga" means "Fellowship with Truth," and this Organization has as one of its principal aims the establishment of international good-will, understanding, and fellowship. Swami Yogananda brought the ideals of this Sat-Sanga Order to America, and calls his educational, non-sectarian message by the name of "Self-Realization Fellowship Movement."

The first school to teach the methods of Self-Realization was founded by Paramhansa (originally Swami) Yogananda in India, at Ranchi, Behar. Later, two more schools were started at Puri and Bankura. All are Residential Schools for boys. Since 1920 Swami Yogananda (now Paramhansa) has carried on extensive teaching and organizing in the United States of America.

When Paramhansa Yogananda first made the great discovery of how the individual supply of energy could be connected with the un-limited storehouse of Inner Cosmic Energy, he realized that the right application of this knowledge could overcome the physical handicap of ill health, which has ever been one of the chief obstacles to man's progress throughout the Ages.

But man is more than a body. To be in a state of perfect health does not constitute happiness, nor does it fulfill the purposes of man's destiny. Man's nature is three-fold. Paramhansa Yogananda, therefore, felt that any system which could rightly consider itself of universal and all- round use and application must include methods whereby man could perfect himself in all his varied manifestations -- physical, mental, and Spiritual.

To his own discovery of a method for physical well-being, Paramhansa Yogananda added a scientific technique of concentration and meditation for mental and Spiritual perfection -- a technique which has been used in India for several thousand years by Saints and Sages, and is now incorporated by Paramhansa Yogananda into his Self-Realization Fellowship Instruction in a simple, practice form especially adapted to the requirements and environment of the busy but aspiring Western peoples.

Jesus promised to send the Holy Ghost after He was gone. The Holy Ghost is Sacred Invisible Vibration which is the Word or Om or Cosmic Vibration, the Great Comforter, the Savior from all sorrows. To know how to contact this Cosmic Vibration or Holy Ghost will be taught later in a special technique for quickening your evolution known as "Kriya: (krae ya). This evolutionary technique was given by Supreme Master Babaji, who despite his present incarnation of several hundred years' duration (based on recorded fact), has retained his youth, and he gave this technique to his disciple, Lahiri Mahasaya, who in turn gave it to Swami Sree-Yukteswarji. He in turn gave it to Swami (Paramhansa) Yogananda to bring to the Western peoples, so that, through this supreme method they might be equipped to expand the Cup of their Self-Realization, in order to hold the Ocean of Omnipresent Christ, or Cosmic Consciousness. Hence, this work is the Second Coming of Christ.

DYNAMO OF VOLITION   **THE DYNAMIC POWER OF WILL**

The dynamo of all our powers consists in volition.
All our physical, mental, and Spiritual actions are

initiated and continuously operated by the power of volition. Without volition we cannot walk, talk, think, work, imagine, or feel. The person who refuses to exercise volition or will power will have to lie on a sofa in a state of suspended animation. First, even the slightest movement of the muscles or winking of the eyelids, or any act of thinking, are all initiated by the use of volition. Therefore, volition, or will power is the spring of all our actions.

A wish implies a helpless desire of the mind. A desire is a stronger wish; it is often followed by fitful efforts to manifest itself into action.

An intention, or a determination, is a definite, strong desire once or twice very forcefully expressed through action for the accomplishment of a certain purpose. A determination, however strong, is often discouraged after one, or a number, of unsuccessful efforts to accomplish something. But a volition consists in a series of continuous, never-discouraged, unceasing determinations and acts revolving around a desire, until it becomes dynamic enough to produce the much craved result. The phrase, "Will and act until Victory," is the slogan of all volitive activity. No matter how impossible to accomplish a thing, impossible in appearance, the man of volition never stops repeating conscious acts of determination as long as he is living.

WILL POWER GOVERNS Does not will power govern the physique? Coercion or compulsion **THE UNIVERSE** can never bring about growth. It is freedom bring about growth. It is freedom that accelerates evolution. Too much dependence upon what is external or objective throttles the possibility of progress and nips in the bud the potent factors of evolution. Evolution presupposes the existence of a power of growth from within, and of a subject that will grow by adjusting itself to its environment and adjusting the environment to itself. Without a technique like that offered by Self-Realization Fellowship, one's will power remains untrained and atrophied.

The exercise of will power by the study of Self-Realization Instructions opens up limitless possibilities for all-round success. No body movement or thinking is possible without willing. We must will to move or think, or imagine. Direction of physical activities and thought force by a developed conscious will power can accomplish many things which might be considered impossible by most people. Using the will does not mean physical or mental strain or strenuousness. Conscious will means a cool, calm, determined, increasingly steady and smooth flowing effort of the attention and the whole being toward Oneness with a definite goal.

PHYSICAL PERFECTION Self-Realization Instructions combine the basic laws, **THROUGH WILL POWER** utilized by the ancient Hindu Yogis, with the discoveries of modern physiological science. Some Western athletes have learned to control certain of their muscles by will, but have failed to see the scientific principles underlying such control. The Yogis of India have a large number of postures which they practice in order to strengthen and develop their will power. The will develops the body, and, at the same time, one is developing his will by exercising it as taught in Self-Realization Praecepta. The physical and mental development are intertwined and help each other. This technique is distinctly different from other systems of technique, inasmuch as they teach one how to concentrate his attention, not upon instruments, muscles, or body movements, but upon the awakened energy which is the direct giver of power, strength, and vitality to all the tissue in the body. Hence the faithful student will find that the technique invariably and consciously develops his will power along with his bodily strength.

EVOLUTION OF The evolution of this great force must be carefully studied. **WILL POWER** The baby's first cry at birth is the first announcement of the birth of will power. The baby cries because it wants to remove the feeling of discomfort, due to first painful opening and activity of the lungs. This is called "automatic physiological volition." Then, when the baby grows old enough to talk and unthinkingly follows the wishes of its mother, it is said to possess "unthinking will." The mother calls him a "good boy" because he obeys her in an unthinking way.

Then the baby grows older and begins to think for himself, and if the mother denies something which the baby thinks he should have, then he first manifests obstinacy by offering resistance to the mother's will. Suddenly the mother becomes angry and calls her boy "naughty." In the first act of obstinacy the baby finds the birth of his "blind will."

BLIND WILL This will is called "blind will" because it is not often guided by wisdom. Most youths have this blind explosive will which, like dynamite, they use to explode in the air without serving any purpose. This blind will makes the youth use up his energy and possibilities on passions, temptations, brawls, fast driving accidents, rash resolutions, ungoverned appetites, and so forth. The bee loves fragrance and sits in the lotus flower and finds its grave in the petals when it forgets to get out before they close upon him. The fish loves the taste of water and dies when taken out of it. The moose loves music and is lured to its death trap by the flute of the hunter. The male elephant loves the sense of touch and is lured by the tame she elephant to the trap, which is true of human beings too. The insect loves sight and beauty and perishes trying to enjoy the white beauty of the candle flame. So each of these animals dies because it is addicted to one single sense of smell, or taste, or sound, or touch, or sight, but man has an attachment to all these five senses and he must watch his step and save himself from his blind will, which urges him to jump into the yawning, burning crevasses of the five sense-lures.

THINKING WILL Then, after using up the blind will, or getting his own nicks, the youth learns what is meant by "thinking will." But this thinking will, if it is used up too much in wrong activities, becomes a semi paralyzed thinking will. But, if this thinking will retains its normal power and is made to revolve around a definite purpose, it becomes "dynamic volition." Every volition must be used only on a wholesome purpose; otherwise, it will weaken itself due to lack of encouragement from Truth. When one knows his volition is worthwhile, then he finds the nature of his purpose more worthwhile, and the tenacity of his volition becomes greater. The man of volition says: "I will use my dynamic volition until success or death comes while fighting for the Truth." He refuses to stop even if he dies; he believes in taking up his determination and activity in some other reincarnations to seek fulfillment if death cuts him off.

A WILL A WAY A strong will, by its own dynamic force, creates a way for its fulfillment. By its very strength, the will sets into motion certain vibrations in the atmosphere; and Nature, with its laws of order, system, and efficiency, thereupon creates circumstances favorable to the individual who exercises will power. Will derives its strength from an honest purpose, lofty motives, and noble solicitude to do good to the world at large. A strong will, therefore, is never stifled; and it always finds a way.

GOD'S WILL AND YOUR WILL Now comes the distinction between human dynamic will and super dynamic volition or Divine Will. One must remember that God did not make up his inert instruments, but instruments endowed with free choice. God's will is not guided by whim or temptation. His will is guided by wisdom. So, also, God made us in His image, made us His children, so that we, like His true children, might guide our will with wisdom, even as He does. To teach people not to use there will is ridiculous denial of the Divine Fathers wish, and is an utter impossibility.

Non-application of will would require the lying in a coffin in a suspended state of animation without using the will involved in moving the muscles or in thinking.

NOT TEMPTATION BY GOD All craving and desire in man should be transmuted and turned toward God, instead of allowing it to try to delude the God in man. Temptation is a delusive, compelling, conflicting, joy-expecting thought which should be used to pursue Happiness making Truth and not misery-producing error. Although God is the creator of consciousness, still the vitiated consciousness in man turns away from Him and tries to lure the Soul to concentrate upon the temporary joy of the senses.

CONTACT GOD FIRST Do not will and act first, but contact God first, and thus harness your will and activity to the right goal. As you cannot broadcast through a broken microphone, so must you remember that you cannot broadcast your prayer through the mental microphone which is disordered by restlessness. By deep calmness, repair your mind microphone. Then again, as you cannot get an answer by just calling someone through a microphone and then running away, so, also, you must not first pray once and run away, but you must continuously broadcast your prayer to God through your calm mental microphone UNTIL you hear His voice. Most people pray in restlessness and do not pray with the determination to receive a response.

IN TUNE OR OUT If one guides his will wrongly, it is productive of evil, but if one guides his will with wisdom, it is in tune with Divine Will, for it is guided also by wisdom. Wisdom-guided, self-initiated human will, and human will guided by God's Wisdom-guided Will, are one and the same thing.

LET THY WILL BE DONE Jesus found His will so much guided by Wisdom that He could say either: "I say unto thee, arise," or "Father, let Thy will be done." Many people misinterpret the real meaning of the saying of Jesus: "Let Thy will be done," and preach a dangerous doctrine of not using the will. Many others and physically lazy, and most people are mentally lazy. They are unwilling even to initiate creative thinking, or self-emancipating thinking, lest they succeed.

DIVINE WILL HAS NO BOUNDARIES The only savior of man is the constantly progressive dynamic will. Human will, however powerful, is still limited by the circumference of the body and the boundaries of the human physical universe. Man's will can initiate successful activities in the body or the earth, or in finding the mysteries of the distant stars. But the Divine Will has no boundaries; it works in all bodies, in all things: God said: "Let there be light," and there was light. God's will works in everything. By deep meditation and by wisdom guided, unflinching, never-discouraged determination, when we can revolve our volition around all our noble desires with success, then our will becomes Divine Will. Man's will can ordinarily work within the boundaries of his own little circle of family, environment, world conditions, destiny, and prenatal and postnatal cause and effect- governed actions; but Super-Dynamic Volition can change the course of destiny, wake the dead, put the mountain into the sea, and change the course of the solar or stellar systems.

REALIZE THAT YOU POSSESS SUPER-DYNAMIC DIVINE WILL Therefore, for absolute control of your life and for destroying the roots of failure due to prenatal and postnatal causes, you must exercise your will in every undertaking, until it leaves its mortal delusion of being human will and becomes all-powerful, Divine Will. You do not have to acquire this Super Dynamic Divine Will, but you only need to know that you already possess it in the image of God within you.

17

THE APOLOGUE
"The Big Frog and the Little Frog"

A big, fat frog and a little frog fell into a milk pail. They swam and swam for hours trying to get out. They swam and swam for hours trying to get out, but they could not, due to the slippery sides of the milk pail. The big frog, all exhausted, moaned: "Brother little frog, I am going to give up and lie down to die."

The little frog thought to himself: "To give up is to be dead, so I will keep on swimming." Two hours passed and the tiny legs of the little frog were all tire out and he thought he could do no more, but as he looked again at the dead frog, he shook his head and repeated: "To give up is to be dead meat, so I will keep on paddling until I die, if death is to come, but I will not give up trying, for while there is life there is still hope."

So, intoxicated with determination, the little frog kept on paddling with his little feet. After a while, when he felt that he was completely paralyzed and all was over, and that he was going to drown, he suddenly felt a big lump under him. To his great joy, he saw that it was a lump of butter when he had churned by his incessant paddling. And the little froggie, beside himself with joy, leapt out of the milk pail to freedom.

So, remember, we are all in the slippery milk pail of life, trying to get out of our troubles and in-harmonies like the two frogs. Most people give up and fail like the big frog, but in order to succeed we must learn to persevere in our effort toward one good, as the little frog did. We shall churn an opportunity by our God-guided unflinching will power, and will be able to hope out of the milk pail of failure onto the shore of eternal success. Not to give up is to develop will power, and to win in everything we undertake.

HEALTH CULTURE

HEALING COLDS BY PROPER DIET   When you catch cold, fast for two days. Remember that during a cold the extra poisons of our body are being thrown off. If you add more food to your system, you help to obstruct the poison eliminating system of Nature by clogging up the circulation with extra food chemicals.

If you cannot bear up under a complete fast, eat apples or pears or grapes, but refrain from eating acid fruits. Do not eat anything at night. Do not drink hot or cold water. Drink only two glasses of tepid warm water daily. I do not believe that to drink too much water during a cold is good, for the extra water taken comes out constantly through the mucous membrane, making the nose run too much and causing irritation and accumulation of pus there. Fasting during a cold is very good, for it helps Nature to effect (sic) her own cure without interruption from any source. It is very good to use some laxative suitable to your system at the beginning of a cold.

A good four hour sunbath with the rays of the sun falling directly on the epidermis of the body has been known to cure a cold in one day. Sensitive skinned people should protect their skins by smearing olive oil, or something similar, over their bodies before taking a sunbath. The best hours for sunbaths are between 11 a.m., and 3 p.m.

HEALTH HINT Food should not be eaten according to hereditary, national, and individual habits. There are individual or hereditary habits of eating foods which are bad from the point of view of general dietary laws of food combination or food chemistry. Such specific bad habits of eating food should be gradually overcome. Bad habits of eating make the human system demand wrong foods. In such cases, the right food, although disagreeable to the system, should be taken in very small quantities first, and then gradually increased until the system responds to normal food. One should learn to eat Nature's foods, such as fruits and green vegetables, and drink at least a glassful of good milk each day.

FORTNIGHTLY INSPIRATION

Making others happy, through kindness of speech and sincerity of right advice, is a sign of true greatness. To hurt another Soul by sarcastic words, looks, or suggestions, is despicable. Sarcasm draws out the rebellious spirit and anger in the wrongdoer. Loving suggestions bring out repentance in him. Repentance consists in thoroughly understand one's own error and in abandoning it.

Repent of your indifference to Him without whom you cannot live or speak, or have entertainment or bridge parties. Try to cultivate His acquaintance, being introduced to Him by the right Preceptor. All earthly friends, who seems so real, will be unreal someday, will pass away, and the One who seems intangible will prove to be your only true lasting friend. It is worthwhile to know God, for all your life's labor will then not be spent in vain, as is the case with those who labor day and night for everything except God.

Talk to Him with a crying silent Soul in the depths of the night, steadfastly, deeply, determinedly. Be like the naughty babies who are not allowed in the apartment houses, who cry persistently. Cry for God and do not stop until He comes to you.

FORTNIGHTLY AFFIRMATION

"I shall tune my free will with the Infinite Will of God and my only desire shall be to do the Wisdom-guided Will of Him who sent me."

WILL!

POWER!

SUCCESS!

YOGODA SAT-SANGA FORTNIGHTLY INSTRUCTIONS
BY
PARAMHANSA YOGANANDA
(To be Confidentially Reserved for MEMBER'S USE ONLY)
"Thy Self-Realization Will Blossom Forth From Thy Soulful Study"

COME INTO THE GARDEN OF MY DREAMS

"In the garden of my dreams grew many dream blossoms. The rarest flowers of my fancy all bloomed there. Unopened buds of earthly hopes audaciously spread their petals of fulfillment, warmed by the light of my dreams. In the dim glow, I spied the specters of beloved, forgotten faces, spites of dear, dead feelings, long buried beneath the soil of mind, which all rose in their shining robes. I beheld the resurrection of all experiences, at the trumpet call of my dream angels.

As we rest, and wake a little, to slumber again so from beneath the cover of fleeting dreams of birth and death, we rise for a while and fall asleep again, and ream another earthly dream of struggle.

On the sledge of incarnations we slide from dream to dream. Dreaming, on a chariot of astral fire we roll from life to life. Dreaming, we pass through dreams, failures, victories. Dreaming, we sail over trying seas, eddies of laughter, whirlpools of indifference, water of mighty events, deaths, births dreams.

In the chamber of Thy Heart I shall behold the making of the noblest dreams of life. 0 Master Weaver of Dreams, teach me to make a many-hued carpet of dreams, for all lovers of Thy pattern of dreams to walk over, as they travel to the Temple of Eternal Dreams. And I will join the worshipping angels of living visions that I may offer on Thy altar a bouquet of my newborn dreams of Thee."

PRAYER TO PRECEDE THE PRAECEPTUM STUDY

DEMAND FOR PROSPERITY "As Thou art my Father, I am Thy Child. Thou art the Spirit; I am made in Thy Image! Thou art the Father who owns the Universe.

Good or naughty I am Thy Child, and, as such, have the right of possession over all things; but I have been truant and wandered away from Thy Home of Cosmic Plenty. Help me to learn, first, to identify my consciousness with Thy Universal Consciousness. Rescue my consciousness, shipwrecked on the tiny island of the body. Expand me, and make me feel that I am again Thy Image. And when, by Thy Grace, I shall find that, like Thee, I am everywhere, then I shall have dominion over all things, as hast Thou."

THE TRUE SOURCE OF PROSPERITY

RIGHT DESIRES Do not wander aimlessly, lost in the jungle of life, constantly bleeding your happiness with the thorns of new desires. You must find the goal of your life and the shortest road which leads you there. Do not travel unknown roads, picking up new troubles. I am not telling you to be desireless, speechless, ambitionless, and useless in the world. All I am telling you is to culture the right desires and drop the useless ones.

ALL-ROUND WELFARE Too much wrong ambition is just as bad as too much passive contentment. As human beings, we have been endowed with needs and we must meet their demands. As man is a physical, mental, Spiritual being, he must look after his all-round welfare, avoiding one-sided, over-development. To possess wonderful health and a good appetite, with no money to maintain that health and to satisfy that hunger is agonizing. To have lots of money and lots of indigestion is heart- rending. To have lots of health, and lots of wealth, and lots of trouble with self and others, is pitiable. To have lots of health, wealth, and mental efficiency, but no knowledge of the ultimate Truth, and with a lack of peace, is very useless, disturbing, and dissatisfying.

YOUR GOAL OF LIFE Most people live almost mechanically, unconscious of any ideal or plan of life. They come earth, struggle for a living, and leave the shores of mortality without knowing why they came here, and what their duties were. No matter what the goal of life is, it is obvious that man is so undermined with needs that he must struggle to satisfy them. The believer and the disbeliever in God must both struggle to meet their needs. Therefore, it is very important to know that man should concentrate on his needs and not create a lot of useless extra desires.

Efficiency through Concentration:

After establishing that the goal of life is maximum efficiency, peace, health, and success, let us consider the surest way to prosperity. Prosperity does not consist just in the making of money: it also consists in acquiring the mental efficiency by which man can uniformly acquire health, wealth, wisdom, and peace at will.

Great wealth does not necessarily bring health, peace, or efficiency, but acquirement of efficiency and peace are bound to bring a properly balanced material success. Most people develop mental efficiency as the by-product of their efforts for material success, but very few people know that money is made for happiness, but happiness cannot be found just by developing an insatiable Soul- corroding desire for money.

Man often forgets to concentrate on his little physical needs and on his great need of developing mental efficiency in everything, and of acquiring Divine contentment. Man is so busy multiplying his conditions of physical comfort that he considers very many unnecessary things as a necessary part of his existence.

SUCCESS THROUGH CONCENTRATION Mental efficiency depends upon the art of concentration. Man must know the scientific method of concentration, by which he can disengage his attention from objects of distraction and focus it on one thing at a time. By the power of concentration, man can use the untold power of mind to accomplish that which he desires, and he can guard all doors through which failure may enter. All men of success have been men of great concentration, men who could dive deeply into their problems and come out with the pearls of right solutions. Most people are suffocated by distraction and are unable to fish out the pearls or success.

CONCENTRATION IS NOT ALL, HOWEVER However, one may be a man of concentration and power and may dive deep into the sea of problems but still may not find the pearl of success at all. There are many men who have powerful concentration but they do not know where to strike success. This is where another factor

tor in acquiring prosperity comes into consideration. Brilliant people with efficient minds also have starved or have had only meager success.

THE LAW OF CAUSE AND EFFECT AND LAW OF ACTION   All prosperity is measured out to man according to the law of cause and effect which governs not only this life, but all past lives. This is why intelligent people are often born poor or unhealthy, whereas, an idiot may be born healthy and wealthy. Men were originally sons of God made in his image, having free choice and equal power of accomplishment, but by the misuse of his God-given reason and will power man became controlled by the natural law of cause and effect and law of action (Karma) and thus limited his life. A man's success depends not only upon his intelligence and efficiency but upon the nature of his past actions. However, there is a way to overcome the unfavorable results of past actions. They must be destroyed and a new cause set in motion.

GOD THE REAL SOURCE THE SECRET OF SUCCESS AND POWER God is the secret of all mental power, peace, and prosperity. Then why use the limited impossible human method of prosperity?

By visualizing prosperity, or by affirmation, you may strengthen your subconscious mind, which may in turn encourage your conscious mind, but that is all that visualization alone can do. The conscious mind still has to achieve the success just the same and is hindered by the law of cause and effect. The conscious mind cannot initiate a new cause which will bring positive success in any direction, but when the human mind can contact God, then the super-conscious mind can be sure of success, due to the unlimited power of God and due to creating a new cause of success.

The man of powerful concentration must ask God to direct his focused mind on the right place for right success. Passive people want God to do all the work and egotists ascribe all their success to themselves. Passive people do not use the power of God in intelligence and egotists, though using God-given intelligence, forget to receive God's direction as to where the intelligence should be used. I can blame inertia in the cause of failure, but it hurts me to see intelligence egotists fail after making real intelligent effort.

ESTABLISH YOUR ONENESS WITH GOD The surest way to prosperity lies, not in begging through wrong prayer, but in establishing first your Oneness with God and afterward demanding the Divine Son's share. That is why Jesus said that men of the world wrongly and unsuccessfully seek bread first, but that they should seek the Kingdom of God first, then all things, all prosperity, unasked, would be given added unto them. This is easier said than done. You have heard this before, but you must learn to demonstrate this truth in your life. You must remember that Jesus actually knew and felt it when he said: "I and my Father are One." That is why He could command storms to stop, turn water into wine, wake Lazarus from sleep, and heal the physical and mental sufferers, and could feel the multitude. He was Spiritually efficient, and hence He knew the art of mental and physical efficiency.

"UNSELFISH SELFISHNESS" Neither man nor nations should depend upon individual or national strength only, but should remember that all prosperity flows from God. When industrial selfishness begins to reign supreme and the Spiritual laws of including others in your prosperity and acting each for all and all for each, are broken, then the entire financial system of a country is thrown into confusion. Since Spiritual and financial laws govern our lives, we must seek prosperity not by the selfish physical method alone, but by the combined law of unselfish-selfish activity. Every work we do is in a sense selfish, but when we try to make others happy and wealthy while we try to become so ourselves, it is called "unselfish selfishness."

GOD'S WILL AND YOUR WILL Broadcast your message "My father and I are One" until you feel this overpowering, all-solacing Bliss of God. When this happens, you have made the contact. Then demand you celestial right by affirming: "Father, I am Thy Child, guide me to my right prosperity."

CONTACT GOD FIRST Do not will and act first, but contact God first and thus harness your will and activity to the right goal. As you cannot broadcast through a broken microphone, so must you remember that you cannot broadcast your prayer through the mental microphone which is disordered by restlessness. By deep calmness, repair your mind microphone. Then again, as you cannot get on answer by just calling someone through a microphone and then running away, so also, you must not run away but you must continuously broadcast your prayer to God through your calm mental microphone until you hear His voice. Most people pray in restlessness and do not pray with the determination to receive a response.

Through prayer and right meditation you can know that you are a Divine Child and as such you can claim unlimited prosperity and can create at will anytime, anywhere, what you need. Jesus, being a true Son of God, had atomic control of all matter and earthly prosperity. That is why he could feed five thousand people with five loaves of bread, just like the very many Indian saints who were and are capable of miraculous deeds.

Every morning mentally say: "Father, bless me that I may know that all prosperity flows from Thee."

THE APOLOGUE

"Two Blind Men who sought Riches from God and a King"

Akbar, the Great, sometimes called "Guardian of Mankind," the Mogul Emperor of India, was the greatest Asiatic monarch of modern times, and one of the greatest kings of India. He won the title of "Guardian of Mankind" because of the benevolence of his rule and at the same time the devoted zeal in which he sought to reign in lost sections of the once vast empire which had broken away under long periods of misrule before Akbar ascended the throne.

He fostered religious tolerance among the many conflicting religions. During his reign; his greatest achievement consisted in bringing the two warring religions, Hinduism and Mohammedanism, into harmony. He sometimes dressed as a Mohammedan and went into the mosque to pray, and sometimes he dressed as a Hindu and went to worship in the Hindu temple. This broadminded king went about showering good on needy individuals and social groups everywhere.

It so happened that the Emperor Akbar was in the habit of riding on a richly decorated chariot drawn by eight horses. Heralds and bodyguards used to trumpet his arrival in all quarters of the city. In spite of this pomp and splendor it was the strict order of the Emperor to stop the procession anytime, anywhere, if any of his subjects wanted to offer him a petition.

One day, as the King's procession passed along the boulevard, His Highness met two blind men, sitting about twenty yards apart, shouting for alms. This attracted the King's attention and he stopped his carriage in front of the first blind man, who was shouting: "To whom the King gives, he alone can be rich." After listening to the first blind man, the King ordered his carriage to stop in front of the second blind man who was shouting:" To whom God gives, he alone can be rich."

For a month the King heard the two blind men shouting their respective demands for riches from him and from God, whenever his procession passed along the boulevard. At last, one day the King, feeling quite flattered by the first blind man's utterance that: "To whom the King gives, he alone can be rich," ordered a very large loaf of bread to be baked with the inside stuffed with solid gold. This loaf the King gave to the first blind man, completely ignoring the second blind man, who believed that God alone could make him rich.

Soon after the King went on a hunting trip, and when he returned and once again passed along the boulevard in his usual way, he come across the first blind man to whom he had given the

23

loaf. This blind man was still shouting: "to whom the King gives, he alone becomes rich." Then the King asked: "What did you do with the loaf I gave you?" The blind man replied: " Your Royal Highness, the loaf you gave me was too large and not well baked, so I sold it to the second blind man for ten cents. I was happy to get even that much money."

The King looked about for the second blind man but he was nowhere to be seen. Upon inquiry, the Emperor found out that the second blind man had given the loaf to his wife, who had opened it up and found the gold. With this she bought a home and invested the money in dividend paying securities.

Upon learning this, the King, with inner humbleness but with outward wrath) rebuked the first blind man, saying: " You fool, you gave away my gold-stuffed loaf to your friend who depended upon God and not upon me for wealth. From now on you must change your motto and shout, like your friend: " To whom God gives, he alone can be rich."

This story of the two blind men has a wonderful moral. So many millions of people today think that all wealth comes from the banks, factories, and jobs, and through personal ability. The great depression has proven that the most prosperous nation on the face of the globe, as America, is a starved notion. When the wealthiest country on earth, without any national catastrophe whatsoever, can be suddenly thrown into poverty, it proves that there are Divine Laws other than physical laws, which govern the physical, mental, Spiritual, and financial phases of life.

Every day strive to be healthy, wealthy, wise, and happy, not by taking away the health, wealth, and happiness of others, but, by analyzing and planning everything you do, in order to make others better and happier while you are trying to be better and happier yourself. Learn to include the happiness and welfare of others in your own happiness.

The happiness of the individual, the family members, and the nation depends entirely upon the law of mutual cooperation, unselfish selfishness, and living up to this motto: " Father, bless us, that we may remember Thee always, and let us not forget that all things flow from Thee always.

HEALTH CULTURE

VITAMINS You may eat a whole dinner, very palatable, very satisfying and filling, and yet you may be eating a dead meal. Without the presence of vitamins in food, your meal is dead. It is a meal which you eat to deceive yourself. For, instead of nourishment you invite disease.

Diseases are born of our ignorance of the laws of the body and mind. Right eating, moderation, and exercise will practically banished disease from the face of the earth. Vitamins are the brains of the food you eat. They direct the digestion and absorption of food, while the food builds the different tissues. No matter what you eat, never forget to include vitamins in your menu. Vitamins are condensed Life Force. They are subtle electricity stored to replete the body battery with fresh energy. They are tabloids of energy.

PEARLS OF HEALTH LAWS 1. A carrot a day (with a part of stem and roots unscraped only thoroughly washed). Chew it well. Nature made it hard to strengthen your teeth by chewing. It is sweet and luscious once you get used to the taste. You will soon find cooked carrots absolutely tasteless, in addition to there being only the corpse of the carrot from which the vitamin soul has departed.

2. A lemon a day.
3. An orange a day.
4. An apple a day.

5.   A glass of almond milk or any nut milk. (Grind two tablespoonful of nuts thoroughly and mix with water.
6.   Chopped green leafed vegetables daily.
7.   Unsulphured dates and raisins one handful daily.
8.   Avoid white flour and overeating.
9.   Keep colon clean.
10.   Whole wheat bread, fresh cheese and a glass of milk are beneficial if you work hard during the day.
11.   One should not have a starvation meal or eat less than one needs of the right articles of food.
12.   Adding one quart of milk a day or six tablespoonful of almonds with water or milk, would help the gathering of strength to fight hard work. (See footnote)

FORTNIGHTLY INSPIRATION

Many persons have dived in the Ocean of Thy Abundance again and again to seek the pearls of opulence, power, and wisdom, but only a few divers have found them. These few persons have praised the wondrous riches of Thy Sea because they dived well and found the secret treasure nook. Those who dived in the wrong places blamed Thy blue brine of abundance as devoid of the most desired treasures. Many persons perish diving in the Sea of Treasures, being devoured by monsters of selfishness, greed, faithlessness, doubt, idleness, and skepticism.

Heavenly Father, teach me how to dive in Thy Ocean of Plenty again and again if I do not find the pearls of Thy Perception by one or two divings. I will not say that Thy Ocean of Everything is empty, for Thou wilt show me that the fault is with my diving. I will put on the divine apparel of faith, power, and fortitude, and Thou wilt direct my mind to dive in the right place, where Thy bounty is hidden.

FORTNIGHTLY AFFIRMATION

"Father Divine, this is my prayer: I care not what I may permanently possess, but give to me the power to acquire at will, whatever I may daily need."

"AUM"

PEACE! PROSPERITY! PEACE!

NOTE: Out of the 12 items of health food, try to take as many as you can find easily and afford for without any worry.

YOGODA SAT-SANGA FORTNIGHTLY INSTRUCTIONS
BY
PARAMHANSA YOGANANDA
(To be Confidentially Reserved FOR MEMBER'S USE ONLY)
FRIENDSHIP

Is friendship the weaving of the red strings
Of two hearts?
Is it the blending of two minds into a spacious One mind?
Is it the spouting of love founts together
To strengthen the rush of love on droughty Souls?
Is it the one rose grown 'twixt twin mind-branchlets
Of one compassionate stem?
Is it the one thinking in two bodies?
Friendship is noble, fruitful, holy
When two separate Souls march in difference
Yet in harmony, agreeing and disagreeing,
Glowing, improving diversely.
With one common longing to find solace
In true pleasure.
When ne'er the lover seeks
Self-comfort at the cost of the one beloved
Then, in that garden of selflessness
Fragrant friendship perfectly flowers.
Ah, friendship! Flowering, heaven-born plant!
Nurtured art thou in the soul of measureless love.
In the seeking of Soul progress together
By two who would smooth the way each for the other.
And thou art watered by attention of affection
And tender dews of inner and outer sweetness
Of the inmost, selfless heart's devotion.
Ah, friendship! Where thy soul-born flower falls
There on that sacred shrine of fragrance
The Friend of all Friends craves to come
And to remain!

PRAYER TO PRECEDE THE PRAECEPTUM STUDY
O Divine Mother, teach me to use the gift of Thy Love in my heart to love all of Thy children. Father Divine, teach me to enter through the portals of family love, or through the love of my friends into the mansion of wider social love. Teach me, then to pass through the doors of social love into the wider mansions for international love.
Into the endless territory of Divine Love in which I may perceive all animate and inanimate objects as breathing and living by Thy love. Teach me to love Thee more than anything else, for it is Thy Love with which I love everything.

FRIENDSHIP
HOW TO ATTRACT FRIENDS
Friendship is God's Love shining through the eyes of your loved ones, calling you home to drink His nectar of all differences and selfishness dissolving Unity. Friendship is God's trumpet call, bidding the Soul destroy the partitions which disparate it from all other Souls and from Him. True friendship unites two Souls so completely that they reflect the Unit of Spirit and Its Divine qualities.

True friendship is broad and inclusive. Selfish attachment to a single individual, excluding all others, inhibits the development of Divine Friendship. Extend the boundaries of the glowing kingdom of your love, gradually including within them your family, your neighbors, your community, your country, all countries, in short, all living sentient creatures.

Be also a Cosmic friend, imbued with Kindness and affection for all of God's Creation, scattering love everywhere. Such was the example set by Christ, Swam Shankara and my Masters - Babaji, Lahiri Mahasaya, and Swami Sriyukteswarji.

Consider no one a stranger. Learn to feel that everybody is your kin. Family love is merely one of the first exercises in the Divine Teacher's course in Friendship, intended to prepare your heart for an all-inclusive love. Feel that the life blood of God is circulating in the veins of all races. How does anyone dare to hate any human being of whatsoever race, when he knows that God lives and breathes in all? We are Americans, or Christians, or Hindus, or other nationalities, for just a few years, but we are God's children forever. The Soul cannot be confined within man-made boundaries. Its nationality is Spirit; its country is Omnipresence.

This does not mean that you must know and love all human beings and creatures personally and individually. All you need do is to be ready at all times to spread the light of friendly service over all living creatures which you happen to contact. This requires constant mental effort and preparedness; in other words, unselfishness. The sun shines equally on diamond and charcoal, but one has developed qualities which enable it to reflect the sunlight brilliantly, while the other absorbs all the sunlight. Emulate the diamond in your dealings with people. Brightly reflect the light of God's Love.

To have friends, you must manifest friendliness. If you open the door to the magnetic power of friendship, a Soul or Souls of like vibrations will be attracted to you. The more friendly you become toward all, the greater will be the number of your real friends. When perfect friendship exists either between two hearts or within a group of hearts in a Spiritual Organization, such friendship perfects each individual. In the heart, purified by friendship, one beholds an open door of unity through which one should invite other Souls to enter - those who love him as well as those who love him not.

Friendship should not be influenced by the relative positions of people. It may and should exist between lovers, employer and employee, teacher and pupil, parents and children, and others. God's effort unites strife-torn humanity manifests itself within your heart as the friendship instinct.

SERVICE TO FRIENDS

True friendship consists in being mutually useful, in offering your friends good cheer in distress, sympathy in sorrow, advice in trouble, and material help in times of real need. Friendship consists in rejoicing in the good fortune of your friends and sympathizing with them in adversity. Friendship gladly forgoes selfish pleasures or self-interest for the sake of a friend's happiness, without consciousness of loss or sacrifice, and without counting the cost. Human love and friendship have their basis in service on the physical, mental, or business plane. They are short-lived and conditional. Divine Love has had its foundation in service on the Spiritual and Intuitional planes and is unconditional and everlasting.

The greater the mutual service, the deeper the friendship. Why does Buddha or Jesus have such a wide following? Because They, like the other great Masters, were unequaled in Their service to humanity. Hence, to attract friends, you must possess the qualities of a real friend. Idiots may become friends, but their blind friendship may end in a sudden blind hatred. Help your friend also by being a mental, aesthetic and Spiritual inspiration [to] him. Never be sarcastic to a friend. Do not flatter him unless it is to encourage him. Do not agree with him when he is wrong. Real friendship cannot witness with indifference the false, harmful pleasures of a friend. This does not mean that you must quarrel. Suggest mentally, or if your advice is asked, give it gently and lovingly. Fools fight. Friends discuss their differences.

LOVE YOUR ENEMIES

The secret of Christ's and Pralhad's strength lay in their love for all, even their enemies. Far better to conquer by love the heart of a person who hates you than to vanquish such a one by other means. To the ordinary man such a doctrine seems absurd. He wants to return ten slaps for the one he has received and add twice as many kicks for good measure. Why should you love your enemy? In order that you may bring the healing rays of your love into his dark, hatred-stricken heart. When it is so released, it can behold itself as pure golden love. Thus will the flame of your love bum the partitions of hatred and misery which separate your Soul from other Souls and all Souls from the vast sea of Infinite Love.

Practice loving those who do not love you. Feel for those who do not feel for you. Be generous to those who are generous only to themselves. If you heap hatred upon your enemy, neither he nor you are able to perceive the inherent beauty of your Soul. Jealousy is self-love and the death of friendship. Avoid doing anything which brings harm to yourself or to another. If you are self-indulgent, or if you encourage a friend in his vices, you are an enemy disguised as a friend. By being true to yourself and a true friend to others, you gain the friendship of God. Once you make your love felt in the love of other people, it will expand until it becomes the one Love which flows through all hearts.

There are people who do not trust anyone, and who utterly doubt the possibility of ever having true friends. Some, in fact, actually boast that they get along without friends. If you fail to be friendly, you disregard the Divine law of self-expansion, by which alone your Soul can grow into the Spirit.

When necessary, if humility and apologies on your part bring out your enemy's good qualities, by all means apologize. The person who can do this will have attained a definite Spiritual development, for it takes character to be able to apologize graciously and sincerely. It is the consciousness of his own inferiority which makes a man hide behind a display of pride. Do not, however, encourage a wrongdoer by being too humble and apologetic.

You need not fawn on your enemy. Silently love him. Silently be of service to him whenever he is in need, for love is real only when it is useful and expresses itself through action. Thus will you rend the veils of hatred and of narrow-mindedness which hide God from your sight. Constant contact with the Infinite in meditation fills one with Divine Love, which along enables one to love one's enemies.

Always remember that you need the inspiration of better company in keep yourself constantly improving, and you should share your goodness with people of inferior qualities who need your help. A Saint once said: "Your outward good company is of paramount importance, as it influences your mind and reason which, by repetitions of thought and action, form good habits.

FRIENDS OF PAST INCARNATIONS

Make every effort to rediscover your friends of past incarnations, whom you may recognize through familiar physical, mental, and Spiritual qualities. Rising above considerations of material or even Spiritual gain, perfect your friendship, begun in a preceding incarnation, into Divine Friendship. There are people with whom you come in daily contact, yet with whom you do not feel in sympathy. Learn to love them and adapt yourself to them. There are others who give you the instantaneous feeling that you have known them always. This indicates that they are your friends of previous incarnations. Do not neglect them, but strengthen the friendship existing between you. Be on the lookout for them always, as your restless mind may fail to recognize them. Often they are very near you, drawn by the friendship born in the dim distant past. They constitute your shining collection of Soul jewels; add to it constantly. In these bright Soul galaxies you will behold the One Great Friend smiling at you radiantly and clearly. It is God who comes to you in the guise of a noble, true Friend, to serve, inspire and guide you.

Each individual has his own standard of physical and mental beauty. Wat seems ugly to one may appear beautiful to another. Looking at a vast crowd, you like some faces instantaneously; others do not attract you particularly. The instant attraction of your mind to the likeable inner and outer features of an individual is your first indication that you have found a friend of the past. Your dear ones whom you loved before will be drawn toward you by a prenatal sense of friendship.

Do not be deceived by physical beauty. Ask yourself whether or not a face, the manner of walking, in short, everything about a person, appeals to you. Sometimes overeating and lack of exercise may distort the features of a friend, and thus he may escape your recognition. Sometimes a beautiful woman may all in love with an ugly man, or a handsome man with a physically unattractive woman, due to the loving friendship of a past incarnation. A fat, distorted body may harbor a real friend. Therefore, to be sure that your eyes have not deceived you regarding the physical characteristics of your supposed former friend, ascertain whether you are mentally and Spiritually congenial. Delve deeply into a person's mind and guard yourself against being prejudiced by little peculiarities, in order to find out whether your tastes and inclinations essentially agree. Seek your friends of past incarnations in order that you may continue your friendship in this life and perfect it into Divine Friendship. One lifetime is not always sufficient to achieve such perfection.

Ugliness of disposition and. selfishness drive away all friends of former incarnations, whereas friendliness drawn them toward you. Therefore, be ready always to meet them half way. Never mind if one or two friends prove false and deceive you.

DIVINE FRIENDSHIP

Friendship is the universal Spiritual attraction which unites Souls in the bond of Divine love and may manifest itself either in two or in many. The Spirit was One. By the law of duality it became two positive and negative. Then, by the law of infinity applied to the law of relativity, it became many. Now the One in the many is endeavoring to unite the many and make them One. This effort of the Spirit to unify many Souls into the One works through our emotions, intelligence, and intuition and finds expression through friendship. When Divine Friendship reigns supreme in the temple of your heart, your Soul will merge with the vast Cosmic Soul, leaving far behind the confining bonds which separated it from all of God's animate and inanimate Creation.

When you behold, assembled all at once beneath the canopy of your perfected universal friendship, the Souls of the past, present, and future, the busy stars, the amoeba, the whippoorwill, the nightingale, the dumb stones, and the shining sea sands, then the friendship thirsts of your heart will be quenched forever. Then God's Creation will ring with the emancipating song of all difference-dissolving celestial friendship. Then the Divine Friend will rejoice to see you come home after your evolutional wanderings and roamings through the pathways of incarnations. Then He and you will merge in the Bliss of Eternal Friendship.

The building of wisdom and Spiritual and intuitive understanding by mutual effort alone can bind two Souls by the laws of everlasting, universal Divine Love. When true friendship exists between two Souls and they seek Spiritual love and God's love together, when their only wish is to be of service to each other, their friendship produces the flame of Spirit. Through perfected Divine Friendship, mutually seeking Spiritual perfection, you will find the One Great Friend.

No man who fails to inspire confidence in other hearts, and who is unable to extend the kingdom of his love and friendliness into other Soul territories, can hope to spread his consciousness over Cosmic Consciousness. If you cannot conquer human hearts, you cannot conquer the Cosmic Heart. All this may seem very complicated, but when you touch the Infinite, your difficulties will melt away. Divine love will come to you. Beautiful intuitive experiences of universal friendliness will play like fountains in your mind. Keep in mind this prayer: "Heavenly Father, Let those that are our own come unto us, and finding them may we find friendship with all, and thus find Thee."

THE APOLOGUE
THE MAN WHO REFUSED HEAVEN

Long, long ago there lived, in India, a holy man who spent his days on the peaceful banks of the holy river Ganges. (This river is considered holy by the people of India because many Saints meditate under the shady banyan trees on its banks.

Years passed in deep contemplation, but the Spiritual aspirant found that, although he was surrounded by a celestial environment of beautiful scenery and good people, good books, and devotional temple services, yet his mind constantly dwelt on mentally harming and robbing people.

As often as he tried to meditate on God, the holy man found that in the inner chamber of his mind many undesirable thoughts entered constantly torturing him with the misery or temptation. No matter how he tried to ward off these uninvited thoughts, the more they made forceful inroads into his peace.

At last he vowed: "I will not stop praying until I find definite release from these disturbing thoughts stab my peace during meditation. One hour passed, two hours passed, and still the bandits of restlessness kept piercing the holy man's meditation. Finally, at the end of three hours, the disturbing thoughts suddenly vanished from his temple of meditation, and in their stead he beheld a beautiful vision of a Saint standing lifelike before him.

This beautiful Saint not only appeared to be living but spoke with celestial softness: "Son, in a former life you were a bad man, but before you died you resolved to be good. That is why you were born in this life with a holy resolution to be good and also with bad thoughts which you incurred in your past life. It is a shame that amidst the holy surroundings of the Ganges, good friends, and regular meditation, you have been living in the inferno of inward restlessness." The Saint went on after a gentle pause: "According to the decree of your past actions of your previous life and because you have not made a greater effort to live peacefully in your present Spiritual surroundings, it is metaphysically ordained that unless you work very hard at meditation now, at death you will have to choose between living in Heaven with ten fools, or living in Hades with one wise man. Which of the two do you prefer?"

The Spiritual aspirant replied: "I prefer to live in Hades with one wise man, for I know from my own experience that the ten fools would make a Hades of Heaven. Whereas, I believe that if I were with one real wise man, even in the stygian darkness of Hades, he would help me to make Heaven of it."

So, if you have a heavenly home but are constantly fighting

with the mothers of your family and friends, you are living in a self-created Hades. On the other hand, no matter what inharmonious surroundings you may have, if you meditate or sit in silence for a few minutes every day and live in harmony, you will always live in Heaven and will carry your own portable paradise within your breast wherever you go.

HEALTH CULTURE

DIETARY LAWS To have faith in G o d ' s healing power through the mind, and obey dietary laws, is better than just to have faith in God and mind and disregard dietary laws. Every day, for beneficial results, eat green-leafed vegetables, including a carrot with part of its stem, and drink a glass of orange juice (including pulp) with a tablespoonful of finely ground nuts. Mix good salad dressings made of thoroughly ground nuts, cream, a few drops of lemon juice, orange juice, and honey, with all salads.

A little curry sauce with boiled vegetables, once in a while, is a good salivary stimulant.

ONE FRIEND
Many clouds do race to hide Thee —
Of friends and wealth and fame —
And yet through mist of tears I see
Appear Thy Golden Name.
Each time my father, mother, friends
Do loudly claim they did me tend. I
wake from sleep to sweetly hear That
Thou alone didst help me here.

FORTNIGHTLY AFFIRMATION
"I will try to please everyone by kind
considerate actions, all the time trying to
remove the cause of misunderstanding knowingly
or unknowingly offered by me."

FRIENDSHIP! MEDITATION! GODLINESS! PEACE!

YOGODA SAT-SANGA FORTNIGHTLY INSTRUCTIONS
BY
PARAMHANSA YOGANANDA
(To be Confidentially Reserved FOR MEMBER'S USE ONLY)

THE DIVINE GYPSY

I will be a Gypsy —
Roam, roam and room,
I will sing the song that none has sung!
I will sing to the sky,
I will sing to the winds,
I will sing to my red clouds
I will roam, roam and roam—
King of the land through which I roam-
By day, the shady trees will be my tent.
At night, the stars shall be
My candles, twinkling in the firmament,
And I will call the moon to be my lamp
And light my silver, skyey camp
I will be a Gypsy-
Roam, roam and roam.
I will eat the food which chance may bring;
I will drink from crystal sparkling spring;
I will doff my cap and off I'll go.
Like a wayward brook of long ago,
I will roll o'er the green
And scatter the joy all my heart
To binds, leaves, winds, hills, — then depart
To stranger and stranger lands.
From East to West.
0! I will be a Gypsy- Roam, roam and roam!
But always, when I lay me down to rest.
I'll sing to Thee my Gypsy song.
And pray to Thee my Gypsy song and prayer.
And find Thee, always, everywhere.

PRAYER TO PRECEDE THE PRAECEPTUM STUDY

0 Spirit, teach to heal the body by recharging it with Thy Cosmic Energy, to heal the mind by concentration and smiles, and the Soul by meditation born intuition. Make me feel that my heart is throbbing in Thy Breast, and that Thou art walking through my feet, breathing through my breath, wielding my arms of activity, and weaving thoughts in my brain. 0, make me Thyself, that I may behold the bubble of me, floating in Thee.

THE ART OF REJUVENATION

PART 1.

PHYSICAL BODY CONSTANTLY CHANGING

We now come to the Instructions on Recharging the Body Battery, by which you may learn how to draw more and more life-sustaining, energy from the ether, and depend less and less upon solids, liquids, sunshine, and gases for sustenance. However, we shall first give a few hints about the outer source of energy for sustaining the human body battery, before passing on to the method of recharging the recharging the body with energy from the Inner Source. With the knowledge furnished you in this series of Instructions, you will be able to eliminate the interruptions which might otherwise come through the demands of your body, and gradually become perfect physically as well as mentally and Spiritually. Instantaneous perfection in body, mind, and Soul must inevitably appear when perfect understanding is reached. It is the inevitable Law of God. Change does not mean annihilation. It means certain changes of motion which we, as human beings, fear and dislike. The nature of matter is change. The nature of Spirit is changelessness. The first process in rejuvenating the physical body is to supply it with the sixteen elements of food chemicals which it needs, plus sunshine from regular sun baths and good oxygen, and from regular, proper breathing. While walking every day, inhale, counting one to twelve. Hold the breath twelve counts, then exhale, counting one to twelve. Do that twenty four times every time you walk. Everyone must have at least a half hour sun bath twice a week, or preferably every day.

The human body, which looks so compact and solid, is in fact nothing but a bundle of motions. It is a bundle of forces whirling together in ultra-rapid motion. The solid flesh is made of very tiny cells, particles of water, and other chemicals. This superstructure of flesh and bones has, on the external side, been made dependent upon the ultraviolet rays in the sunshine, and upon oxygen, good food, and pure liquids, such as water, fruit juices, and so forth.

Ordinarily, people concentrate upon food, air, and sunshine only in order to keep the body well, but a time comes to everyone when health fails in spite of all the outer means of good food and air supplied to it. Then it is realized that the body battery has to be recharged by the Inner Source also.

"MAN SHALL NOT LIVE BY BREAD ALONE"

Jesus said: "Man shall not live by bread alone, but by every word which proceedeth out of the Mouth of God."

"Bread," or in other words, any kind of food, alone does not support life. If it alone supported life, you could put it into the body of a dead man, lay him out in the sun, and expect him to come to life. The power which creates Life, the force which enables the body organs to be converted into energy — that is the direct source of Life.

An automobile battery depends for its life not upon its indirect outer source of distilled, water alone, but upon the vibrating electric current which flows into it from the dynamo through the mouth of the wires (the direct Inner source). Jesus, centuries ago, gave utterance to the great Truth when He said that man's body battery is charged by "the word of God" (Inner Energy), and not by outer sources alone. Like the automobile battery, it can be said: Man's body battery does not live by the indirect outer source only of bread, oxygen, solids, liquids, sunshine, and so forth, but by the vibrating life current which flows into the body from the invisible Dynamo of Cosmic Energy surrounding the body, through the "Mouth of God," or through the medulla oblongata and the will (the direct Inner source).

Self-Realization Instruction teaches that just as an automobile battery needs both distilled water and electricity to keep it alive, so the body battery needs recharging with Life Force through the medulla as well as food and the physical means of sustaining life.

It is electricity that changes the distilled water into the force that recharges a battery, and it is energy that converts oxygen, solids, and liquids into the force that keeps us alive, but solids and liquids develop into what they are by this same energy, and when you put them into your stomach, they must again be converted into energy before they are of any use to the body; furthermore, when the energy that is in them is taken out, the residue of this mass of material is forced out of the body as waste material, through the pores, the intestines, and the kidneys. Just as distilled water, the outer source of sustenance alone will not sustain life in the battery or bring life back, so oxygen, solids, liquids, and sunshine alone, will not help a dead body battery.

GOD THE ORIGINAL SOURCE OF ENERGY, OR LIFE FORCE

The medulla is the original source of intake of the Life Force as it comes from God. The medulla is the "Mouth of God" because that is where God breathes the Life Force into you. Do not confuse this with the passage that says: "God breathed into his nostrils the breath of life and man became a living Soul." You shall learn all about that in the Praeceptum on the "Garden of Eden" also.

Every part of the body can be operated upon by the surgeon, except the medulla. Have you ever heard of a surgeon suggesting the possibility of operating upon the medulla? No. If you were to touch it with but the tiniest point of the smallest needle, you would be dead instantly. Heart? Of course, the heart is quite commonly operated upon. The brain? Cerebral operations are far from rare. The spine? Yes, they puncture the spine sometimes and get what they call good results occasionally. But the medulla? Never. Why? Because it is the Center of all the Centers of Life. It is the one Center through [which] the Life Force enters the body. All other centers heart, brain, and the centers of the spine, such as [the] cervical, dorsal, lumbar, sacral, and the coccygeal, are but minor Centers, receiving the Life Force through the medulla, and acting merely as distributing Centers.

HOW TO RECHARGE THE BODY WITH ENERGY

Science has proved that everything is being recharged by Cosmic Energy. The human body is surrounded by a halo of Conscious Cosmic Energy. The medulla oblongata is the antenna of the receiving station which receives the radiographed energy from the Cosmic Consciousness, and Cosmic Energy, through the human body radio operator the will. Just as ships on the sea, without wire connections, can be controlled by radio, so God's Intelligence, through vibrations of Cosmic Energy is supplying our bodies with Life Force without visible connections.

God originally created Cosmic Vibration of Energy which, when once started, became perpetual, and you can, by your wireless will power, draw upon it and bring it into your body through the medulla. This Cosmic Energy, the same energy through which you and everything else in the universe were created, surrounds and permeates all Creation within and without all the time. It enters through the "Mouth of God" and is the invisible "Word" which sustains life of all kinds.

You will find in this series of Instructions the knowledge by which you will learn to live more and more by calling upon the eternal supply of Cosmic Energy, which is ever available to us, which is within and without, and is always all about us, and thus recharge[s] the body at any and all times with vitality. With this knowledge, the body may be made fit in all respects, and a perfect body, free from disease, presents less resistance to the methods and practices by which Self-Realization is reached, and by which the human consciousness, as well as the body, is raised to the fatigueless state.

The material human consciousness cannot grasp the Universal Christ Consciousness within itself, no matter how desirous it is to do so, but when the student, by the methods of Self-Realization, through concentration and meditation, enlarges the caliber of his consciousness and raises its quality, he can perceive the Universal Consciousness in all atoms. This is what is meant by "received Him." Thus, according to Jesus, all Souls can actually find their Souls One with Christ Consciousness, by intuitive Self- Realization. They can know themselves as "Sons of God."

On the internal side, these living cells, which constitute the flesh, bones, and all tissues, are kept rejuvenated by thoughts and by biological forces. In the inner Spiritual source, the body motions are constantly flooded and rejuvenated with the motions of consciousness, including subconsciousness, superconsciousness, Christ Consciousness and Cosmic Consciousness. The vital sparks are condensed sparks of God's thoughts. Therefore we see that the physical body is really a bundle of motions.

You should depend more and more upon the limitless supply of the inner source of cosmic consciousness and less and less upon the other sources of the body energy. Eating all the time will make your hot body get old quicker, and the only way to keep the body really rejuvenated is to unite human consciousness and Cosmic Consciousness through meditation. The mind must never have suggested to it the human limitations of sickness, old age, and death, but it should be constantly, inwardly told: "I am the Infinite, which has become the body. The body as a manifestation of Spirit is the ever-youthful Spirit."

REJUVENATION OF THE SOUL

Self-Realization is the KNOWING, in all parts of the body, mind, and Soul, that we are now in possession of the Omnipresence of God; that we do not have to pray that it come to us; that we are not merely near It at all times, but that God's Omnipresence is our Omnipresence; that He is just as much a part of us now as He will ever be, and that all we have to do is to improve our KNOWING.

Self-Realization may be, and is, attained by some people who are struggling with sick and otherwise imperfect bodies, but it cannot be attained unless you can learn to concentrate and meditate uninterruptedly upon God. Since it is difficult to concentrate and meditate while the aches and pains of the body continually have the attention of the mind, the path of Self- Realization is made much easier if the imperfections of the body and the harmonious operations of its functions are arranged so that the mind need not at any time be interrupted in meditation through the demands of the physical body.

By constantly holding the peaceful aftereffects of meditation in mind, by feeling the immortality in the body, by believing in Eternal life instead of beholding the illusory changes of life, and by feeling the ocean of Immortal Bliss God underlying the changeable waves of experiences of past lives and the waves of perceptions of childhood, youth, and age in this life, the Soul can find not only perpetual rejuvenation in the Soul, but also in the body. Just as soon as the body is found to be, not isolated from Spirit, but a number of rising, falling waves of vibrating currents in the ocean of Cosmic Consciousness, then the perpetual rejuvenation of the Spirit can be implanted in the body if so desired.

(The Principles and Technique of Rejuvenation will be continued in the next Praeceptum).

THE APOLOGUE
THE BOATMAN AND THE PHILOSOPHER

Long ago a learned Hindu Philosopher who was thoroughly theoretically-versed in the four vast Hindu Bibles, wanted to Cross to the other side of the Holy River Ganges in India. The river, though often muddy, is called the Holy River because its waters are very healthful to the bathers and because Saints of India sit on its picturesque banks under the shady banyan trees and meditate upon the Infinite. The vibrations of the Holy Saints are picked up by super-sensitive Souls who silently stroll by its banks in deep contemplation. The famous author, Keyserling, speaks of this fact. Thoughts are things. Every house is decorated with the furniture of good or evil thought vibrations. For this reason you can feel almost instantaneously the good or bad vibrations of a home, place, or country.

To return to the story, a lone boatman was carrying the Hindu Philosopher across the Holy River Ganges in a rowboat. The proud Hindu Philosopher, knower of the four Hindu Bibles, finding nothing to occupy his mind, thought of showing off his knowledge a little bit to the boatman. Thinking this, the Hindu Philosopher asked: "Boatman, have you studied the First Hindu Bible?" The boatman replied: "No, sir, I don't know anything about the First Hindu Bible. To this the Hindu Philosopher, looking very vise, pityingly remarked: "Mr. Boatman, I am sorry to declare unto you that 25 per cent of your life is lost." The boatman swallowed this insult and kept on quietly rowing his boat. When the boat had gone some distance across the Ganges, the Hindu Philosopher's eyes sparkled with unholy wisdom and he exclaimed loudly: "Mr. Boatman, I must ask you, have you studied the Second Hindu Bible?" This roused the boatman and he replied: "Sir, I tell you definitely that I know nothing about the Second Hindu Bible." To this the Hindu Philosopher in cool amusement replied: "Mr. Boatman, I am very sorry to declare unto you that 50 per cent of your life is lost."

The boatman angrily settled down to his work at the oars. Now the boat had reached the middle of the river and the wind was blowing a little strong, when for the third time the Hindu Philosopher's eyes glistened with superiority and he demanded: "Mr. Boatman, tell me, have you studied the Third Hindu Bible?" By this time the boatman was beside himself with wrath and shouted: "Mr. Philosopher, I am sorry you cannot find anybody else to practice your knowledge upon. I told you, I don't know anything about the Hindu Bibles."

The Philosopher, in great, gloating triumph, with a mimicry of wisdom resounding in his voice, nonchalantly declared: "Mr. Boatman. I am sorry to announce unto you that 75 per cent of your life is lost." The boatman kept mumbling and somehow swallowed the words of this impossible Philosopher.

Ten more minutes passed, when suddenly a demon of a storm seared the veils of the clouds and sprang ever the waters of the river Ganges, lashing it into furiously excited waves. The boat began to rock like a little floating leaf in the tumultuous madly raging current of the river. The Philosopher kept shivering and trembling, while the boatman with a smile of assurance on his face looked at the Hindu Philosopher and asked: "Mr. Philosopher, you pelted me with so many questions, may I ask you one?" Receiving an affirmative reply, the boatman asked "O, Mr. Hindu Philosopher, knower of the Four Hindu Bibles, you established that 75 per cent of my life was lost; now can I ask you a question: Do you know how to swim?" To this the Hindu Philosopher tremblingly replied: "No, no, dear boatman, I cannot swim." Then the boatman, with victorious indifference smilingly replied: "Mr. Hindu Philosopher, knower of the Four Hindu Bibles, I am sorry to declare unto you that 100 per cent of your life is soon going to be lost."

Just at that moment , as if by way of fulfillment of the prophecy of the boatman, a furious gust of storm upset the boat, drowning the Philosopher, and the boatman, by powerful strokes, overcome the waves and reached the shores of the Ganges in safety.

You realize the moral of the story that, no matter if you are prosperous or powerful, until you learn the art of right behavior and right living, you will drown in the sea of difficulty. But, if you know the art of swimming across life's tumultuous river, by initiating the right actions at the right time, then, with powerful strokes of will power, you can buffet all tests of life and reach the shores of complete contentment.

HEALTH CULTURE

HEALING LAWS God wants His children to enjoy health and happiness, but they create disease and sorrow by breaking His laws. God is harmony, and when man, made in His image, tries to lead an Inharmonious life, he hurts himself. God never punishes man. Man punishes himself by reaping the results of his self- created wrong actions.

There are diseases which result from breaking hygienic laws and the consequent bacterial invasion. There are maladies which result from disobeying the mental laws of Being, and the consequent attack of mental bacteria of fear, anger, worry, greed, temptation, and lack of self-control. -There are diseases which arise from the Soul's ignorance. Do not forget, that ignorance is the mother of all physical, mental, and Spiritual diseases. Abolish ignorance by contacting God and forthwith body, mind, and Soul will be healed of all maladies.

DIETARY HINTS 1 . Fast one day a week on orange juice and take a suitable laxative (which is not a drug) prescribed by your doctor.

2. Include the following every day, combined with your regular diet for each meal: In the morning, orange juice and ground nuts. Luncheon should be the heaviest meal of the day. Combine with your lunch, 16 leaves of uncooked spinach, any fresh salad, any kind of cooked vegetable, and any protein except meat or fish. Milk should be between meals. Whole wheat bread and butter. At night, fruits of any kind and nuts.

3. A three day fast once a month on orange juice with a laxative each day will expel almost all poisons, and will do much to make the body strong, healthy, and youthful to the last days of life.

FORTNIGHTLY INSPIRATION

"0, Conscious, Cosmic Energy, it is Thou who dost directly support my body. Solid, liquid, and gaseous foods are converted and spiritualized into energy by Thy Cosmic Energy, and it supports my body. Help me to learn, 0 Spirit, to live more and more by direct Cosmic Energy and less and less by food. Being energy, burning in the bulb of the senses, I recharge myself with Thy Cosmic Energy."

FORTNIGHTLY AFFIRMATION

"0 Eternal Energy! awaken within me Conscious Will, Conscious vitality, Conscious Health, Conscious Realization. Good-will to all. Vitality to all. Good Health to all, Realization to all. Eternal youth of body and mind abide in me forever, forever, forever!"

ETERNITY

Oh, will that day arrive
When I shall ceaselessly ask,
And drive Eternal questions
Into Thine ear, O Eternity,
And have solution
How weak weeds grow and stand unbent,
Unshak'n beneath the trampling current;
How the storm wrecked titanic things;
Uprooted trees;
And quick disturbed the mighty seas;
How the first spark blinked,
And the first tree;
The first goldfish;
The first blue bird so free
And the first crooning baby
In this wonder house made
Their visit and entry.
They came, I see;
Their growth alone I watch.
Thy Cosmic Mouldering Hand
That secret works on land and sea;
I wish to seize,
O Eternity.

"Bless me, that I may behold nothing but that which is good. Teach me; that I may touch nothing but purity. Train me that I may listen only to Thy Voice in all good speech and in the beauty of songs. Direct me to inhale only the breath of purity—exuding perfumes from flowers of spirit. Invite me to indulge in wholesome tastes of soul-nourishing food. Teach me to touch that which reminds me of Thy touch."

THE ART OF REJUVENATION
PART II.
RELATION OF WILL POWER TO ENERGY

Self-Realization is the KNOWING, in all parts of the body, mind and Soul, that we are now in possession of the Omnipresence of God; that we do not have to pray that it come to us; that we are not merely near it at all times, but that God's Omnipresence is our Omnipresence; that He is just as much a part of us now as He will ever be, and that all we have to do is to improve our KNOWING.

To those who can consciously realize this at every moment, no instruction can be given, for all knowledge is theirs; it is all theirs; it is all there is of religion. For those who are not immediately able to comprehend this and consciously yield their existence to the recognition of this Truth, whose very simplicity forms the greatest bar to its acceptance and understanding, certain suggestions and methods are available by which complete understanding may be realized, and these methods comprise the work of the YOGODA SAT-SANGA.

The material human consciousness cannot grasp the Universal Consciousness within itself, no matter how desirous it is to do so, but when the student, by the methods of Self-Realization, through concentration and meditation, enlarges the caliber of his consciousness and raises its quality, he can perceive the Universal Consciousness in all atoms. This what is meant by "Received Him." Thus all Souls can actually find their Souls One with Cosmic Consciousness, by intuitive Self-Realization. They can know themselves as "Sons of God."

THE PHYSICAL BODY

The physical body is a combination of cells which are made of moving molecules. These cellular molecules are made of whirling atoms, protons, and electrons. These cellular and molecular atoms and electrons in turn are made of semi-intelligent sparks of God's thoughts. Therefore, we see that the physical body is a bundle of motions. On the surface of this body is found the chemical motions and dance of cells. Below the surface of the waves of the chemical and cellular motion is found the dancing waves of molecular motion. Below the molecular motion move the waves of atomic motion. Below the atomic motion is found the electro-protonic motion. Below the electro-protonic motion is found the dancing waving sparks of the vital forces. Below the surface of the vital sparks lie the waves of sensation. Below the waves of sensation lie the waves of thought, feeling, and will-force. Below all the above layers of waves the Ego is found to remain hidden.

On the surface, the body appears to be a solid mass, occupying a small portion of space, but we see that these cellular, waves are manifestations of a vaster area of dancing molecular waves. Likewise, the molecular waves are manifestations of a vaster area of atomic waves. The atomic waves are manifestations of vaster electro-protonic waves. The electronic waves are manifestations of the vast forces of all forms of sub- consciousness, super-consciousness, and Cosmic Consciousness.

On the surface, the body as chemical motion is small and dependent upon chemicals drawn from the earth, and upon food, water, and sunshine, but on the internal side the body and its chemical cellular motions are nothing but condensed waves of Cosmic Consciousness.

Therefore, the body as a solid substance occupies a very small space, but since the body on the internal side is condensed Cosmic Consciousness, it is very vast and ever Omnipresent.

Tissue is the general name for all the different forms of materials of which the body is composed. Then again, the same invisible force biologically so arranges the cells that some form into hard bones wonderfully worked into a skeleton frame, around which the flesh can cling.

This superstructure of flesh and bones has, on the external side, been made dependent upon the ultra-violet ray in the sunshine, and upon oxygen, good food, and pure liquids, such as water, fruit juices, and so forth. On the internal side these living cells, which constitute the flesh, bones, and all tissues, are kept rejuvenated by thoughts and biological forces.

It is very strange that the chemical motions of the body have to be kept alive and dancing by the forces of food, chemicals, and sunshine, while it would be entirely possible to keep them alive and flooded with vitality from the inner source of Cosmic Consciousness, but the body being motion, cannot live without motion; hence it has to be kept stirred with life externally by food forces, and internally it has to be kept dancing with vitality derived from Cosmic Consciousness.

THE POWER OF WILL Mechanical exercises generally teach one to concentrate upon the muscles and to consider oneself a muscular Being only. They help to stimulate the animal consciousness in man and not his subtle nature. Self-Realization Instruction teaches the science ignored by most exercises. It teaches its students how to concentrate upon their life energy and Will Power, awakening the consciousness of their subtle Spiritual nature. It teaches its students that strength comes from within and not from the muscles, and that Life does not depend solely upon food or exercise, but is sustained from the powers within. For example, a dead man artificially made to exercise with dumb-bells does not become strong, nor does he live if his stomach is stuffed with food, since his Life Energy is absent. Self-Realization Instructions teach one to spiritualize the body, which is the reflection of the Spirit. It teaches one to consider oneself as the Life Energy and not a body consisting of bones and muscles with a certain weight. It shows how by TENSION, energy can be put forth in the body, and by RELAXATION it can be withdrawn from it. Since expenditure of Life Energy is involved in all processes of thought, feeling, and physical activity, Self-Realization Instruction shows how to replenish the reckless expenditure of energy by tapping at its source. It teaches that the seat of Life Energy is the Medulla Oblongata. It shows that this Life Energy can be continually supplied to the body by stimulating it by the power of Conscious Will. The Will serves to bridge the gulf existing between the Life Energy in the body and the Cosmic Energy surrounding it. It teaches one how to work without fatigue by keeping in touch with Cosmic Life Energy.

All limbs and muscles are moved by the exercise of Will and Life Energy. The flow of Life Energy into the sensory nerves is caused by Divine Will and your own Will; into the motor nerves by your own Will. The greater the Will, the greater the flow of Life Energy into a particular body part. Angry men and angry animals manifest abnormal strength. This abnormal strength is not due to their muscles growing stronger within the short period of their anger. Their Will is stimulated by anger and causes an extra flow of Life Energy or strength into their muscles and bodies.

Most mechanical physical culture systems ignore the above facts, and because they use only unconscious mechanical will, their exercises consist of muscle - bumping. Such exercises do not cause a sufficient flow of Life Energy into the muscles and tissues used. If you follow the teachings of Self-Realization Instruction, you will learn how to vitalize every body cell.

RELAXATION AND TENSION

The activity of life consists principally in expressing motion and consciousness in the muscles, limbs, and bodily organs. Relaxation means the release of the energy and consciousness which have been employed by the entire body, or any of its parts, during mental or physical activity. Man receives sensation coming from outside stimulation through his eyes, ears, nose, tongue, and skin surface by means of the impulses which travel through the sensory nerves, and he responds to sensations by sending energy back through the strings of motor nerves which causes tension or contraction of the muscles.

Tension results from willing to send energy to any muscle. Lift your right arm. Now ask yourself what powers are used in the lifting of the arm. You will say: "Will power." But think, if your arm became paralyzed, your will to lift it would still be present, but still you would not be able to raise it. Why? Because the energy could not flow freely through the nerves into the muscles of the arm. But if the arm were healed, you would again be able to lift it by willing.

Look at your right arm resting at your side, throbbing with energy. Can you lift it without willing? No, you cannot. Therefore, remember that you use both ENERGY and WILL in the lifting and moving of the limbs or any part of the body.

ENERGY AND WILL

Experiment: Lift your right arm forward, shoulder high, parallel to the ground with palm up. Close your left hand and place it on your upturned right palm, pressing downward as if your left hand weighed about five pounds. Resist this pressure by tensing the right arm. Increase the pressure of the left hand to ten pounds. Will to hold it and increase the tension by willing to send more energy to the right arm. Now increase the pressure with the left hand to fifteen pounds and will to hold it by increasing the tension in the right arm to hold the greater weight. You can do this weight lifting exercise mentally without pressure or use of weights, as shown in the following:

Relax and drop your arms to your side. Again lift your right arm parallel to the ground with upturned palm. Hold it there. Now realize that a certain amount of Will and Energy holds your arm in this position. If you take the will away from the uplifted right arm, the arm will fall, drawn by gravity, and hang by your side; or it will fall if the nerves ore suddenly cut, or paralyzed, or if the energy is withdrawn.

Now raise your right arm and tense it as much as is required to hold an imaginary weight of five pounds. Then tense it stronger, to hold an imaginary increased weight of ten pounds. Then tense stronger still to hold an imaginary increased weight of fifteen pounds. Now relax and drop your arm.

When holding actual or imaginary pressure or weight of five pounds, you have to will to hold it, and accordingly you use the amount of Energy necessary to hold it. Likewise, when you will to hold an increased weight of ten or fifteen pounds, you increase your Will and the amount of Energy sent to the arm in order to hold the greater weight.

It may now be seen that we experience weight according to the degree of Will and amount of Energy spent in lifting it. This experiment of lifting imaginary weights proves that an act of pure consciousness or Will produces actual Energy in a body part. "Will is the invisible switch of consciousness which sends Energy to any body part and produces tension in that part.

If you touch the two poles of an electric battery, your hands will be energized and tensed. If you drink milk or eat food when tired, you will feel added Energy in your body. You produce this Energy in the body through electricity or food, through some outward material agency introduced in the body. But in tensing or energizing your right arm, or any body part, with Will, you produce Energy in the arm or the body part purely by the power of consciousness or will. By imagining that you are sending Energy to the right arm, you may succeed in sending a faint current there, but it is only by Willing that you can perceptibly send Energy. By energizing through tension, the great link between consciousness, Will, Energy and the body is found. By willing to energize the right arm (1) you rouse Energy felt as power and then (2) you create tension in the muscles. This shows that consciousness (Will), is the main factor in creating changes in the flow of Energy to muscles or to any body parts.

Also, in lifting weights by Will Power, the great relation between Will and Energy is found. The greater the Will, the greater the amount of Energy and Tension in any body part.

(Technique of Rejuvenation continued in next Praeceptum)

THE APOLOGUE
(For the Entire Family)
THE MOUSE WHO BECAME A TIGER

A dark forest inhabited by wild animals, encompassed the holy city of Benares, in India, in the bowels of this deep jungle lay a beautiful Hermitage where lived a great, God-known Saint who possessed many miraculous powers. This holy man had no one near to him in this the dangers of ferocious tigers and wild beasts of the forest in order to visit the great Saint, and all brought offerings of fruits and flowers. No disciple ever goes empty handed to his Master, who gives the disciple priceless Spiritual treasures. Everyone who came to visit the Saint marveled at the great friendship between him and the mouse, and everyday threw tidbits to this Sage's pet, who was universally known as the Saint's Mouse.

One day, when a group of students were visiting the great Master at this secluded Hermitage, they found the mouse being chased by a cat, and he ran squeaking at the feet of the Master Sage for protection. The Sage stopped the cat from its work of crime, and right before the wondering gaze of his students, changed the little trembling mouse into a huge, ferocious cat. The metamorphosed mouse henceforth fearlessly went unmolested in the company of cats. The mouse was happy and only resented it when some of the old disciples would exclaim: "0, look at the Saint's glorified mouse-cat."

One day, while the same group of students was visiting the Master, the cat was being wildly pursued by jungle dogs and came mewing at top speed for protection at the feet of the Sage. The Sage exclaimed: "I am tired of saving you from the vicious dogs. From now on, be thou a wild dog. The disciples were amazed to see the bewilderment and disappointed retirement of the wild dogs, when they suddenly, right before their eyes, saw the mouse-cat changed into a dog. The mouse-dog became friendly with the other wild dogs, playing with them and eating the same food with them in a scornful sense of superiority.

On another occasion, while the group of students was studying with the Master, to their utter dismay they found a full-grown Royal Bengal Tiger chasing the mouse-dog, who was racing for shelter at the feet of the sage. The Master, by his miraculous powers, petrified the tiger and exclaimed: "Mr. Mouse, I am sick of constantly protecting you from your enemies throughout the day and night, so you must be a tiger henceforth." No sooner had the Saint said this than the mouse-dog became transformed into a very wild tiger. The students, relieved of their fear, laughed heartily, exclaiming: " Look at that Saint's wild tiger.

He is only a glorified mouse. As days went by and the visitors to the Hermitage found out that the fearsome tiger patrolling the place was no other than an uplifted mouse through the miracle of the Saint, then, often some sarcastic students would be heard saying to who were afraid of this tiger: "Don't be nervous. That is not a tiger. It is only a mouse glorified into a tiger by the Master."

The mouse who became a tiger got tired of this popular affront constantly hurled at him.

So he thought: "If I could only kill the Saint then the constant memory of my disgrace as his transformed mouse could be removed." Thinking this, the mouse-tiger sprang to try to kill the Sage, to the great consternation of his disciples.

In an instant, beholding the audacious ingrate motive of his transformed pet, the Sage loudly commanded: "Be thou a mouse again," and lo, the roaring tiger was transformed into a squeaking little mouse.

Now remember, dear friends, most of you forget that by using God- given will power you have changed from a little human mouse, squeaking with failure and fear, into a brave tiger of industry and power, but forget not that if you try to be antagonistic to that power, you may change again from a tiger of power to a mortal mouse of failure. So, never forget God while you perform your duties but, no matter what duties you are performing, always, in the background of your mind, hum a silent devotional song of love to your beloved Heavenly Father.

HEALTH CULTURE

HEALING LAWS All that is necessary in rejuvenating the body is to supply it with the sixteen elements of food chemicals which it needs, plus sunshine from regular sunbaths and good oxygen, and from regular, proper breathing. While walking every day, inhale, counting one to twelve. Hold the breath twelve counts, then exhale, counting one to twelve. Do that twenty four times every time you walk. Everyone must have at least a half hour sunbath twice a week, or preferably, every day. The mind must never have suggested to it the human limitations of sickness, old age, and death, but it should be constantly, inwardly told: "I am the infinite, which has become the body. The body as a manifestation of Spirit is the ever-youthful Spirit."

DIETARY LAWS

Lunch for People with Sedentary Habits

Eat a raw ground vegetable salad, a different one every day. Grind the vegetables. Use one handful of any ground nuts with vegetable salad. Six prunes, dates, or figs (unsulphured). Very small portion of cooked vegetables. Eat a little fresh cottage cheese.

Lunch for People with Normal Health

A big raw vegetable salad every day with orange and cream or nut dressing. Use a new vegetable every day. Grind the vegetables. A piece of whole wheat bread or one bran muffin and bread. One cooked vegetable. Six unsulphured prunes or such dates or such figs. Drink no water with meals. Occasionally you may eat a piece of fish broiled, if you are a non-vegetarian. Eat your biggest meal at lunch time. One tablespoonful of honey. Juice of one lemon.

FORTNIGHTLY INSPIRATION

If the poor win victories by satisfying the demands of real necessities, they receive contentment and may live and die rich.

That is real prosperity. But to live in poor contentment and die spiritually poor in spite of material riches, is real poverty. Be prosperous by smiling, no matter what happens. Do not be afraid to sell the bonds of smiling when the market of happiness is low. Keep smiling while planning and acting for success, and your smiles will fetch priceless treasures in the end. Wise, persevering activity, with unfading smiles, brings sure success.

FORTNIGHTLY AFFIRMATION

"I am youthful, I am youth, I am healthy, I am health, I am strong, I am strength, I am joyful, I am joy, I am successful, I am success, I am peaceful, I am peace, I am Immortal, I am Immortality."

HEALTH! PEACE! IMMORTALITY!

YOGODA SAT-SANGA FORTNIGHTLY INSTRUCTIONS
BY

PARAMHANSA YOGANANDA
(To be Confidentially Reserved FOR MEMBER'S USE ONLY)

God! God! God!

From the depths of slumber,
As I ascend the spiral stairway of wakefulness,
I will whisper:
God! God! God!
Thou art the food, and when
I break my fast Of nightly separation from Thee,
I will taste Thee, and mentally say:
God! God! God!
No matter where I go, the spotlight of my mind
Will ever keep turning on Thee;
And in the battle din of activity,
My silent war cry will be:
God! God! God!
When boisterous storms of trials shriek,
And worries howl at me,
I will drown their noise by loudly chanting:
God! God! God!
When my mind weaves dreams
With threads of memories,
Then on that magic cloth will I emboss:
God! God! God!
Every night, in time of deepest sleep,
My peace dreams and calls, Joy! Joy! Joy!
And my joy comes singing evermore:
God! God! God!
In waking, eating, working, dreaming, sleeping,
Serving, meditation, chanting, divinely loving,
My Soul will constantly hum, unheard by any:
God! God! God!

PRAYER TO PRECEDE THE PRAECEPTUM STUDY

"I come to Thee with the song of my smiles. The taper of my happiness will merge with Thy Blaze of Bliss. The aroma of Thy Scented Flame and its murmuring joyous waves come floating to me. In Thy enchanting Light I will swim forever. Teach me to drown in Thy Divine Light and life, rather than live in a mirage paradise of earthliness and die."

THE ART OF REJUVENATION
PART III.

(Review the preceding Parts, I and II, to continue the thread of thought and to strengthen the foundation for the Technique of Rejuvenation.)

All Scriptures, such as the Bhagavad Gita or the Christian Bible ha[ve] a three-fold meaning. In other words, the Scriptures deal with the three factors of human existence; namely, the material, the mental, and the Spiritual. Hence, all true Scriptures have been so written that they serve to be beneficial to the body, mind, and the Soul of man. True Scriptures are like the wells of Divine waters, which can quench the threefold material, mental and Spiritual thirsts of man.

Self-Realization may be, and is, attained by some people who are struggling with sick and otherwise imperfect bodies, but it cannot be attained unless you can learn to concentrate and meditate uninterruptedly upon God. Since it is difficult to concentrate and meditate while the aches and pains of the body continually have the attention of the mind, the path of Self-Realization is made much easier if the imperfections of the body and the harmonious operations of its functions are arranged so that the mind need not at any time be interrupted in meditation through the demands of the physical body.

You will find in this series of Praecepta the knowledge by which you learn to live more and more by calling upon the eternal supply Cosmic Energy, which is ever available to us, which is within and without, and is always all about us, and thus recharge the body at any and at all times with vitality. With this knowledge, the body may be made fit in all respects, and a perfect body, free from disease, presents less resistance to the methods and practices by which Self Realization is reached, and by which the human consciousness, as well as the body, is raised to the fatigueless state.

People usually concentrate upon food, air, and sunshine only in order to keep the body well, but a time comes to everyone when health fails in spite of all the outer means of good food and air supplied to it. Then it is realized that the Body Battery has to be recharged by the Inner Source also.

THE BODY BATTERY

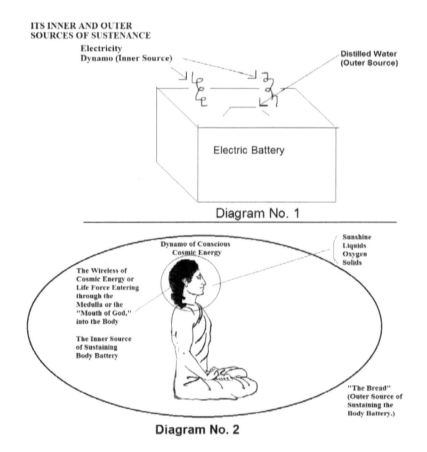

ITS INNER AND OUTER
SOURCES OF SUSTENANCE

Electricity
Dynamo (Inner Source)

Distilled Water
(Outer Source)

Electric Battery

Diagram No. 1

Dynamo of Conscious
Cosmic Energy

Sunshine
Liquids
Oxygen
Solids

The Wireless of
Cosmic Energy or
Life Force Entering
through the
Medulla or the
"Mouth of God,"
into the Body

The Inner Source
of Sustaining
Body Battery

"The Bread"
(Outer Source of
Sustaining the
Body Battery.)

Diagram No. 2

An automobile battery depends for its life not upon its indirect outer source of distilled water alone, but upon the vibrating electric current which flows into it from the dynamo through the mouth of the wires (the direct Inner Source). Self-Realization Instruction teaches that just as an automobile battery needs both distilled water and electricity to keep it alive, so the Body Battery needs recharging with Life Force through the medulla as well as food and the physical means of sustaining life. Just like the saints of India, Jesus centuries ago, gave utterance to the great Truth that man's Body Battery is charged by the "Word of God" (Inner Energy) and not by outer sources alone.

IMPORTANCE OF RELAXATION

TESTS OF PHYSICAL RELAXATION When you are sitting or lying down completely relaxed with breath expelled, let somebody lift your hands or feet a little way, then drop them. If they fall with a thud, without your gradually lowering them, you are relaxed. Let someone lift you up and shake your whole body. If your limbs register no resistance but fly loosely hither and thither like the limbs of a rag doll, you are relaxed.

In perfect relaxation, no muscles are consciously willed to become energized and tensed. Do not tense any part, especially the neck, arms, torso, and legs. By relaxing the muscles and limbs, you help to remove motion and decay from the outward body.

TESTS OF MENTAL RELAXATION   You have attained mental relaxation when you can remain without thought for any length of time desired, and when you can bring the consciousness back into the body at will. When you can remain calm at all times in spite of severe trials, and when you are launched in undying faith in God and your Guru, then you are mentally relaxed.

FIVE STAGES OF MENTAL RELAXATION   1. Most people are so restless all the time that they cannot close their eyes and keep the eyeballs still, keep the body motionless, or concentrate upon one thing at time even for a little while. Such people develop a second nature, which is "Restless all the time without ever being restful." This is the first state.

2.   Then, by the practice of meditation, the above-mentioned all-the-time-mentally-restless person succeeds in becoming "once in a great while restful; not restless all the time." This is the second state of mental relaxation.

3.   Then, by further practice of concentration and meditation, the student reaches the place where he is able to become restful easily, or easily restless at anytime, anywhere. This is the third state.

4.   By deeper practice of concentration and meditation and the higher Lessons from his Guru-Preceptor, the student reaches the fourth state, in which he is "restful most of the time, and only once in a while restless." This is the opposite of the second state. By scientific meditation, you can reverse your nature from restlessness to calmness.

5.   By the practice of the highest Lessons from his Guru- Preceptor, when the student becomes One with God in Samadhi, (Oneness in which the devotee, meditation, and God become one), he reaches the last, or fifth, state of relaxation and Self- Realization, in which he is "restful all the time without ever becoming restless." This state is the reverse of the first state, and can be attained only by being able to invoke Samadhi at will, anytime, anywhere.

SPECIAL KINDS OF RELAXATION

1.   Imperfect Muscular Relaxation. Most people are imperfectly relaxed or partially tensed. In this state the energy and consciousness are only partly or imperfectly withdrawn from certain muscles, limbs, and organs, but not from the five senses of touch, taste, smell, hearing, and sight. This is termed imperfect relaxation. People cannot live in a state of continual partial tension because they became fatigued. This state is termed imperfect muscular relaxation.

2.   Partial Muscular Relaxation. Throwing the breath out (exhaling completely), and remaining without breath as long as it can be done comfortably, calms the action of the lungs and diaphragm, and slows the heart action, and thereby helps to remove the greater amount of motion and decay from the active internal organs of the body. The state when the body, limbs, lungs, and diaphragm are inactive, and the heart is partially calm, is called almost perfect inner and outer muscular and motor relaxation.

3.   Unconscious Sensory Motor Relaxation. In sleep, the consciousness is switched off from the muscles and the inner organs and from the bulbs of the five senses. The Life Energy is switched off from the senses, muscles, and motor nerves, and partially from the heart, lungs, and diaphragm. This state is called unconscious sensory motor relaxation.

4.   Conscious Sensory Motor Relaxation. By the studious practice of the Meditation and Concentration Techniques for a number of years, one can consciously withdraw energy and the mind from the senses and muscles while still remaining conscious.

5.   Unconscious Perfect Sensory-Motor-Organic Relaxation. Death is spoken of as unconscious perfect sensory-motor-organic relaxation. It is the forced switching off of the consciousness and of the life current from the entire body, limbs, muscles, senses, organs, heart, spine, and so forth. Just as the electricity retires into the dynamo when a bulb is broken, so, when the body completely stops activity, the life current, and consciousness, return to the dynamo of Cosmic Energy and Cosmic Consciousness, It must be remembered that as long as the wires to a certain point are not destroyed, a broken bulb at the end of them can be replaced by a new bulb. In the same way, as long as the earthly wires of Soul desire running out of the dynamo of Spirit remain undestroyed and connected with the earth and its attractions, it is necessary for new body bulbs to be replaced as often as one body bulb breaks (goes out at death). But when all the wires of earthly desire are cut, then reincarnation of the Spiritual current in the bulb of flesh ceases, just as the destruction of certain wires completely withdraws and stops all currents from returning through them to the dynamo. Death signifies the complete destruction of the body bulb, but not of the desire wires behind it.

6.   Conscious-Sensory-Motor-Organic Relaxation. Conscious-sensory-motor-organic relaxation consists in the switching off and on at will of the Life Current and of the consciousness in the limbs, muscles, inner organs, lungs, diaphragm, and especially in the heart and spine. This kind of conscious, higher relaxation, by the brake of calmness, is to be taught in later Praecepta.

   The above six forms of relaxation are best illustrated by the various stages of bright, semi-bright, less bright, dim, more dim, completely dim, lights as produced in a bulb to which the dimming apparatus is attached. The various stages of relaxation represent the withdrawing or dimming of the consciousness and Life Current from the bulb of the body. In full bodily activity, as in running, the Bulb of Life is fully brightly ablaze with life. In the imperfect relaxation, it is semi- illumined with life. In perfect relaxation, the life-light is less bright. In sleep, the life-light is dim and calm. In meditation, the life- light is more dim and calm. In conscious trance, the Life Energy retires from the body bulb, but is ready to be switched.

on again at will. In death, the body bulb is broken, but in conscious sensory motor relaxation one learns to switch off consciousness and Life Current from the body and to switch them on again at will. This power gives victory over death.

The Principles and Technique of Rejuvenation will be concluded in the next Praeceptum).

THE APOLOGUE
(For the Entire Family)
THAT MORAL BACKBONE

Long ago there lived a poisonous hooded snake near a rock outside a village. This reptile killed many of the children in the village with its death-dealing fangs, and every attempt of the villagers to kill this sly snake failed, so, as a last resort, the villagers visited their holy man, who lived in a secluded spot in the village, and demanded: "Holy Master, please use your Spiritual powers to prevent the snake from continuing its gruesome work of murdering our little children." Thereupon, the Saint agreed to comply with their request.

Finally, the holy man went near the place where the snake lived, and by the magnetic power of His Divine love induced the snake to come out. Then the Saint commanded: "Mr. Snake, desist from biting to death my dear people of the village. Practice non- violence." With humbled hood the snake promised. The Saint then went on a pilgrimage, and after a year, as he was returning to the village, he passed by the rock where the snake lived and he thought of the snake, wondering if it had kept its promise. To his astonishment he found the snake lying in a pool of blood with seven stitches in its back.

When asked what was the matter with him, the snake in a feeble voice replied: "Holy Preceptor, I have seven stitches in my back as a result of your teachings. Ever since the village children found out that I was harmless, they have pelted me with stones whenever I went out in search of food. I ducked in and out of my hole many times, but still I received seven fractures in my spire. Master, at first they fled at sight of me, but now, due to your teachings of non-violence, I have to flee from them."

The Hindu Master patted the snake on the back and healed him, and then smilingly rebuked him, saying: "You little fool, I told you not to bite, but why didn't you hiss?"

So, remember, when you are too much imposed upon by people and friends who want to get the best of you, do not be spineless, and yet do not inject the poison of injury into them, but, rather, scare them by 'hissing' them out of your sight.

HEALTH CULTURE

HEALING LAWS Obey God's physical laws of hygiene and proper eating, and keep yourself mentally disinfected by the strong faith that nothing can harm you, that you are always protected. There is a Syrian proverb: "The enemy of man is his stomach." Remember that this bodily machinery has been given to you to enable you to accomplish certain works on this material plane, and that you should guard it and take care of it as your previous possession. The chief abuse of the body lies in overloading it with unnecessary food.

Eat sparingly and notice the great change in your health for the better. The proper combinations and quality of food should also not be overlooked. A supply of raw fruits, vegetables, and nuts should be included in the regular diet.

FASTING Fast one day a week, or at least half a day. If you feel unable to do that, live for one day on nothing but orange juice (when available), or some other light food. This plan will give needed rest to the body-machine, which overworks incessantly through over-eating or wrong eating. Do not think that satisfied hunger means satisfied body needs. Learn the laws of rational, scientific diet, and live on simple and wholesome food.

Reducing by fasting sometimes upsets the stomach. This condition can be prevented by frequent drinking of a small glassful of buttermilk or orange juice mixed with a small amount of lemon juice.

FORTNIGHTLY INSPIRATION

Realize that you really are not a fleshly Being and that in reality you are neither a Hindu nor a Christian, nor any of the other limited sense-bound things you appear to be. It is wrong to say that we are mortals, whereas we are essentially made of immortal stuff. It is the truth that we are Gods, and it is wrong to call ourselves weaklings. It is only by realizing our Oneness with God that we can completely break our self-created imaginary limitations of accidents, failure, lack, disease, and death. God has everything -health, efficiency, and wisdom - and to be One with Him is to have claim over everything which He has, as His own Child.

FORTNIGHTLY AFFIRMATION

"The Lord is my strength and song, and He is become my salvation: He is my God, and I will prepare Him an habitation."

HEALTH! STRENGTH! POWER!

YOGODA SAT-SANGA FORTNIGHTLY
INSTRUCTION PARAMHANSA YOGANANDA
(To be Confidentially Reserved FOR
MEMBER'S USE ONLY)

'TIS ALL UNKNOWN

Each rosebud dawning day,
In hourly opening petal rays
Doth fair display
Its hidden beauty.
The petal hours unfolding smile, My
drooping, lagging heart beguile.
Day spreads its petals all
Of novel hopes and joys withal.
The rosebud's there, —
"Today" is here;
In time the rosebud blooms, —
While lazy day oft glooms. Forsake
Thy sleep
0, Lazy Day!
Open Thou with thy full blown ray
To chase my gathered gloom away!
The rosebud opened,
The day now smiled
In fullness fine;
Still I opine
'Tis all unknown
Just why the rose was blown,
And the day was drowned in night
Then raised again to light
Of glorious dawn.
So swiftly marching o'er the lawn!

PRAYER TO PRECEDE THE PRAECEPTUM STUDY

"Divine Mother, ignite our earthliness with the flame of Infinity. With the torch of our devotion, blaze our dark indifference, our restlessness and our ignorance. Inflame out minds with Thy Thoughts! Inflame our hearts with Thy Love! Inflame our Souls with Thy Joy!"minds with Thy Thoughts! Inflame our hearts with Thy Love! Inflame our Souls with Thy Joy!"

THE ART OF REJUVENATION
PART IV.

(Review the preceding Parts, I, II, and III, to continue the thread of thought and to strengthen the foundation for the Technique of Rejuvenation.)

"TENSE WITH WILL: RELAX AND FEEL"

We now come to the Technique of Recharging the Body Battery, by which you may learn how to draw more and more life-sustaining energy from the other, and depend less and less upon solids, liquids, sunshine, and gases for sustenance.

Food contains a limited part of Life Energy, hence we can extract strength from food, but if the internal supply of Life Energy is exhausted, food is of no use. Therefore, we should not only utilize the advice presented in the Health Culture Division of the Fortnightly Praecepta for the sustenance of the human body from the Outer Source of Energy, but should also emphasize and daily apply the method of recharging the body with Energy from the Inner Source.

INNER SOURCE OF ENERGY The exercises in The Art of Rejuvenation show how to recharge the body battery, by Will, thus supplying Energy from the inner source. Now comes the question: "How can we recharge the body battery?" First, lift your arm, then drop it. What lifted your arm? Will Power and Energy. Now close your eyes. Can you lift your arm without willing to do so? Can Will Power alone do it?

No. It requires Will Power and Energy. But how do Will Power and Energy do this? The answer is: By flowing into the different parts of the body. We want healthy muscles, bones, marrow, blood, and tissues, and in each of these the Energy is like a battery. The supply of Energy depends upon the chemicals you take into the body and the Energy taken in through the medulla. Good health does not consist in energization of the muscles alone. The cells in every body part must be energized. To teach you how to recharge the cells in every body part is the purpose of this series of Praecepta.

Now lift your am. What is holding your am up? Will power and Energy, you say. Good. If you do not use Will Power to keep it up, it will drop. So also with Energy. Will Power is the switch which controls the flow of Energy. EXERCISE IN Sit on a chair. Tense the whole body and then relax, GENERAL TENSION keeping the body motionless. Then bend forward with arms down, and, clasping your hands together, hold an imaginary cord which is tied to on imaginary weight of 25 pounds. Now tense the hands and add the strength of the tensed hands to that of the tensed forearms. Then add the tensed upper arms; then tie to them, tensed chest, abdomen, haunches, thighs, legs, and feet. Then will to lift the 25 pounds and send enough Energy and Will Power to lift it one inch from the ground. Now tense harder and continue lifting the weight higher. It is very heavy. Now the imaginary weight has left the ground about an inch, two inches, six inches, on to one foot. Then drop your imaginary weight, relax your whole body, and sit back on your chair, relaxed and motionless.

When you grow stronger, lift imaginary weights of 30 to 40 pounds. The best way to know what the exact degree of Will Power and the exact amount of Energy is required to lift an imaginary weight of 25 pounds (or any amount) is to actually lift that weight and feel how much Will and Energy are required. Then relax. Then try to employ the exact amount of tension required to lift an imaginary weight of the some number of pounds.

SCIENTIFIC TENSION AND RELAXATION Tension results when Energy is sent by Will to any muscle. There are varying degrees of tension, depending upon the amount of Energy sent to the muscles. We shall consider three degrees, which we shall call low, medium, and high tension. Low is a small amount of Energy; medium is more; and high is as much as possible. The withdrawal of Energy from the muscles is called relaxation. This may also be in three stages or degrees, resulting in partial or complete relaxation.

Usually, you must relax before you tense. The popular method of relaxation results when you tell a person to relax while he is sitting, standing, or lying down, and he usually moves his limbs, and while keeping them tensed tries to rest. Then he thinks he is physically relaxed. Even as an automobile standing at your door with the engine running, burns energy, so also, many people while sleeping, sitting, or lying down, are partly tensed, (low, medium, or high) according to their degree of mental nervousness, and are thus burning energy even when their bodies are apparently at rest.

When you move your body or arm to relax it, and keep moving it, you have not relaxed (withdrawn Energy) but are really tensing (sending Energy) to it instead.

Now, after learning the art of producing relaxation and tension in any of the 20 body parts, the student must learn the greatest exercise of recharging the whole body.

SELF-REALIZATION EXERCISES

MECHANICAL AND WILL MOVEMENTS OF MUSCLES COMPARED

Example 1.

1. Extend the right arm in front.
2. Place the left hand upon the right biceps muscle.
3. Bend the right arm at the elbow, observing the automatic contraction of the biceps through the mechanical movement.

N. Note that the action of the WILL is in the bending of the arm B. and not in the contraction of the biceps.

Example 2.

1. Relax the right arm loosely at the side.
2. With the left hand grasp lightly the biceps of the right arm.
3. Close eyes,
4. Then, without bending right arm at the elbow, tense the biceps slowly to the maximum of force with WILL.
5. Sense the tension.
6. Permit no mechanical movement of the arm.
7. Then relax slowly.

N.B. Note that this tensing of the biceps, if done successfully by the novice, is the direct action of the WILL on the muscles. If the novice is not successful with the upper arm, let him make the experiment with the forearm, which may be easier for some people.

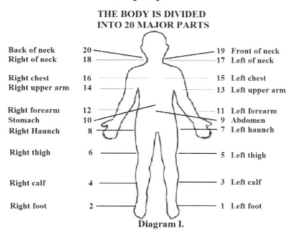

THE BODY IS DIVIDED INTO 20 MAJOR PARTS

Back of neck	20		19	Front of neck
Right of neck	18		17	Left of neck
Right chest	16		15	Left chest
Right upper arm	14		13	Left upper arm
Right forearm	12		11	Left forearm
Stomach	10		9	Abdomen
Right Haunch	8		7	Left haunch
Right thigh	6		5	Left thigh
Right calf	4		3	Left calf
Right foot	2		1	Left foot

Diagram I.

EXERCISE A. At dawn, when your consciousness first awakens in the body, practice the following exercise by lying on your back with closed eyes. Dogs and cars stretch and relax upon awakening, but man strips, his muscle gears by lumping from sleep to the floor, and by suddenly throwing the body in action in response to an alarm clock or telephone bell.

Lie down on the bed on your back, tense the whole body, (all 20 body parts simultaneously); hold tension, counting 1—2—3; then quickly relax and exhale. Feel the Energy and Will Power slipping away from the body. Remain perfectly still like a jelly fish without feeling the bones and flesh, and without moving any muscles as long as you like, and without breathing as long as you can comfortably do so.

THE TECHNIQUE OF REJUVENATION INDIVIDUAL

EXERCISE 1. TENSION AND RELAXATION

1.   Gently tense and relax each body part from 1 to 20, mentally saying: "My children, wake up." Hold the relaxation for a half minute without moving.

2.   Place the attention on the center of the instep of the left foot.

3.   Slowly tense the left foot, low, medium, and high, drawing the toes under.

4.   Keep it tensed. Continue on adding tension, low to high, with Will Power in the above mentioned same manner in all the 20 body parts, from feet to head (1 to 20) by tensing left foot, right foot, left calf, right calf, left thigh, right thigh, left haunch right haunch, contracting abdomen (below navel) and stomach (above navel). Then tense forearm left, forearm right, upper arm left, upper arm right, left breast, right breast, left of neck, right of neck, front of neck, back of neck, in slow, rhythmic succession.

5.   Gently retense and vibrate whole body, holding all 20 body parts tensed, breath held, mentally counting 1 to 6 and quickly noting mentally whether all body ports are tensed or not.

6.   Exhale and slowly relax the chain of tensed parts, head to feet in inverse order from 20 to 1. If, while relaxing the parts above the waist, you find that you have also unintentionally relaxed the parts below the waist; then simultaneously tense again all the parts below the waist and relax from waist down, one by one.

7.   Repeat the above technique once lying on bed, and twice out of bed, standing.

N.B.   a. The above technique can be practiced lying down or sitting in a chair, or while standing.

b.   Always practice the above technique with closed eyes and very slowly.

c.   Do not tense quickly or relax quickly, but gradually.

d.   Tense low any diseased or weak body part.

e.   To heal anybody part, gently tense and relax that part. Then tense low and hold that tension, counting 1 to 10 mentally, electrocuting the disease with recharged Energy. Then relax, Repeat 10 times, three times a day, or as often as you desire. Practice healing of any body part in the lying posture.

f.   By exhaling or throwing the breath out, you relax the lungs, diaphragm, and abdomen. You can do this exercise sitting, reclining, or standing. Of course, if standing you have to keep certain muscles of the feet calves, and thighs engaged and tensed in order to hold the body upright, or you will fall. Any time you feel tired or nervous tense the whole body gently and relax; that is, withdraw the Energy and Consciousness, and active Will Power, and quickly exhale; keep still, enjoy the quietness of the body.

Master this highly practical Technique of Rejuvenation by FAITHFUL and REGULAR practice for your own knowledge and benefit. Each step of the Self-Realization Exercises will give definite results which you can experience for yourself satisfactory and invigorating results in body and mind if you are

THE APOLOGUE
(For the Entire Family)
BUDDHA AND THE COURTESAN

In India, Buddha is considered one of the incarnations of God. He lived about 500 years before Christ and was the son of a King of India. He was married to a beautiful princess, Gopa, who gave birth to a little son. The royal father of Buddha had surrounded him with every conceivable luxury and beautiful surroundings. The young Prince Buddha grew to think of the world as a place where nothing existed but happy events.

Once prince Buddha secretly went out with his charioteer to see the world for himself, and was shocked to the very depth of his Being to see for the first time in his life a shriveled-up old man, a sick dying man, and a corpse. He looked at his celestially beautiful, healthy body and asked his charioteer if his body too would grow old and decay. Reluctantly the charioteer said: "0 Prince, all human flesh is subject to sickness, decrepitude, and death." After hearing this, Prince Buddha began to brood over the delusion of earthly life, until one night, while his wife and child slept on the altar of peace, with bedimmed tearful eyes he took a last look at them and left in quest of Truth, which would free mankind forever from sorrow and suffering and would give him complete understanding.

The Prince practiced many austerities prescribed by Hindu Yogis, and at last, after seven years of fasting and discipline, and meditation under a Banyan tree in Buddha Gaya, India, he found illumination. Then he ate and nourished his body and began to preach in India his gospel of mercy and equal love for all creatures, man and animal alike, and he taught complete renunciation and Nirvana, or the attaining of the state of desirelessness or freedom from Reincarnation. Later, Buddha's missionaries spread the gospel of Buddha all over India, Japan, China, and all over the world.

This state of "Nirvana," or cessation of dualistic existence, is misinterpreted by many as annihilation. Surely, Buddha didn't want the annihilation of Self. He meant cessation of the deluded Self and the birth of an Eternal Self. However, this doctrine rather emphasizes a negative state of being and the goal of ultimate attainment.

This doctrine of Buddha emphasized attainment of a negative state of Cosmic dissolution, so it was later supplanted by the positive doctrine of Swami Shankara, founder of the great Swami Order by his doctrine of the goal of life being the attainment of "The ever-conscious ever-new blissful state of Spirit."

In the course of his missionary travels, Buddha and his disciples came across a curious incident which, for a time extremely puzzled them as to the character of their Master. [While] Lord Buddha and his disciples were resting beneath the cool shade of a tree, a courtesan, attracted by the glowing body and face of the Master, came to him. No sooner had she seen the celestial face of the Lord Buddha than she fell in love with him, and, in the ecstasy of an overwhelming love, with open arms she ran to Buddha to embrace and kiss him, loudly exclaiming: "0 Beautiful, Shining One, I love Thee."

The celibate disciples were extremely astonished when they heard Buddha say to the courtesan: "Beloved, I love Thee too, but do not touch me now not yet."

The courtesan replied: "You call me Beloved and I love you, then why do you object to my touching you?"

The great Buddha replied: "Beloved, I tell thee again, I will touch thee later, but not now. I will prove my true love for thee." The disciples were extremely shocked and some thought that the Master had fallen in love with the courtesan. Years later, as Buddha was meditating with his disciples, he suddenly cried out: "I must go, my Beloved, the courtesan, is calling me; she needs me now and I must fulfill my promise to her."

The disciples ran helter and skelter to follow their Master Buddha, who was madly in love with the courtesan, and was racing to meet her. The disciples ran after their Master with the vague hope of rescuing him from the temptress, the courtesan.

The great Buddha, with his worried disciples, came to the same tree where they had met the courtesan, and what do you think they saw? There lay the courtesan with her beautiful body honeycombed with putrefying odorous small pox sores. The disciples cringed and stood far from her, but the Master Buddha took her decaying body on his lap and whispered in her ears: "Beloved, I have come to prove my love to thee, and fulfill my promise to touch thee. I waited a long time to demonstrate my true love, for I love thee when everybody else has ceased loving thee. I touch thee when all thy summer friends do not want to touch thee anymore." Saying this, Buddha healed the courtesan and asked her to join his family of disciples.

Personal love is limiting, selfish, and considers its own comforts usually at the cost of everything else. Divine love is unselfish and seeks the happiness of the o b e ct of love, and is not limited or partial. God loves the wicked and the good alike, for they are His children, so all those who aspire to know Him must prove to Him that their love too is like His love. When a Soul proves to the Heavenly Father that he loves his good or evil brothers equally, then the Divine Father will say: "My noble son, thy love I accept, for thou dost love all with my love, even as I do." To love those who love you is natural, but to love those who do not love you is to be supernatural and to know God in All.

HEALTH CULTURE

HEALTH LAWS To have a healthy body one must maintain bodily cleanliness inside as well as out. Poisons or waste products are eliminated through four organs and each must have proper care and attention. These four organs of elimination are the skin, the lungs, the kidneys, and the bowels. They will be treated separately.

THE SKIN. About one quarter of the water taken into the body is eliminated, along with a large quantity of waste products, through the pores of the skin. To keep the skin functioning properly wear light, loose clothing. Take a warm bath each night to wash off the accumulated waste of the day and to allow the skin to breathe at night. Take a cool or cold shower in the morning to keep the skin in tone and to help it to react properly as a heat regulator.

DIET LAWS The normal medium in which the body performs its functions is alkaline. When, as a result of improper diet, overwork, lack of rest, lack of fresh air, and so forth, the body becomes acid, we are ill. The alkali which the body needs at this time to neutralize the acid condition is supplied through food and drink. The alkaline chemicals neutralize and eliminate the acids formed by activity and by an excess of acid-producing foods. Alkalinity means health and immunity to disease.

In order to keep the body in an alkaline condition at least eighty per cent of our diet should be chosen from the foods which have an alkaline reaction. A few of the foods which have an alkaline reaction are tomatoes, lettuce, cucumbers, beets, spinach (palak), carrots, pears, figs, oranges, peaches, buttermilk, apples, grapes and dates.

FORTNIGHTLY INSPIRATION

God is Infinite Omnipresence. He is present in everything equally. His light shines equally in wisdom-sparkling-diamond souls as well as in charcoal mentalities dark with ignorance. Because God has given us independence to choose between error and Truth, we can keep our minds transparent with purity of knowledge and love or dark with dogma and inharmony. God has so endowed man with his own power of liberty that man can shut God out or receive Him through his logic and right struggle of life. That some people know less than others is not due to God's limiting the flow of His power through man, but to man's not allowing His Light to pass through. Ignorance-stricken people may be healed of delusion's diseases by contacting the Christ Consciousness of Meditation and faith.

FORTNIGHTLY AFFIRMATION

"I am renewed and strengthened by Thy Life-giving Energy."

STRENGTH! HEALTH! POWER!

YOGODA SAT-SANGA FORTNIGHTLY INSTRUCTIONS
BY
PARAMHANSA YOGANANDA
(To Be Confidentially Reserved for MEMBER'S USE ONLY)

SMILE FOREVER

Smile when the roses are budding;
Smile when the petals of pleasure are falling.
Smile when vigor is throbbing in your breast;
Smile when you have dreaming wrinkles
In your brow.
Smile because you find happiness in peace
    And not in passing possessions.
     Smile because you [are] fearless,
Smile because fear is ashamed to cause you
    Apprehension and failure.
Smile when trials burst upon you;
Smile when the goblin of poverty stalks,
    Smile when all hope threatens to leave you.
    Smile when you are crying
    And smile when you are laughing.
    Smile when you are losing
    And smile when you are winning.
    Smile when you are good
And smile when you are bad.
Smile at the sad past, for it is no more;
    Smile, thinking of the joy of yester-years.
Smile at the past; smile today. Smile
tomorrow, and you will qualify To
smile forever and forever.
Smile newly with the ever new smile of God
    Every second, every minute.
Smile every day in the year.
    And keep smiling in God forever.

PRAYER TO PRECEDE THE PRAECEPTUM STUDY

"Father, teach me to be calmly active and actively calm. Let me become the Prince of Peace, sitting on the Throne of Poise, directing the Kingdom of Activity.

"0 Spirit, teach me to enjoy Thee in Spirit, that I may enjoy the world and my earthly duties with Thy Joy. 0 Spirit, help me to train my senses so that they may enjoy all good things. Teach me to enjoy earthly pleasure with Thy Joy."

THE ART OF REJUVENATION
PART V
MENTAL RELAXATION

Mental relaxation signifies complete mental rest. You can achievethis by practicing going to sleep at will. Relax the body and think of the drowsiness you usually feel just before you fall asleep.

Then try actually to reproduce that state. Use imagination, not will, to do this. Most people do not relax even while they sleep. Their minds are restless; hence they dream. Therefore, conscious mental relaxation is better than relaxation which is the byproduct of physical passive relaxation or sleep. In this way you can either dream or keep dreams off your mental moving-picture screen, as you choose. No matter how busy you are, do not forget now and then to free your mind completely from worries and all duties. Just dismiss them from your mind. Remember, you were not made for them; they were made by you. Do not allow them to torture you. When you are beset by the greatest mental trials or worries, try to fall asleep. If you can do that, you will find, when awakening, that the mental tension is relieved and that worry has loosened its grip upon you. Just tell yourself that even if you died, the earth would continue to follow its orbit, and business would be carried on as usual; hence, why worry? When you take yourself too seriously, death comes along to mock you and remind you of the brevity of material life and its duties.

Mental relaxation consists in the ability to free the attention at will from haunting worries over past and present difficulties; consciousness of constant duty; dread of accidents and other haunting fears; greed; passion; evil or disturbing thoughts at will and keeping the attention fixed on the peace and contentment within.

Hence, the devotee who aspires to develop uniformly and steadily in spirituality must always calm the mind with the practice of concentration, keep the breath quiet by proper breathing exercises, preserve the vital essence by self-control and good company, and keep the body quiet and not in perpetual motion and restlessness.

Let go of your worries. Enter into absolute silence every morning and night, and banish thoughts for several minutes each time. Then think of some happy incident in your life; dwell on it and visualize it; mentally go through some pleasant experience over and over again until you forget your worries entirely. Metaphysical super-relaxation consists in freeing the entire human consciousness from its identification with the body, money, possessions, name, fame, family, country, the world, and the human race and its habits. Super-relaxation consists in disengaging the attention by degrees from consciousness, subconsciousness, the semi-superconsciousness state felt after meditation, and true self-consciousness, and identifying it completely with Cosmic Consciousness. Mental relaxation and semi-super relaxation consist in releasing consciousness from the delusion of duality and resting the mind, keeping it identified with one's own real nature of unity in Spirit. You have hypnotized yourselves into thinking that you are human beings, whereas in reality you are gods.

PHYSICAL RELAXATION

When doing these techniques, you probably for the first time feel the difference between flesh and energy. When you tense all the body parts, you are furnishing energy to all parts of the body. When you tense and then relax all parts, and throw the breath out, you have relaxed all parts of the body. When you tense the whole body and then relax, exhaling the breath, cast away all restless thoughts. Remain without thinking as long as you can, and remain without breathing as long as you can without discomfort.

Try to remain one minute at a time without thinking, especially if you are worried. Then try to remain several minutes with a quiet mind. Mental relaxation consists in withdrawing the attention from the perception of the body and the thoughts. You can relax mentally by diverting the attention from worry to peace through meditation. Mental relaxation is the ability to release attention at will from worries, duties, responsibilities, and so on.

When you wake up in the morning, don't jump out of bed suddenly. First go through the routine of energizing your body while in bed.

First relax all parts and then give them a breakfast of energy. Do not jerk. Then get up and repeat the routine three times on your feet.

When you have learned how to concentrate, you will learn how to withdraw the energy from the body in this way and turn it on God.

Close your eyes. Tense the whole body and then relax. There is no greater method of relaxation than the one you are learning. Any time you are tired or worried, tense and relax the whole body, throw your breath out, and you will become calm. When there is low tensing, tension is not removed, but when you tense high and then relax, you have perfect relaxation.

SCIENTIFIC TENSION AND RELAXATION

Raise the right arm forward parallel to the ground, grasp the forearm just the elbow with the fingers of the left hand, and press gently. Then gently tense and relax the right forearm by closing the right fist, and then relax by opening the fingers again. Hold the right forearm still with drooping palm and fingers.

1.   Low Tension - Partly close the fingers of your right hand and watch the low tension of the muscles in the forearm.

2.   Medium Tension - Close the fingers half way. You now have medium tension.

3.   High Tension Close - your fingers tightly. You now have high tension.

It is possible to tense the forearm or the upper arm without closing the fingers. It is also possible to tense almost any muscle in the body separately. Hold the tension with will and keep the eyes closed. Open your fingers a little bit. You now have low relaxation.

Then open the fingers half way. You now have medium relaxation. Open the hand and let your fingers relax and the hand droop. You now have complete relaxation. Feel the gradual withdrawal of energy and loosening muscles during relaxation. (Relax and Feel).

Try the above with any part of your body, while lying on your back on a hard bed, or on a blanket on the hard floor. Of course, while you relax the forearm or upper arm, be sure to let it hang loosely by your side and do not lift it up. If you tense and relax with your arm raised, you cannot have perfect relaxation because in lifting the arm you have to tense, or contract the muscles which raise the arm.

You can practice these exercises either standing or lying down, and you will become calm, in addition to gaining great strength, strength is valuable, of course, but, above all, calmness is necessary to enable you to learn concentration and meditation. Without concentration and meditation, Self-Realization is impossible.

Physical and mental relaxation are very successfully accomplished by practicing the above exercises while lying on a blanket on the floor, early in the morning after the bath.

Then performing this exercise, keep your mind on the medulla and imagine the energy flowing into your body through the medulla and from thence to every part of the body. By keeping the mind thus fixed upon the medulla, you will soon The Medulla or learn to draw energy from the ether and send it to all parts of the body at will "Mouth of God" without the physical process of tensing and relaxing. Always hold this thought: "I am calmly active; actively calm. I am the Prince of Peace sitting on the throne of Poise."

SPREADING RIPPLES OF PEACE

Fix your mind in between the eyebrows on the shoreless lake of peace. Watch the eternal circle of rippling peace around you. The more you watch intently, the more you will feel the wavelets of peace extending from the eyebrows to the forehead, from the forehead to the heart, and on to every cell in your body. Now the ripples of peace have left the banks of your body and peace is flooding over the vast territory of your mind. Now the flood of peace overflows the boundaries of your mind and moves on in Infinite directions all around you everywhere. Meditate, dwell on, and feel this.

THE APOLOGUE
(For the Entire Family
THE BANDIT AND THE BULL

Once upon a time a very evil bandit named Rakusha lived with his gang in a cave hidden away in the dark breast of the hills of northern India. This rapacious robber was noted for his cruelty and lived by pillage, murder, and plunder. He was by nature very vicious. It is said that the tiger will go on killing animals even though it may be gorged to the throat with meat just for the fun of killing. This tiger-bandit excelled in the art of cruelty and shunned and ridiculed every Spiritual low that he happened to think of. He was the incarnation of wickedness. A sample of his supreme perversity can, in a small measure, be seen from the following event which took place.

Once this master-bandit started with his band on a mission to plunder a poor little village at the outskirts of a forest. As he passed through the forest, he carried on an orgy of killing the song-birds just for the thrill of it. When he arrived at the end of the forest, he perceived a dirt road half a mile long leading into the v i l l a g e . This road was shaded with an avenue of tall trees. One of the bandit gang remarked that the avenue of tall trees afforded shade to the travelers from the heat of the sultry Oriental sun. "Well," the bandit-leader remarked: "All of you get busy and cut down the bark of the trees and let them die, so that they may no longer be liberal with their shade to the villagers."

His orders were obeyed, and as the band of robbers were about to enter the village they found that they had to walk over loose bricks laid in a muddy puddle of water. After they had crossed this puddle, the bandit-king thought: "Let me remove the bricks lest anyone else utilizes the comfort of walking over them and thus miss the contact of the mud." However, on second thought, he refrained from doing this, as he suddenly remembered that he had to walk over the bricks on his way back to his den beyond the forest.

In the meantime, as this bandit and has followers were entering the village, a few Saints happened to be going out of the village and they were delighted to walk on the bricks in the mud puddle, thus saving their shoes from getting soiled. Now, fix in your minds this incident of the holy men crossing the mud puddle, using the bricks unwillingly left there by the bandit-king for his own selfish purpose.

The bandits plundered the village, slaughtering the men, women, and children, and once again started on their return. Once again the bandit-king had to walk on the bricks over the mud puddle, but, after he and his gang were through using the bricks, the leader with his long spear, pushed the bricks into the deepest holes of the mud puddle, lest anyone else should try to use them.

Now the scene changes. Shortly after this, the bandit-leader was treacherously killed by one of his subordinates, who wanted to be at the head of the robbers' roost. It is said in the Hindu scriptures that every man has two Angels, with two recording books, invisibly residing at his left and his right shoulders. The Angel on the left side writes in his book all the misdeeds of the man, and the Angel on the right side records all his virtuous actions; so, when the Soul of this most notorious atrocious robber was being escorted to the darkest and most hideous part of Hades, the leader-in-charge of Heaven and Hades, to make sure that no injustice was done, asked the two Angels to look into their records. The Angel on the left side said: "Honored Sir, the book of sin is so full of this man's wicked deeds that I had to write all around the margin of all the pages of my book."

The Angel on the right said: "All the pages of my book are blank. I cannot find a single record of good action performed by this cruel bandit." Being asked to thoroughly reexamine his book, the Angel on the right exclaimed:" Ah , I find on the last page a single indirect virtuous action. This bandit once unwillingly left a few bricks in a puddle of mud so that he might recross over them, and he has a reward coming to him because a few holy men happened to use those bricks to cross the puddle."

Then the Angel in charge of Heaven and Hades said to the bandit Soul: "You have two hours of complete freedom in Heaven or Hades. Pray let me know your last wish." The bandit Soul, still gorged with wickedness, thought it over and harshly growled: "Get me a flying bull from Hades with long, sharp pointed horns." The ferocious flying bull arrived. The bandit got on the bull's back and, being assured that the bull would do just as he commanded, said: "Mr. Bull, charge all the keepers of Hades." There was wild havoc. Hades had never had such uproar and confusion.

Hearing of this confusion, the Angel in charge of Heaven and Hades, with his flying assistants, arrived on the scene to save the attacked Keepers of Hades. The bandit Soul, in great glee, stopped pursuing the Hell Keepers and at once ordered the bull to drive his long horns into the body of the Angel leader in charge of Heaven and Hades. Seeing this inevitable doom approaching him the Angel and his assistants began to fly all over space, racing to find shelter behind Heaven's safe gates. The Keepers in Hades sent telepathic broadcasts to Heaven, telling the Angels about this terrible outrage caused by the super-bandit. Super Angels flocked to the rescue of the fleeing Angels, but, according to the decree, none could withstand the attack of this flying bull, who was working havoc under the supreme command of this very wicked bandit Soul. The scene was extremely embarrassing and ludicrous, to see even the most powerful host of Angels, including the Keeper of Heaven and Hades, with his assistants, fleeing for their lives toward Heaven.

The bull entered the Pearly Gates hot on the heels of the

fleeing Angels. Heaven was in an uproar. At last, just as the fleeing Angels and the bandit on the flying bull reached the Golden Throne of His Majesty, the two hours had passed, and suddenly the bull stopped his outrageous activity of goring the Angels at the command of the bandit Soul. The Angels shook their fists, and the Keeper of Heaven and Hades rolled up his sleeves and approached the powerless bandit and shouted:

"So, getting the powerful bull from us, even in this other world you had a to follow your wicked ways. We will give you and your flying bull overtime work in the worst part of Hades. Heaven is too good for you."

Suddenly, the Angels and all were frozen into stillness as the Heavenly Father exclaimed: "No, you will not throw the wicked bandit and his bull back into Hades, because they are already free, for they have reached Heaven. It doesn't matter how anyone gets here, even if it is by only a very little goodness, he shall never go back to Hades again."

And so, dear friend, by this story you will learn that, no matter what you have been in the past, if you sin no more and cultivate even a little goodness, that may be the portal to the Heaven of eternal goodness and freedom. The idea is, do not keep brooding over the distance between you and Truth, but keep walking toward it by doing some good every day, and you will finally reach your goal.

HEALTH CULTURE

YOUR SKIN: A PICTORIAL BAROMETER OF YOUR KIDNEYS A truly beautiful skin is a symbol of in internal cleanliness. It accommodates the internal flushing system known as the urinary tract and shares its burdens when, through ignorance and neglect, we have trespassed the Law's governing physical equilibrium.

The eliminative channels carrying off the bodily waste might be compared to the sanitation principle of a metropolis. Visualize the devastating chaos that would ensue were congestion to cripple the whole sewerage system of a big city.

Use an abundance of specific skin goods in salads, as carrots, cucumbers, spinach, parsley, celery, & watercress.

A SKIN-BEAUTY SALAD Upon a large plate, place a few leaves of deep green lettuce leaves. In generous mounds, place on the lettuce leaves some grated cucumber (with skin), minced parsley, chopped celery, raw spinach leaves, and add lemon juice, honey or brown sugar to taste.

FORTNIGHTLY INSPIRATION

No matter what causes it, whenever a little bubble of joy appears in your invisible sea of consciousness, take hold of it and keep expanding it. Meditate upon it and it will grow larger. Watch not the limitations of the little bubble of your joy, but keep expanding it until it grows greater in volume. Keep puffing at it with the breath of concentration from within, until it spreads all over your face, heart, entire body, mind, and over the Ocean of Infinity in your consciousness.

Keep puffing at the bubble of joy until it breaks its confining walls and becomes the Sea of Joy. The bubble of your life cannot die, whether floating in birth, or disappearing in death In the Ocean of Cosmic Consciousness, for you are indestructible consciousness, protected in the bosom of Spirit's Immortality.

FORTNIGHTLY AFFIRMATION

"I relax and cast aside all mental burdens, allowing Cod to express through me as Perfect Peace, Love, and Wisdom."

PEACE! LOVE! WISDOM!

YOGODA SAT-SANGA FORTNIGHTLY INSTRUCTIONS
BY PARAMHANSA
YOGANANDA

IN THE LAND OF DREAMS

Each night, as my Spirit roams
In spheres of slumber vast,
I become a hermit and renounce
My title, body-form, possessions, creeds
.... Breaking the self-erected prison walls
Of flesh and earthly limitations;
I am on all-pervading Son of God,
No longer caged in brittle, dingy clod,
Nor tied by tangible cords of birth, Or man-made
smallness, social standing
And duty-shadows of earth.

There in Sleepland's ether eternal, I have no
country, no homeland dear;
Nor Occidental nor Oriental,
Race hound behind the bars of inheritance. In
Dreamland's limitless acres,
My Spirit revels in freedom
Its only religion freedom Gypsying gaily there,
Pilfering joy from everywhere.

There, no lordling god o'er shadows me.
For there is none but MYSELF to rule myself.
Behold, the slave-god hath become the God!
The sleeping mortal, the awakened, deathless Lord!

PRAYER TO PRECEDE THE PRAECEPTUM STUDY

"Come Thou to my aid, Divine Friend, and usher me on the hard path of my life. The fire of ambition has been waxing strong, fed by the fuel of my rainbow dreams. As often as old dreams faded, fresh die hard hopes burst into new, thirsty flames, that swallowed up many a sturdy tree of my fresh powers."

DREAMS

THE PHENOMENA OF DREAMS

The greatest lesson of dreamland is that we must not take our earthly experience too seriously, for it is nothing but a series of vast dream movies shown to us to entertain us. The Heavenly Father meant to entertain us. His immortal children, with a variety of earthly movies. We must behold comedies, tragedies, and news reels of life movies, with an entertaining joyous attitude.

In the dreamland we forget our names, bodies, nationalities, possessions, and all our frailties. God gave the Soul and mind the power to materialize thoughts in the dreamland and create a miniature Cosmos, even as He does.

The phenomena of dreams shows to us that the mind can reproduce an exact copy of our worldly experience and material life. God shows that we, being His children, can create even as He does. God froze His thoughts into substance and we perceive the dream of the Cosmos with its various sensations.

In the dreamland the Soul becomes free to create a Cosmos after its own fancy; it can move in a new body, new world, enjoy ice cream or hot tea, move in the hot desert of Sahara, or in the bleak regions of Alaska, or the Himalayas. Here in dreamland the Soul can be a poor man or a king; here it can satisfy all its unfulfilled earthly desires by materializing them into dream experiences. Here the Soul can create, if it will, a perfect world, free from poverty, sickness, wickedness, and ignorance. Here it can be a part of anything it thinks it cannot be in its earthly life. Here the Soul can perceive the birth of a baby or the death of a man; here it can cry or smile, hear songs, smell flowers, touch, feel, think, reason, meditate, and perform every activity, even as it does in its earthly life.

We must prove ourselves to be God's immortal children, who can learn and be entertained by the Cosmic movies. We must prove ourselves to be true sons of God by appreciating the lessons of the Cosmic movies without losing the unchangeable joyous poise of our Inner Being the true reflections of immortal unchangeable God.

SIGNIFICANCE OF DREAMS

All dreams have some significance. Even meaningless dreams are the outcome of a disordered, purposeless life. But all dreams are not true. Yet all dreams signify the state of your consciousness. The superconscious individual always beholds true dreams whenever he wants to behold them.

The worldly man has worldly dreams, the active man has dreams of activity. The evil man has dreams of evil. Do not try to explain the meaning of every dream just remember the above classification of dreams, and put your dreams under the classification which you think proper.

Imaginative people have fanciful dreams. Matter of fact people have common worldly dreams. Worried fearful dreams show that you attract worry and fear. They warn you not to worry lest you attract the objects of worry or fear, not only through the conscious mind, but a consciously reinforced subconscious mind. Dreams of wealth, industries, activity, and battles, signify material success. Dreams of ocean, boats, great fires, and floods, all signify much Spiritual development. Dreams of sex signify that you must make conscious efforts to dislodge the conscious and subconscious mind of acquired conscious and subconscious sex impulses.

All dreams have some significance according to the following classifications:

(a) Meaningless weird dreams, and comedy and tragedy dreams. Meaningless weird dreams are born due to the chaotic memory of the subconscious mind. Subconscious optimism brings forth comedy dreams. Subconscious pessimism turns out tragedy dream films.

(b) Superconscious dreams. The all-seeing superconsciousness, or intuition, films some future events and drops the superconscious film into the subconscious mind. This superconscious film becomes projected into a true dream. People who meditate, who live mostly in superconsciousness, often have superconscious dreams,

(c) Superconscious, subconscious, and conscious symbolical dreams. Dreams always tell the state of your mind, hence, adjust your life and actions according to the kind of dreams, not that you have, but that you should have.

It is better not to dream at all, but to be able to produce true dreams in vision at will, which will be taught in a future lesson. While you are resting, you don't want to be imposed upon by dreams.

You don't want to keep your movie house of dreams fully working when you want rest, if dreams come too often, you must meditate and calm yourself, then this condition will disappear. The more calm you become, the less you will dream. You should be able to dream true dreams at will, or be able to produce visions of distant events by the all- seeing power of the superconsciousness within you.

THE LAP OF IMMORTALITY

If you have assurance with the Infinite, you will know whether or not Nature shatters your body and you are still on the lap of immortality, still on the lap of that Infinite assurance. Resurrect yourself from the consciousness of human habits and the human thoughts thereof. Live every second in that consciousness it is the lost thing, that which alone will live forever. This is not to frighten you, but to quicken your understanding, quicken your efforts, so that you will not keep your Soul buried under false satisfaction.

We have no existence but in the universal. The body you see is nothing but materialized electricity. How could electricity be sick? It is a delusion, but simply saying that it is delusion is not enough.

If in a dream you see a wall and you see your body strike the wall, you will have a broken skull in dream. Self-Realization Fellowship teaches that it is only by coming in contact with God that one sees that God is the universe and that the body is nothing but condensed electricity. Science has said that electricity is nothing but energy or frozen Cosmic Consciousness. We must not call it Mind. Mind is different. To say that everything is Mind is wrong, it is Cosmic Consciousness which makes us feel different things; consciousness of Matter and consciousness of Spirit.

Resurrect your Soul from the dreams of frailties. Resurrect your Soul in eternal wisdom. What is the method? The answer is: Relaxation, self-control, right diet, right fortitude; undaunted attitude of mind. Don't acknowledge defeat. To acknowledge defeat is greater defeat. You have unlimited power; you must cultivate that power. Meditation is the greatest way of resurrecting your Soul from the bondage of body and all your trials. Meditate at the feet of the infinite. Learn to saturate yourself with Him. Your trials may be heavy, may be great, but the greatest enemy of yourself is yourself.

You are immortal; your trials are mortal; they are changeable; you are unchangeable; you can unleash the eternal powers and shatter your trials.

Resurrect yourself from, weakness, disease, ignorance, consciousness of disease, and, above, all, from frailties of habits that beset your life.

That forced silence on the last day will be a mystery sleep, in which your nightmare and your beautiful dreams of earthly life will bid farewell, at least for a time. Then, maybe, after a short rest on the downy bed of blissful oblivion we shall wake up in another dream of another life, on a new star, or a new earthly setting. Then, maybe, we shall be deluded into thinking that we are awake while we are still dreaming. Will this sleeping and deluded waking in dreams continue until we know that we can really awaken in God?

As in dreaming, we divide our minds into thoughts of many things, such as minds, mountains, Souls, sky, and stars, and make every reality out of the tissue of fancy, so has God transformed His dreaming mind into a star-chequered savanna of the blue with the indwelling planetary family, earth, and us sorrowing, laughing, coming, and dying.

May God make us fearless by letting us know that we are waking and dreaming in Him, and that we are His all-protected, ever-happy Self.

Let us unite our evading life with His Imperishable Life. Let us blend our flickering, stale happiness into His enduring ever-new Blessedness.

THE APOLOGUE
(For the Entire Family)
THE MAN WHO BECAME A BUFFALO

By the side of a mountain overlooking a beautiful flower- decked valley in India, was a cozy hermitage. This hermitage was a cave, carved into the rocky ledge of the mountain. Here dwelt a great Master with a devoted disciple. When the dawn wiped away the darkness from the face of the hills, the hill sides smiled brightly with many colored blossoms. The Master and the disciple sang hymns together with the rising sun, which reminded them of the awakening of wisdom after a long sleep of ignorance. They smiled when Nature smiled after her silence of the night.

While dawn still lingered o'er the valley, the Master would ask the disciple to sit upright in the perfect meditating posture, and listen to his sermons with absorbing attention. Thus, every day the disciple eagerly devoured the lessons falling from the lips of his Master.

One day, however, the Master noticed that his young disciple was absent minded and restless, so he gently inquired: "Son, today your mind is not on my sermon, and it seems to be wandering o'er the hills elsewhere, pray tell me, what is the reason for your absentmindedness?" The disciple respectfully replied: "Honored Master, I cannot concentrate on your lessons today, for my mind is helplessly thinking about the newly acquired, tame buffalo which is grazing on the green verdure of the valley."

The Master, instead of scolding the disciple, calmly asked, him to retire into the silence chamber, lock his door, and think of nothing but the buffalo. One day passed, and the next morning the Master looked through the little window in the silence chamber. The disciple was still meditating upon the buffalo, so the Master asked: "Son, what are you doing?" The disciple answered: "Sir, I am grazing with the buffalo in the field. Shall I come?" The Master replied: "No, Son, not yet; go on grazing with your buffalo."

Another day passed and, on the third morning, the Master asked through the window of the Chamber of Silence: "Beloved Child, what are you doing?" To which the disciple, in the state of ecstasy, replied: "Heavenly Master, I behold the buffalo in my room, and I am feeding it. Shall I come to you with my buffalo?" The Master replied: "Not yet, my Son. Go on with the vision of the buffalo, and of feeding it."

Another two days passed in the meditation and visualization of the buffalo and, on the fifth day, the master spoke through the window of the Silence Chamber where the disciple was alone in complete ecstasy "Son, pray tell me, what you are doing now." The disciple bellowed, imitating the buffalo's voice: "What do you mean? I am the buffalo. I am not your Son." To this, the Master replied: "All right, Mr. Buffalo, you had better come out of the Silence Chamber." The disciple bellowed: "How can I get out through the narrow door? My horns are so big, and my body is so large." Then the Master went into the Silence Chamber and brought his disciple out of his trance. The disciple smiled to find himself walking on all fours, trying to imitate the buffalo of his vision.

Then the disciple, after a light repast, went to listen to the sermon of his Master. The Master asked the disciple many deep, Spiritual questions, all of which he answered correctly, as never before.

The Master remarked: "Now, your concentration has reached the perfect state, when you and your mind can be one with the object of study."

Likewise, remember, when you think of a great business man and his ability, or when you think about God, think deeply; concentrate deeply, until you feel you have become that business man or have become One with God.

HEALTH CULTURE

A LOVELY SKIN While a lovely skin depends primarily upon good health, and the essentials of its acquisition and maintenance, start with purification from within, there are numerous aids to the complexion which we shall give in the Praecepta from time to time. Pimples mean clogged pores; unsightly growths indicate excess carbohydrates in the diet (starches and sweets); wrinkles are Nature's hunger-cries for food iodine and oil. A dry skin wrinkles faster than that which is well lubricated.

Oil, particularly olive oil, as an aid to skin beauty, has been used throughout the Ages. It is chronicled that chief among Cleopatra's secrets of beauty and rejuvenation was the generous use of oil of the olive. Secure a good brand of yellow olive oil. Use with strained lemon juice, half of each. The lemon prevents unseemly hair growth and assists the oil in penetrating. Another excellent facial skin builder and a good base for powder is oil of almonds.

FORTNIGHTLY INSPIRATION
COME INTO THE GARDEN OF MY DREAMS

In the garden of my dreams grew many dream-blossoms. The rarest flowers of my fancy all bloomed there. Unopened buds of earthly hopes audaciously spread their petals of fulfillment, warmed by the light of my dreams. In the dim glow I spied the specters of beloved, forgotten faces, sprites of dear, dead feelings, long buried beneath the soil of mind, which all rose in their shining robes. I beheld the resurrection of all experiences, at the trumpet-call of my dream- angels.

O King of my dreams and of countless dream-worlds, in the garden of Thy dream galaxies let me be a tiny star, or let me twinkle by Thy side Thy loved dream-star in the chamber of Thy Cosmic Dreams. Or, if I be not held by the string of Thy Love as a tiny star-bead of life in the garland of Thy Dreams, then give me the humblest place in the Heart of Thy Dreams.

In the chamber of Thy Heart I shall behold the making of the noblest Dreams of Life. O Master Weaver of Dreams, teach me to make a many-hued carpet of Dreams for all lovers of Thy Pattern of Dreams to walk over as they travel to the Temple of Eternal Dreams. And I will join worshiping angels of living visions, that I may offer on Thy altar a bouquet of my newborn Dreams of Thee.

FORTNIGHTLY INSTRUCTIONS

"My dreams of perfection are the bridges that carry me into the realm of pure ideas."

DREAMS! PEACE! DREAMS!

YOGODA SAT-SANGA FORTNIGHTLY INSTRUCTIONS
BY
PARAMHANSA YOGANANDA
(To Be Confidentially Reserved For MEMBER'S USE ONLY)

MY DEVOTION

O Thou Mother of all conscious things,
Be Thou consciously receptive to my prayers.
Through Thee I know all that I know;
And Thou knowest all I know.
So Thou knowest my prayers.
And knowing and feeling Thee constantly thus,
O know Thou art I, I am Thou.
My little wavelet has vanished in Thee.
1 know Thou alone existed;
And Thou alone dost exist now and ever will.
Thou art impersonal, invisible.
Unseen, formless, omnipresent.
But forever I want to worship Thee
As both personal and impersonal;
By my devotion -
I beheld Thee
Sometimes as Krishna,
Sometimes as Christ,
Personal, visible and imprisoned
In the little space
Hidden within the temple of my love.
O Invisible, just as Thou, didst freeze
Thy unseen Infinitude
Into the sea of cosmic finitude.
So do Thou appear unto me -
Visible and living -
That I may serve Thee,
I want to see Thee as the ocean of life
With and without the ripples
Of finite creation.
O creator of all things,
I want to worship Thee both as personal
And impersonal.

PRAECEPTUM PRAYER

"Teach me, Thou, to conquer myself by myself. Bless me, that my discrimination may be the charioteer of the steeds of my five senses, holding properly, the reins of my mind. Let my Soul, in the little chariot of the body, on the wheels of discipline, drive triumphantly over the speed-way of many earth-lives, until on the last lap of the last race, it shall find itself safe in the limitless Royal Chariot of the King of Kings!"

PLAIN LIVING AND GOD-THINKING

Do you realize how you spend your life, very few of us know how much we can put in our life if we use it properly, wisely, and economically. First, let us economize our time - lifetime ebb away before we wake up, and that is why we do not realize the value of the immortal time which God has given us. Too much time is spent in rushing, in racing, in getting nowhere. Very few of us stop, think, think at all - they just eat, sleep, and die.

It is important to differentiate between your needs and your wants. Your needs are few, while your wants can be limitless. In order to find freedom and Bliss, minister only to your needs. Stop creating limitless wants and pursuing the will-o'-the-wisp of false happiness. The more you depend upon conditions outside yourself for happiness, the less happy you will be.

Fostering the desire for luxuries is the surest way to increase misery. Don't be the slave of things or possessions. Boil down even your needs. Spend your time in the search of lasting happiness or Bliss. The unchangeable, immortal Soul is hidden behind the screen of your consciousness, on which are painted dark pictures of disease, failure, death, and so forth. Lift the veil of illusive change, and be established in your immortal nature. Enthrone your fickle consciousness on the changelessness and calmness within you, which is the throne of God; then let your Soul manifest Bliss night and day.

Happiness can be had by the exercise of self-control, by cultivating habits of plain living and high thinking, and by spending less money, even though earning more. Make an effort to earn more so that you can be means of helping others to help themselves, for one of the unwritten laws decrees that he who helps others to abundance and happiness always will be helped in return by them, and he will become more and more prosperous and happy himself. This is a law of happiness which cannot be broken. It is better to live simply and frugally and grow rich in Reality.

True Desirelessness

The Soul's nature is Bliss, a lasting inner state of ever- now, ever-changing joy, which eternally entertains without changing the one entertained even when passing through the trials of physical suffering or death. Desirelessness is not a negation. It is rather the attainment of the self-control you need in order to regain your eternal heritage of all-fulfillment lying within your Soul. First, give the Soul the opportunity to manifest this state, do your duty to your body and mind and the world. You need not give up your ambitions and become negative; on the contrary, let the everlasting joy, which is your real nature, help you to realize all noble a m b i t i o n . Enjoy noble experiences with the Joy of God. Perform real duties with Divine Joy.

You are immortals, endowed with eternal joy. Never forget this during your play with changeable mortal life. This world is but a stage on which you play your parts under the direction of the Divine Stage Manager. Play them well, whether they be tragic or comic, always remembering that your real nature is eternal Bliss and nothing else. The one thing which will never leave you, once you transcend all unstable mental states, is the joy of your Soul.

WHAT IS GOD?

The usual conception of God is that He is Superhuman, Infinite, Omnipresent, and Omniscient, but in this general conception there are many variations. Whatever conception we have of God, if it does not influence our daily conduct; if our everyday life does not find an inspiration from it, and if it is not found to be universally necessary, then that conception is useless. If God in not conceived in such a way that we cannot do without Him in the satisfaction of a want, in our dealings with people in earning money, in reading books, in passing an examination, in the doing of the most trifling or the highest duties, then it is plain that we have not felt any connection between God and life. God may be infinite, Omnipresent, Omniscient, Personal and Merciful, but these conceptions are not sufficiently compelling to make us try to know God. We have no immediate and practical use for those conceptions in our busy, rushing lives.

We read about God in the various Scriptures. We hear of His presence and praise in the sermons of religious men and Saints. We imagine Him behind the veils of beauty of Nature. We think about His existence through the logic within us, but all of these windows through which we try to see God are fitted with opaque glass of uncertain inference drawn from untested, unscrutinized data.

We cannot have full or direct knowledge of God through the limited powers of the intellect, which gives only a partial and indirect view of things. To view a thing intellectually is not to see it by being one with it. It is to view it by being apart from it. Intuition is the direct grasp to Truth. It is in this Intuition that Bliss Consciousness, or God Consciousness, is realized. God is Bliss. He is ever-existent. When we wish Eternal Bliss, or God, we also wish Eternal, Immortal, Unchangeable, Ever-Conscious Existence.

It must be remembered that finding God does not imply complete neglect of the various physical and Spiritual battles of life.

On the other hand, the climbing Spiritual aspirant must learn to conquer in order to make the Temple of Life free from the darkness of ignorance and the weakness of disease, so that God's perfect Presence may be perceived. As [a] house full of jewels cannot be seen in the dark, so the presence of God cannot be felt while the darkness of ignorance, overpowering disease, or mental inharmony prevails.

HOW TO KNOW GOD

To know God is to love him. Knowledge of God must precede the ability to love Him, At least, we must have some little conception of what He really is. We are told, "He is Love," but we only know human love; how then can we conceive of that wondrous love that makes all mankind free. You know the taste of an orange, and you have only to think of oranges which you have tasted in the past in order to recall that taste clearly. Can you think of God with a similarly clear conception? The answer is: "No."

Wood, stone, animals - all things are but different manifestations of God with varying rates of vibration. Our own feelings may be an expression of God, but they are not God. The wave may be a manifestation of the ocean, but the wave cannot be called the ocean. Is electricity God then? No, for we cannot switch Him on and off. He is ever-burning Cosmic Spirit.

Sage Patanjali says: "His Voice is Pranava or OM". The Bible says: "The Word was God." What is the Word? Do you really know any Supreme Being? Have you soon Him? Do you not believe about Him only what you have been told from earliest childhood? Some people say: "He is Omnipresent." Yet space alone is not God. In all of space we do not see any one Intelligence. When you move through space, space does not talk to you. Space is the thing which you are in. Space does not mean "intelligence."

When my Master asked me, "What is God?" I said: "God is Spirit." When he asked: "Then, what is Spirit?" I answered: "Spirit is Infinite Intelligence." "Yes," he said, "but Infinite Intelligence is God, so you see you are talking and reasoning in circles, [and] that way you will never get anywhere." Substituting different names for God does not explain Him.

In the same way, when you are asked what water is, you say: "It is H20 or aqua, or pani, or jal," and try to explain what water is. If you really know what God is, then you can explain Him satisfactorily to a new inquirer. But when you try to analyze or explain God without knowing Him, you only bring your ideas about God to the fore. What is God? That was one of the questions I thought I was sure of, until I found that I could not make a satisfactory explanation. But from my Master's explanation I really learned about God, and found Him for myself. God has been a reality to me ever since.

FORCE AND A CONTROLLING INTELLIGENCE

There are two things in this universe: First, Force and second, Intelligence controlling that Force. You cannot mention any one thing that does not have intelligence. The human body is simply a combination of 16 elements, and nothing more. With intelligence added, it becomes a live and thinking Being. Now I ask you, can intelligence come out of nothing, is it not reasonable to suppose that somewhere there is some sort of factory that produces that intelligence? We humans are only one of the many products of that factor of Cosmic Intelligence. GOD IS THAT INVISIBLE FACTORY OF INTELLIGENCE from which stars, planets, and all manifest things are born, created and harmonized.

Why do all the seasons come on time? Why do we have hunger in the body and food outside to satisfy that hunger? If there were no Cosmic Intelligence, maybe we would have hunger but no food. But throughout the universe, in spite of the many mischievous pranks of Nature, there always seems to be a rhythm, and this rhythm and all things are products of the one factory of the one all-running Intelligence. But when we speak thus, still we do not explain what that Intelligence is. Here is the explanation:

GOD IS THE SUPREME INTELLIGENCE THAT GOVERNS EVERYTHING

Some people do not realize that there is a difference between Force and Intelligence. Electricity is a force, but unless we put it into a lamp, it does not give a light that can be used. Intelligence puts it into the lamp. All the forces of Nature cannot satisfactorily work by themselves without the guidance of Intelligence, The cosmic Factory of Intelligence works in a coordinated way. Steam has power to make things move and fire converts water into steam. These are only two of Nature's forces, but they, of themselves, in their unharnessed natural state, do not accomplish anything purposefully useful, but when harnessed to Intelligence, and directed rightly, they can be made to be of great service to mankind. The earth and the whole of the universe seemingly has been routine (*sic*) so that human life is made possible This Cosmic routine, "The rhythm of the spheres," is the product of Intelligence.

The surest sign that God exists is the increasing heart-bursting Joy felt in Meditation. When your mind is free from prejudice, when narrow-mindedness vanishes, when you unreservedly sympathize with everybody, when you hear the Voice of God in the chorus of churches, tabernacles, temples and mosques, when you realize that life is a Joyous battle of duty, and at the same time a passing dream, and above all, when you become increasingly intoxicated with the Joy of Meditation, and in making others happy by giving them God-peace, then you will know that God is with you always and you are in Him.

THE APOLOGUE
THE MAN WHO WOULDN'T BE KING

Long ago, there lived a few saints in a retreat at the outskirts of a jungle valley. Here they ate the fresh fruits from trees and drank with the cup of their hand, the living water of the sparkling mountain springs. Here blew the zephyrs of ceaseless peace and their diamond-eyes glittered with celestial smiles. Joy throbbed in their bosoms, giving perpetual solace.

And yet, one day, one of the saints thought he had too much of Spiritual happiness and wanted a little taste of Kingly happiness. He wanted to be a King for a day. With this desire scorching his heart, he set out in quest of regal happiness, and left the satisfying, peaceful nook of the hermitage.

On the way he felt and thought: "Heavenly Father, I am Thy child, surely Thou wouldst guide me to the place where I can enjoy Kingly happiness for a day." Thinking this as he walked some distance from the hermitage, his eyes fell upon a stately, palatial mansion.

"Ah, I see the Heavenly Father has made my dream come true," he exclaimed, and began hurrying toward the mansion.

He passed by the gates and wasn't stopped by any of the guards he walked all over the flower-bedecked garden, and he met no one. He went into the dining room of the palace and found steaming hot delicious food invitingly awaiting at the table but not a trace of waiter servants. Encouraged by all this strange array of edible food, he thought within himself: "Methinks, the Lord is good to me and has materialized this palace and wonderful food fit for me. It is just as I wanted. My dreams have come true."

Being sentimentally convinced, he proceeded to enjoy the preliminaries of being a God-sent King for a day. He took his bath in the royal bathroom, dressed, and sat down for dinner. At this time the servants of the palace, who had been out gambling among themselves, rushed in, in great excitement and shouted: "Who are you, eating the food of our King who is out hunting and is expected to arrive any minute?" The Saint, still thinking that it was test of the Lord, and thinking himself to be a cosmopolitan friend, replied, in a calm, loving tone: "I am a friend of the great King; I have come here at His command to enjoy royal happiness for a day."

The servants, taking Saint to be an august guest of the King let him finish the royal dinner and ushered him to sleep in the royal chamber. They did not understand that the Saint referred to God as the Great King and not to their King who was out hunting.

Two hours passed. The herald of the King arrived with a message from his Highness, stating that he was detained and would arrive at the end of three hours and would like to have steaming hot food prepared. The servants worryingly asked: "Didn't His Highness send a guest to enjoy his dinner and bed?" The King's herald was frothing at the mouth with rage when he found that this beggar-saint without Invitation had devoured the King's food and was audaciously snoring on the royal bed. So, he urged the servants to run out and bring sticks and broomsticks with which to rout the beggar-Saint.

The Saint was awakened from his dream of royal happiness by sticks and staves mercilessly falling upon him, but the more the servants beat him and scolded him, the more he laughed without cessation. The servants became furious at his increasing laughter and flogged him to unconsciousness and threw him beyond the palace gates.

The unconscious Saint was picked up by a brother Saint and was taken back to the hermitage. The brother forced milk into the mouth of the unconscious Saint, and by way of testing his recovery of consciousness, asked: "Do you know who is feeding you milk?" The beaten Saint laughingly replied: "The same God who beat me for trying to be a King for a day - that same God is feeding me milk."

The brother/hermits were glad to see their chastised brother Saint's faith in God unchanged in prosperity, as in the form of a repose in the king's bed, and in adversity, as in the event of his punishment. This beaten Saint wasn't like those who worship God during prosperity and disbelieve in God during adversity.

Meanwhile, the King of the palace returned to his mansion and demanded hot food and was very wrathful to learn of the beggar who had eaten his food and who had laughed when he was being beaten. The whimsical King took a fancy to the strangeness of the story of the beggar Saint who had laughed while being beaten, and ordered his servants to find this beggar. The servants searched high and low until they, returning home in despair, galloped by the Saints' retreat and wore attracted by the loud laughter of the beggar Saint. They dismounted, kidnapped the beggar Saint, and took him before the King.

When the King and the Saint met, the Saint began to laugh louder than ever, as if unable to hold his merriment within the cup of his heart. The King repeatedly asked the Saint under threat of death the reason for his laughter while being beaten. When threats failed, the King used entreaty, and, being driven mad by curiosity, offered his throne to the beggar if only he would explain his laughter while being beaten.

At last, seeing the King humbled, the beaten beggar Saint replied: "Look, I was thrashed by God for craving the delusive enjoyment of Kingly material comfort for a day, but my laughter increased because I got off easy: I thought: "If I merit so much beating for just one day of being King, think how many more beatings are coming to you for indulging in Kingly material happiness for years? I was beaten for forgetting God for just one day, and think how much beating you yet must have for forgetting Him every day - all the time! No, thank you, I would not be King, for I have ever-fresh happiness in God, which does not end with the lashings of worries."

HEALTH CULTURE

SKIN BEAUTY The face of the average individual (particularly one whose consciousness has not yet been awakened to Self-Realization) is a complete reflection of all the physical and emotional upheavals that transpire within. The remainder of the body-skin, we know, does not register the degree of wear and tear that is taking place, at least not to the unpracticed eye.

Beauty is never pictured with ugly skin, blotches, unsightly enlarged pores, wrinkles, and so forth. The latter condition at once suggests uncleanliness, and we must remember that the Spirits demand a cleansed, radiant vehicle with which to demonstrate at its highest capacity. In poetry, painting, and song, reference is often made by the artist of the Skin-Beautiful. There is, unquestionably an Important tie between the Inner and Outer Man enclosed within the boundaries of the skin, the medium through which "Our Light So Shines," suggesting, as it were, the finishing touch of the Creator of the finished Man, the end, termination; a case wherein is contained all that is the YOU, to have and to hold and to care for until the final deliverance to succeeding realms along the Path.

DOs

Give your skin a daily air bath, as well as a sun bath.

Apply lemon juice as a bleach to discolorations, then add a drop of olive oil. Fresh cucumber juice is also a splendid food for this purpose.

Daily friction baths with a rough towel. Work up a good perspiration by some sort of exercise. Also, an occasional sweat bath is recommended.

An excellent astringent can be made at home thus: Beat egg white until stiff; cover face and neck with it and leave it on for four or five minutes. Wash off with cool water. After a few applications, notice effect upon former flabby skin tissue. (Not meant for vegetarians)

DON'Ts

It is often advisable to discontinue the use of dairy products if the skin is too oily. For a period, at least.

Don't drink city water while the skin and kidneys are inoperative. Distilled water dissolves and flushes, and does not add further to whatever encumbrance of hard deposits already exists in the bloodstream.

Don't take too frequent or prolonged tub-baths unless expressly for therapeutic purposes.

While they do relax, they also have a tendency to dry up the skin, besides being demagnetizing.

Best time to take hot baths is at night, unless, course, in an emergency. Never wear rubber in clothing, as this interferes with circulation.

Never use the lard-based cold creams sold on the market. Prepare your own. Use either almond oil, olive oil and lemon, or the vegetables oils as a foundation.

PRAECEPTUM INSPIRATION
THINK OF GOD IN EVERY ACTION

Learn to love God as the Joy felt in meditation. Choose only good paths before you start the race to the goal of Realization.

Then think of God as you start on the path of your material or Spiritual duty. Then think of God with each footfall of your advancing feet as you make your way carefully and joyously over the broadening road of fulfillment. Then think of Him after you have traveled far on your life's path and finished your progressive action. Ask God to be with you, when you, by your own will, choose good action.

Then think of God before you eat body-nourishing food; then think of Him while you are eating it. Then, when you have finished eating, think of God, Change your centre from material desires to a desire for God. Ask God to make your peace, silence, joy, and meditation His holy altars, where your Soul may meet and commune with Him in the Holy of Holies. Let your prayer be: " Make my understanding the temple of Thy guidance."

PRAECEPTUM AFFIRMATION

"Teach me to open the only gate of meditation which leads to Thy Blessed Presence."

"AUM"

75

YOGODA SAT-SANGA FORTNIGHTLY INSTRUCTIONS
BY
PARAMHANSA YOGANANDA
(To be Confidentially Reserved for MEMBER'S USE ONLY)

DIVINE LOVE

Thou art the mystic echo from the caverns of heart,
And the inaudible voice of feeling.
Thou art the unseen charmer of Souls,
Thou art the fountain flowing from the bosom Of friendship.
Thou art the Divine Cupid, enticing mystic Souls
To pierce the heart of all living things,
Thou art the silent language of Souls,
And the invisible ink which lovers use
To write letters on the pages of their hearts,
Thou art the mother of all affections,
And in Thy breast of love throbs the heart of God.
Love is the silent conversation between two hearts,
And it is the call of God to all creatures,
Animate and inanimate
To return to His house of Oneness.
Love is the heart-beat of all life,
And the angel of incarnation.
Love is born in the garden of Soul progress,
And it sleeps behind the darkness of outer Attachments.
It is the oldest and the
Sweetest nectar, preserved in the bottle of Hearts.
Love is the light which dissolves all walls
Between Souls, families, and nations.
Love is the unfading blossom of pure friendship
In the garden of both young and mature Souls.
Love is the door to heaven, the complete songs of Souls.

PRAECEPTUM PRAYER

"With the love of all human loves, I have come to love Thee, Thou God of all loves. Thou art the protecting father. Thou are the little child, lisping love to his parents. Thou art the mother, showering infinite kindnesses. Thou dost flow in the all-surrendering love of the lover to the beloved. Thou art the love of friends. Purify me with the reverence of a servant to his master. Teach me to love Thee with all pure loves, for Thou art the Fountain of Love, heavenly and earthly. Bathe me in the spray of all loves."

THE INNER LAWS OF SOUL MAGNETISM

Magnetism consists in an attractive force inherent in certain bodies. The human Soul has within it such an attracting power. Spirit, or God, created everything by the force of repulsion. He had to repulse vibratory forces out of Himself in order to create dualities and multifarious objects. This repulsed force created finite objects from the Infinite. This ideational repulsed force materialized into Cosmic Energy, which in turn materialized into matter. Originally, this repulsive universal creative force rested in Heaven in the Bosom of God, but being cast out (projected away from Spirit) it becomes a conscious Independent Force, creating delusive finite dualities contrary to the pattern of the One Universal Spirit, God. Being conscious, the Creative Repulsive

Force which went out of Him was conscious.

This delusive finite creative force is spoken of as Satan, or the Satanic creator of evil and misery-producing finite objects. This Satanic Force, like an outgoing lightning, or Universal Energy, fell from Heaven; that is, was repulsed out of the bosom of the Cosmic Spirit, but Spirit or God, tries by universal attractive force to keep attracting all objects created out of Him by this Universal misguided force of Satanic Delusion.

This Satanic Force received independence to create; in fact, created all the anomalies and evils in this finite stricken world. This Satanic repulsive energy wants everything to reincarnate and remain in its finite state through the law of material attachment, instinct, and conscious and unconscious desire. If this Universal force had not been conscious, human beings and all objects after once being created would have, after a certain period, found freedom from the outgoing force and returned to Spirit, Thus, the finite objects, losing their cohesive creative power of repulsive attachment, would have evaporated in their original state of infinitude.

However, this Universal Satanic Force is conscious and independent and therefore keeps everything and everybody deluded with the consciousness of finiteness and unspiritual separateness. That is why objects go through the process of evolution and why Souls reincarnate through the law of cause and effect and the power of desire born of the contact of finite matter. This repulsive force keeps up a steady fight with Spirit and its emancipating attractive force, which tries to constantly call all created objects back to dissolving unity. On the other hand, living objects and Souls are but children of force sent from God; that is why He tries to recall all His truant children back to Himself. Meditation is the only way to go back to God and escape the clutches of Universal Delusion. It is the conscious way of going into the Infinite to forget your finite titles of race, religion, family, fame, name, possessions - all that belongs to the delusive little finite body.

The human soul is the image of God, but the body in which it is encased is partially created and maintained by the finite creating power of Satanic Repulsive Force. God meant well in creating, but Creation, finding itself independent, created imperfect objects, just as it pleased, against the will of God.

Hence, each individual life is the scene of the tug-of-war between God's in-drawing magnetism and Satan's outwardly repulsing magnetism. Man's mind and senses are attracted to finite matter; his discrimination and intuitions are attracted to Soul-pleasing actions and Spirit. The Soul, by the power of discrimination and intuition tries to pull into itself and to harmonious actions, all unifying noble bodily and mental forces. The Satanic Force wants the body projected, and kept away from the influence of Divine magnetism, groveling in finitude and inharmony.

The Soul's power of moving toward God is called Soul Magnetism. Soul Magnetism consists in drawing into itself all good-reminding human experiences. Soul Magnetism is the power by which an individual draws into himself friends, [the] heart's real desired objects, and the acquirement or the power to know everything about everything. It is the Spirit's magnetic drawing power, which is distributed and seated in every heart - -in everything. The sun keeps the planets tied to itself by rays. That is called solar magnetism.

UNIVERSAL MAGNETISM

The electrons are held together to a nucleus by the power of universal magnetism. This is termed electronic magnetism. Because Spirit is in everything, and has in itself this drawing power, therefore all things created out of Him have the individuality of Spirit and His drawing magnetic power, although in an individualized state.

All atoms and molecules have a nucleus which keeps their tiny particles held together. The cohesive power in the atom is called "atomic magnetism." The combination of different atoms, which constitute different elements, is called "elemental magnetism." The power which keeps the body of a planet together is termed "planet magnetism." Its Life Force attracts the sunlight, the oxygen, carbon dioxide gas, and so forth.

ANIMAL MAGNETISM

Animal organisms are held together by animal magnetism. The snake has great magnetic attracting power. It charms and draws little animals to itself by its animal magnetic power. Man, being a rational, moral, aesthetic, Spiritual animal, possesses intellectual, moral, aesthetic, and Spiritual magnetism, as well an animal magnetism. By animal magnetism, a man draws to himself physically-minded people. This animal magnetism is almost hypnotic in its effect.

Young people of opposite sex, living on the material plane, often exchange their animal magnetism, blind one another by emotions and passions, and draw to themselves all kinds of destructive evil habits.

Hypnosis is a crime since the hypnotizer robs his patient of free will, judgment, and consciousness. Hypnosis practiced on an individual repeatedly for any length of time might affect the brain and make mind mechanical, guided automatically by enslaving suggestions. Never allow yourself to be under the influence of any one's animal magnetism or semi-hypnotic power. There is only a shade of difference between animal magnetism and hypnosis. When an individual exercises his animal magnetism on another person, he becomes blinded and prejudiced all the time by his wrong or right judgment.

A person under the influence of animal magnetism may move here and there but may be acting solely under the influence of another individual's instincts and habits. Here the consciousness is apparently free from the influence of hypnosis, but in reality is secretly guided and prejudiced by another person. An individual under the influence of hypnosis becomes unconscious of the surroundings and is only aware of the suggestions of the other individual. A hypnotized person is guided by his subconscious mind, and his conscious mind becomes almost entirely inactive. That is why no one should want to be influenced by animal magnetism or be hypnotized.

The ordinary horseshoe magnet has three poles - positive, negative, and neutral. Through its positive-negative hands, the magnet draws pieces of iron to itself within a certain range, so, in developing magnetism, you must first make up your mind as to what kind of magnetism you want. Then the next thing is to remember that you must choose the specific magnetic person from whom the specific magnetism is to be acquired. When a magnet is rubbed on a piece of non-magnetic iron, the iron becomes magnetic. Likewise, another person's magnetism can be absorbed by close association and loving, respectful attention.

If you think you are a failure and you want business magnetism, you must associate yourself closely with successful businessmen (the kind you want to be), shake hands with them, and mix with them very closely.

In all hand-shaking two magnets are formed. The upper Spiritual magnet is formed with two heads as the two poles, and the lower magnet is formed with the two pairs of feet as the two poles. The junction of the hands in the hand-shake forms the common neutral point, and the common curve of the two lower magnets. Therefore, when shaking hands with everybody you take a chance; it is not good to constantly associate with undesirable individuals with whom you have to shake hands every day.

SPIRITUAL MAGNETISM

In the case of exchanging moral, mental, aesthetic, and Spiritual magnetism, immediate contact is not always necessary. Such magnetism can be derived from a distance by meditating on the visual images and mentalities of different persons possessing different magnetism.

One who deeply meditates on the image and mentality of a Spiritual man attracts his nature and imitates his Spiritual magnetism.

When electricity passes through a wire, it becomes magnetic, so, also, if a man continuously thinks, lives, and dreams about morality, aesthetic objects, spirituality, and friendship, he can develop moral, aesthetic, and Spiritual magnetism from within.

By meditating upon OM and GOD, one can develop Soul and Spiritual vibratory magnetism. This magnetic power has limitless range and power. If you keep yourself morning, noon, and night, dreaming, feeling, and sensing the all-attracting Divine Magnetism, then your power can draw objects of desire from a distance, and can uplift people by the mere sight of contact, or even by your simple wish or your powerfully directed uplifting concentration. By this power you can draw friends from afar - those that had been real friend in a past life. By this power you can make the elements bow to your wish. By the invitation of the Divine Magnetism, you can draw angels, all creative luminous forces, savants, and past Saints to come to you and dance in your joy. By this Divine Magnetism you can draw unto yourself all rays of knowledge, to come and sparkle and scintillate around your Being.

RULES FOR DEVELOPING MAGNETISM

One strongly positive-evil individual plus one negative passive-good individual equals this: The positive-evil magnetism makes a horse-shoe magnet with the negative-good, and the positive-evil magnetism will be predominant.

One weak negative-evil individual plus one strong positive- good individual equals this: The positive-anger magnetism will reign.

A very strong, calm disposition plus a negative, slightly angry disposition, equals this: Magnetism of calmness will be predominant. A strong, positive failure plus a lesser positive failure equals reinforced failure-magnetism.

A strong positive success plus a lesser positive success equals reinforced success.

A strong failure plus a strong success equals a strong failure magnetism, or a strong success magnetism.

A great moral power plus a weak moral power equals a great moral magnetism.

A great Spiritual power plus a great business man equals a great Spiritual magnetism and a great business magnetism.

A weak Spiritual man and a great evil power equal evil magnetism. A great Spiritual power plus a weak evil power equals a great Spiritual magnetism.

A great intellectual power plus great ignorance equals great intellect or great ignorance. A great intellect plus a small intellect plus a small intellect equals a great intellect.

THE APOLOGUE
(For the Entire Family)
THE HIMALAYAN MUSK DEER

Musk is a kind of valuable, extremely fragrant salve found in the navel of the musk deer, a habitant of the highest Himalayan Hills of India. At a certain age, the ravishing odor of musk secretly oozes out of the navel of the musk deer. The deer becomes excited at the attractive odor of musk and frisks about, sniffing under trees and searching everywhere for many weeks to find the source of the fragrance. Finally he grows angry and very restless when he is unable to find the source of the musk perfume, and jumps from the high cliffs into the valley, trying to catch hold of the source of the rare fragrance, and thus plunges to death. It is than that the hunters get hold of him and tear out the pouch of musk.

A Divine Bard once sang: "O you foolish musk deer, you sought for the fragrance everywhere but in your own body. That is why you did not find it. If you only had touched your nostrils to your own navel, you would have found the cherished musk and would have saved yourself from suicide on the rocks below."

Don't you think most people act like the musk deer? As they grow, they seek the ever-fragrant happiness everywhere outside of themselves in play, temptation, human love, and on the slippery path of wealth, until, finally, they jump from the cliff of high hope onto the rocks of disillusionment when they cannot find the real happiness which lies hidden within the secret nook of their own Souls.

If only you would turn your mind inward, in deep daily meditation, you would find the source of all true, lasting happiness existing right within the innermost silence of your own Soul. Don't be like the musk deer and perish seeking false happiness in the wrong place, but, beloved seekers of happiness, awake, and try to find your happiness within the cave of deep contemplation.

HEALTH CULTURE

GROWING YOUNGER Through eating an abundance of alkaline foods, either in bulk, reducing them to juices, or through the process of sun-drying and powdering, we can go far toward arresting physical decay and restoring a condition of Youth to prematurely aging body cells, if, simultaneously, the amount of acid-forming foods are, for a period, eliminated, and when later resumed, used sparingly.

We are, or should be, just beginning to live when the first half of life has passed. The storms and passions of youth, resulting from misdirected sense activity, have subsided, succeeded by a more or less even tempo of maturity and the conservative use of the Life Force. Impulse, eager seeking after pleasure, dramatic striving for self-expression of Personality, has given place to an impersonal quality of desire to lose oneself in service to one's fellow men, in whatever niche we happen to find ourselves placed by Destiny. And with it a conscious seeking to develop that Something Within our own Soul.

That is the period of Life that Browning so aptly referred to when he wrote:

"Grow old along with me!
The best is yet to be,
The last of life, for which the first was made"

My students whom I am endeavoring to guide safely through the many stepping stones of Self-Realization must cease to think in the term of birthdays, or look back at the years passed, with sighs of regret. Follow the Beacon Light that leads onward, upward! Just as, at the last day of school, the diligent student is happily expectant, having learned his lessons, and now passes on to another grade, ready for the next step toward his educational development, so, at the second half of life, we should find ourselves in fuller possession of our faculties and talents, radiant, vitally forceful, efficient, zestful, for new worlds to conquer, and to pass on whatever wisdom we have gleaned through those experiences, study, meditation, and inspiration. Instead, all about us we see broken bodies, "disillusioned" and confused mental slants on Life, and Spiritual floundering.

One grows younger seeking Truth. If the search has been a sincere and persistent one, we are bound to stumble across the very thing that was needed for our rehabilitation, which, ultimately, in the last analysis, whatever the road traversed, is the finding of the Kingdom Within, and working from that base.

Proper exercise, frequent [r]evitalization periods, and an abundance of good fresh air by day and night, meditation, correct mental attitude - these and many more must be included in the curriculum, but the matter of food nourishment plays such an important role in the acquisition and maintenance of Health that we stress it by constant repetition. Oft-times, merely cutting down the quantity habitually eaten daily will alleviate discomfort and suffering, and solve your individual Health problem. Test your Will Power when called upon to resist or accept excess sweets and starches; use your better judgment in the frequency with which flesh food" is partaken.

The phrenologist watches and studies the mouth to determine character. Truly, it can be our undoing if we permit it to affect us; what goes into it in the form of food; what comes out of it in the form of words; what expression rests upon it, contempt and defeat, or Radiance.

A DELICIOUS YOUTH DISH Shred young, small carrots. Put into a steamer with a small quantity of water, or cook in parchment paper. When tender, but not too soft, empty into a platter. Do with butter, or olive oil, or your favorite vegetable oil, and a few drops of lemon juice. Garnish with endive sprays. Finely minced garlic or a dash of fresh herbs, such as thyme, may be added while cooking.

FORTNIGHTLY INSPIRATION

No matter what causes it, whenever a little bubble of joy appears in your invisible sea of consciousness, take hold of it, and keep expanding it. Meditate upon it and it will grow larger. Do not watch the limitations of the little bubble of your joy, but keep expanding it until it grows greater in volume. Keep puffing at it with the breath of concentration from within, until it spreads all over your face, heart, entire body, mind, and over the Ocean of Infinity in your consciousness. Keep puffing at the bubble of joy until it breaks its confining walls and becomes the Sea of Joy.

Silently repeat: The Ocean of Spirit has become the little bubble of my little Soul. The bubble of my life cannot die, whether floating in birth, or disappearing in death in the Ocean of Cosmic Consciousness, for I am indestructible consciousness, protected in the bosom of Spirit's Immortality.

FORTNIGHTLY AFFIRMATION

"As I radiate love and good will to others, I open the channel for God's love to come to me, for Divine Love is the Magnet that will draw all good unto me." "I AM AWAKE AND READY."

YOGODA SAT-SANGA FORTNIGHTLY INSTRUCTIONS BY PARAMHANSA YOGANANDA
(To Be Confidentially Reserved
FOR MEMER'S USE ONLY)

THY MAGIC POWER

Make my eyes behold what Thou dost see.
Make my ears catch the burst of Thy voice
In the billows of all Creation.
Make my speech the fountain of nectared words
Showered o'er Souls scorched with bitterness.
Make my lips utter naught but the songs
Of Thy love and joy.
Beloved, work through me the work of Truth.
Keep my hands busy serving all my brothers.
Keep my voice forever casting seeds of love
For Thee on the soil of seeking Souls.
Keep my feet ever moving on the pathway
Of right action.
Lead me from dark ignorance to Thy light
Of Wisdom.
Lead me from temporary pleasures to
Thy ever-new Joy within.
Make my love Thy love, that I may know all Things as
mine. Father, throb through my heart and make me feel
Sympathy for all living creatures.
Kindle in me the flame of Thy wisdom and burn
The dark forest of my mundane desires.
Let Thy reason be the preceptor of my reason.
Think through my thoughts, for it is
Thy Magic Power which uses my mind as Thy mind,
My hands as Thy hands, my feet as
Thy feet, my Soul as Thy Spirit, to
Perform Thy Holy Works.

PRAECEPTUM PRAYER

"0 Spirit, let not my insatiable sense-cravings be fed with wrong actions. Teach me to discipline them, that they may want only true happiness. Let me, then, learn to wisely govern the finite forces Thou has entrusted unto me, that each possession with two-fold potency may be used only for good. Let me, 0 Spirit, co-operate with Thy Will until all of my thoughts shall conform to Thy harmonious Plan."

DESTROY DEPRESSION BY SUBSTITUTING PROSPERITY

According to the Law of God and of Divine brotherhood this earth was to be the home where all the wealth of the mines and other resources would be equally distributed by equal labor. And the law of Divine birthright was established, which is, that all men are the children of God, and made in the image of God; all nations are of one blood, and all men are descended from the same stock. If you love the world and consider it as your own family, and believe in it and love it, recognizing no difference between different nationalities, then you will establish your legitimate Astral right of owning your share of the earth's capital.

Those who seek prosperity for themselves alone are bound to be poor for some time, or to suffer from mental inharmony, but those who take the world as their home and who really think and work for group or world prosperity, start the Astral forces to work, leading them to the place where they can find their legitimate prosperity.

This is the surest secret law. Prosperity is not dependent only upon creative ability, but also upon your past actions, and also upon the Astral law of cause and effect, which has the power to distribute prosperity equally to all without exception. Those who rouse this Astral power to positive prosperity, succeed wherever they go, whether or not they are in prosperous or poverty-stricken environments. Therefore, seek prosperity, not only for yourself and your family, but for a wider group of friends, and for your country, and the whole world.

Destroy luxury. Learn to use cheaper things in an artistic way, then believe that you are a child of God and that as such you have all the prosperity of God and the earth behind you. As a child of God, and especially when, by meditation, you change from a prodigal son to a true son of God, you will know that whatever God has, you have.

1. Cut down luxuries,
2. Think yourself a child of God.
3. Think of all nationalities as your brothers.
4. Seek prosperity for yourself and for others.
5. Develop the creative thought as success every day after deep meditation.

YOUR GOAL OF LIFE

Most people live almost mechanically, unconscious of any ideal or plan of life. They come on earth, struggle for a living, and leave the shores of mortality without knowing why they came here, and what their duties were. No matter what the goal of life is, it is obvious that man is so undermined with needs that he must struggle to satisfy them. The believer and the disbeliever in God must both struggle to meet their needs, therefore, it is very important to know that man should concentrate upon his needs and not create a lot of useless extra desires.

Do not wander aimlessly, lost in the jungle of life, constantly bleeding your happiness with the thorns of new desires. You must find the goal of your life and the shortest road which leads you there. Do not travel unknown roads, picking up new troubles.

Too much wrong ambition is just as bad as too much passive contentment. As human beings, we have been endowed with needs and we must meet their demands. As man is a physical, mental, Spiritual being, he must look after his all-round welfare, avoiding one-sided, overdevelopment. To possess wonderful health and a good appetite, with no money to maintain that health and to satisfy that hunger, is agonizing. To have lots of money and lots of indigestion is heartrending. To have lots of health, and lots of wealth, and lots of trouble with self and others, is pitiable. To have lots of health wealth, and mental efficiency, but no knowledge of the ultimate Truth, and with a lack of peace, is very useless, disturbing, and dissatisfying.

EFFICIENCY THROUGH CONCENTRATION

After establishing that the goal of life is maximum efficiency, peace, health, and success, let us consider the surest way to prosperity. Prosperity does not consist just in the making of money; it also consists in acquiring the mental efficiency by which man can uniformly acquire health, wealth, wisdom, and peace at will. Great wealth does not necessarily bring health, peace, or efficiency, but acquirement of efficiency and peace are bound to bring a properly balanced material success. Most people develop mental efficiency as the by-product of their efforts for material success, but very few people know that money is made for happiness, but happiness cannot be found just by developing an insatiable Soul-corroding desire for money.

Mental efficiency depends upon the art of concentration. Man must know the scientific method of concentration, by which he can disengage his attention from objects of distraction and focus it on one thing at a time. By the power of concentration, man can use the untold power of mind to accomplish that which he desires, and he can guard all doors through which failure may enter. All men of success have been men of great concentration, men who could dive deeply into their problems and come out with the pearls of right solutions. Most people suffocated by distraction are unable to fish out the pearls of success.

Man often forgets to concentrate on his little physical needs and on his great need of developing mental efficiency in everything, and of acquiring Divine contentment. Man is so busy multiplying his conditions of physical comfort that he considers very many unnecessary things as a necessary part of his existence.

The man of powerful concentration must ask God to direct his focused mind on the right place for right success. Passive people want God to do all the work and egotists ascribe all their success to themselves. Passive people do not use the power of God in intelligence and egotists, though using God-given intelligence, forgot to receive God's direction as to where the intelligence should be used. I can blame inertia as the cause of failure, but it hurts me to see intelligent egotists fail after making real intelligent effort.

However, one may be a man of concentration and power and may dive deep into the sea of problems but still may not find the pearl of success at all. There are many men who have powerful concentration but they do not know where to strike success. This is where another factor in acquiring prosperity comes into consideration. Brilliant people with efficient minds also have starved, or have had only meager success.

All prosperity is measured out to man according to the law of cause and effect, which governs not only this life, but all past lives. That is why intelligent people are often born poor or unhealthy, whereas, an idiot may be born healthy and wealthy. Men were originally sons of God made in his image, having free choice and equal power of accomplishment, but, by misuse of his God-given reason and will power man became controlled by the natural law of cause and effect of action (Karma) and thus limited his life. A man's success depends not only upon his intelligence and efficiency but upon the nature of his past actions. However, there is a way to overcome the unfavorable results of past actions. They must be destroyed and a new cause set in motion.

GOD'S WILL AND YOUR WILL

Broadcast your message, - "This Soul of mine is God Himself;" "My Father and I are One" until you feel this overpowering, all-solacing Bliss of God. When this happens, you have made the contact. Then demand your celestial right by affirming: "Father, I am Thy child, guide me to my right prosperity," or "Father, I will reason, I will will, I will act, but lead Thou my reason, will, and activity to the right thing which I should do in order to acquire health, wealth, peace, and wisdom."

Do not will and act first, but contact God first and thus harness your will and activity to the right goal. As you cannot broadcast through a broken microphone, so must you remember that you cannot broadcast your prayer through the mental microphone which is disordered by restlessness. By deep calmness, repair your mind microphone. Then again, as you cannot get an answer by just calling someone through a microphone and then running away, so, also, you must not first pray once and run away, but you must continuously broadcast your prayer to God through your calm mental microphone UNTIL you hear His voice. Most people pray in restlessness and do not pray with the determination to receive a response.

GOD - THE REAL SOURCE OF PROSPERITY

God is the secret of all mental power, peace, and prosperity. Then why use the limited impossible human method of prosperity? By visualizing prosperity, or by affirmation, you may strengthen your subconscious mind, which may in turn encourage your conscious mind, but that is all that visualization alone can do. The conscious mind still has to achieve the success just the same and is hindered by the law of cause and effect. The conscious mind cannot initiate a new cause which will bring positive success in any direction, but when the human mind can contact God, then the superconscious mind can be sure of success, due to the unlimited power of God and due to creating a new cause of success.

THE APOLOGUE
(For the Entire Family)
THE HOLY SQUIRREL

It does not seem possible that we, who are made in the immortal image of God, can cease to exist at death. Neither can we think that imperfect Beings can, at death, all at once merge into the Being of God. It stands to reason that if we are cut off by untimely death in an imperfect state, we have to be reborn on earth in order to wipe away all our stains of error before we can merge in God as His Perfect Image. So, I hope you will understand the moral of the story about the reincarnation of one of India's holy Saints in the body of a Holy Mother Squirrel.

This Saint so loved baby squirrels that he wanted to incarnate as a mother squirrel so that he could actually bestow his maternal affection on the baby squirrels. The story goes that this Saint reincarnated as the Holy Mother squirrel, and with her tiny babies lived on the top of a tree by the sea. It is said that whosoever fed this Holy Squirrel became either prosperous, or was healed of whatever affliction he possessed.

Once upon a time, when the Holy Squirrel had gone far away from the shore in quest of food, a storm lashed the ocean into high waves and swept away the tree with all the baby squirrels. The Holy Mother Squirrel, on her return found the dark work of the sea and commanded: "Ocean, give me back my babies or I will fix you."
When the ocean paid no attention to her warnings, the Mother Squirrel was seen day and night for seven days, to dip her bushy tail into the water and then brush it on the sand.

Seeing this continuous, curious, determined activity, an angel of God appeared and said: "Holy Mother Squirrel, of all the strange things, your action of dipping your tail in the ocean and rubbing it on the sand is the strangest. Prithee, could you tell me the reason for your queer activity?

The Holy Mother Squirrel replied: "Mr. Angel, the audacious sea swallowed my babies in my absence and paid no heed to my request to return them, so I am resolved to run the ocean dry." The Angel laughed and said: "Why, Mother Squirrel, in seven days more you won't have any brush left on your tail with which to attempt to run the ocean dry."

The Mother Squirrel, with the determination of Eternity written on her face, replied: "A thousand million lives or more will I be born again and again as a squirrel and I will grow as

85

many bushy tails as required to dry the ocean." And saying this, the Holy Squirrel went on with her strange activity.

Seven days later, when the brush of her tail had almost disappeared and yet the Mother Squirrel had not stopped her work, the Angel of God came back, and with folded hands said: "Holy Squirrel, your will is law - please stop punishing the ocean and we will return your babies."

Remember, dear friends, that if all mortal methods of seeking happiness have failed you, do not be discouraged, but rouse your slumbering, all-accomplishing Divine Determination. Then you will find that the Divine Laws Of God are bound to give you the Dream happiness that you desire.

HEALTH CULTURE

ORGANIC CHEMICALS The Youth principle is found in the following list of organic chemicals, 6 of the 16 of which the body is composed of: Iron, Silicon, Iodine, Fluorine, Sodium, and Potassium, We are listing the food items under each chemical, for our students to become acquainted with them, and what they stand for. Make them a part of your daily dietary consideration.

IRON - Needed by the anemic; in hemorrhages; retarded mental development. Oxidizes the blood, raisins, red cabbage, spinach, grapes, currants, black cherries, rice bran, bran, carrots, blackberries, whole wheat, lettuce, grapefruit, watermelon, cucumbers, strawberries, beet tops, olives, peas.

SILICON - This is the chemical that has much to do with the building and nourishing of the hair and nails. With the chemical Sodium, it nourishes the ligaments. It is a strong antiseptic and alkalinizer (sic). Needed by the pessimist, the tubercular, and other wasting diseases.
cucumber, endive, steel-cut oats, barley, rye, wheat, lettuce, raw cabbage, spinach, carrots, peas, gooseberries, strawberries, olives, walnuts, figs.

IODINE - Feeds the glands and increases their activity. Prevents body poisons from injuring the brain. Responsible for the creation of Beautiful Thoughts and the Creative ability. Lack of it causes the arteries to break down, wrinkles, varicose veins, and so forth. Iodine stands for refinement, culture, and development of Inner Perception.
sea kelp, pineapple, Irish moss, sea foods, mushrooms, spinach, potato skins, tomatoes, beets, strawberries.

FLUORINE - Contains the properties that cement the bone and tooth structure. Essential in all decaying diseases. Brittle tooth and faulty bone indicate a lack. It is a strong antiseptic. In this list is mentioned Goat's Milk and fresh goat's cheese. The goat is not subject to tuberculosis, and its milk, being so near the consistency of Mother's milk, is recommended in cases where milk is needed and there is an idiosyncrasy to cow's milk.
pineapple, sea foods, mushrooms, spinach, potato skins, tomatoes, beets, strawberries, garlic, watercress, goat's milk, goat's cheese, Swiss cheese, cabbage, mackerel, spinach, sea foods

SOLIUM - With Silicon, nourishes the ligaments. The tennis player, the long distance runner, needs an abundance of this chemical principally found in celery. Gives endurance, energy, and swiftness of movement. Reduces hard deposits in the blood-stream and keeps Calcium in solution, thus preventing stiff joints and hardened arteries. It promotes secretions that insalivate the foods we eat and prepares them for digestion. Is known as the Male chemical, celery, spinach, carrots, tomatoes, leek, walnuts, okra, string beans, pistachio nuts, dandelion, radishes, apples, lentils, peaches, gizzard, cucumber, beet greens, pumpkin, almonds, pecans, olives, salt, watermelon, milk, strawberries.

POTASSIUM - Gives energy to the heart, lungs, and all muscles. It is the great healer of Mother Nature's garden. It is known as the Female chemical, being specially needed by the reproductive organs. Indicated in constipation, and by those easily fatigued. bitter herbs, spinach, watermelon, dandelion, parsley, dill, dried olives, asparagus, potato skins, lentils, celery, peppermint, watercress, lettuce, bran, strawberries, carrots, peaches.

YOUTH COCKTAILS

No. 1. Grind a large juicy cucumber, skin, and all. Strain. Drink juice. This is a powerful rejuvenator, cools the blood, clears the skin, and builds hair and nail cells.

No. 2. With a large spoon, scrape the juice of a watermelon. Drink a glassful of this occasionally. Flushes the kidneys, and has many other curative qualities.

FORTNIGHTLY INSPIRATION
ONENESS WITH GOD

The surest way to prosperity lies, not in begging through wrong prayer, but in establishing first your Oneness with God and afterward demanding the Divine Son's share. That is why Jesus said that men of the world wrongly and unsuccessfully seek bread first, but that they should seek the Kingdom of God First, then all things, all prosperity, unasked, would be added unto them. This is easier said than done. You have heard this before, but you must learn to demonstrate this truth in your life even partially. Rishis and great Spiritual personages of all ages actually demonstrated this in their lives. You must remember that Jesus actually knew and felt it when he said: "I and my Father are One." That is why He could command the storms to stop, turn water into wine, wake Lazarus from sleep, and heal the physical and mental sufferers, and could feed the multitude. He was spiritually efficient, and hence He knew the art of mental and physical efficiency. So you must make the bliss contact of God first by regular, deeper and deeper meditation every day according to the Self-Realization Techniques presented in the Praecepta from time to time. When you make the contact, your status will be changed from that of a mortal beggar to that of a Divine Son and you will automatically gain what you need without the beggary of prayer. The Omniscient Father knows all the needs of a True Son.

Become a True Son of God by constantly feeling Him in the Joy of Silence and as Peace during and Activity.

FORTNIGHTLY AFFIRMATION

"Since our thoughts and words are the seeds we are planting that will bring forth our harvest of the future, I shall begin today filling my consciousness with ideas of undance and all good."

ACTIVITY! PEACE! ABUNDANCE!

YOGODA SAT-SANGA FORTNIGHTLY INSTRUCTIONS
BY
PARAMHANSA YOGANANDA
To Be Confidentially Reserved FOR MEMBER'S USE ONLY)

THE CANDLE OF PEACE

Take the bowl of my mind and fill it
With Thy Understanding,
Take my bottle of emotion and fill it
With Thy Mercy.
Take the empty basket of my Soul and fill it
With Thy Fragrant Wisdom,
Use my life's vessel to dip cupfuls of Thy Love
And pour them into the desire-parched
Throats of others.
Break the walls of my love and flood me
With Thy Omnipresence
'Tis the streak of love's dawn peeping through
The little opening fissure of my heart,
Which bespeaks of the sunlight of Thy Love
Spreading over the dark dungeon of my
Indifference.
The darkness of my love is lit by the gentle
Luminosity of Thy Love,
The empty hall of my Soul is illumined by the
Light of Thy Spirit.
Thou art the Life behind my body,
The Intelligence behind my mind,
The Love behind my feeling,
The wisdom behind my ignorance.
With the little taper of my love I may read
Thy Golden Book, which lay age-long Hidden in me.
Thy Lore has been the invisible
Candle of Peace Dispelling my darkness.
And showing me Thy Secret Messages
Written on the pages of all hearts.

PRAECEPTUM PRAYER

"0 Father, my little prayers are all aroused in reverence, waiting for Thee. My little joys are dancing in tune with the temple- bells of harmony. The muffled drum of my craving beats deep for Thee. My passion, my ignorance, tremblingly wait to be sacrificed before Thy altar. I shall say my prayers with mystic beads made of my crystal tear-drops and polished with my love for Thee. I shall cleanse the altar of my heart with my repentance. Come! I pray for Thy Presence!"

HUMBLENESS VERSUS EGOTISM

Find out on what throne of consciousness your Ego is occupied. Find out what kind of consciousness is predominant in your mind. Are you egotistical? If so, remember that egotism drives wise men and Truth away from you. Try to be humble instead of egotistical, and through the magnetism of humbleness attract the protecting presence of friends, Saints, and gods.

Humbleness is a fertile valley of consciousness where the rain of God's wisdom falls fruitfully. As on a mountain peak no rain can gather, so also, on a high Ego no waters of knowledge can remain. Egotism shuts the door of recipiency through which knowledge enters. Humbleness opens the portals wide and bids all wisdom to come within. Egotism is obvious ugliness written on the face of the egotist, and repels people, whereas humbleness is the fragrance which makes the bearer very attractive to all. Egotism is born of a superiority complex, whereas humbleness is born, not of an inferiority complex, but of wisdom.

Egotism refuses to investigate Truth, whereas humbleness is always ready to learn. Egotism slaps wisdom in the face, humbleness entreats the lotus feet of Truth to enter the innermost sanctum of the Soul. Egotism reveals its smallness by ineffectually trying to make others feel small. Humbleness oozes out greatness of heart and sets an example of greatness for others to follow. Egotism is the brittle imitation-armor of Souls. Humbleness is the inner costume of Saints and gods. Egotism repels friends and Truth. Humbleness attracts friends and understanding. The egotist, like an empty vessel, makes much noise, whereas the humble man is like a cask filled with the precious wine of wisdom.

Egotism reveals a limitation of knowledge, whereas God, who is all wisdom, is humble and never egotistical, because He knows everything. Humbleness is magnetism and is distributor of happiness and invites the all-protecting wisdom of friends and God. The egotist shuts God out, daring to think much of himself in the Omnipresence of God. The humble person knows that there can be nothing greater than God, and therefore he draws God to himself through the fragrance of his humbleness.

The egotistical man has plenty of time to speak to others of his greatness because he is not busy performing great deeds, but the great man is humble because he is so busy doing big things that he has no time to speak of his greatness. The egotistical man watches some of his qualities so gloatingly that he forgets to acquire more good qualities. The egotistical man tries to be satisfied with his small acquirements by making them look big to himself. Consequently he does not progress. Humbleness belongs to the great who cannot stand apart and greedily watch over their greatness. Saints say that the least, or the most humble one, is the greatest in the kingdom of God.

YOU WILL REAP WHAT YOU SOW.

If you want to be loved, start loving others who need your love. If you expect others to be honest with you, then start being honest yourself. If you do not want others to be wicked, then you must cease to be evil yourself. If you want others to sympathize with you, start showing sympathy to those around you. If you want to be respected, you must learn to be respectful to everyone, both young and old. If you want a display of peace from others, you must be peaceful yourself. If you want others to be religious, start being Spiritual yourself. Remember, whatever you want others to be, first be that yourself, then you will find others responding in like manner to you.

If you can find your own faults without developing an inferiority complex, and can keep busy correcting yourself, then you will be using your time more profitably than if you spent it in just wishing others to be better. Your good example will do more change to others than your wishing, your holy wrath, or your words.

Only the little rich man, the inefficient business man, and the man with a little knowledge are offensively and dangerously egotistical. Such egotism not only offends the really rich, the real business man, and the real wise man, but it leads the egotist himself to his doom because of short-sightedness and consequent entanglement in difficulties and failures.

THE LAW OF SERVICE

The law of service to others is secondary to, and born out of the low of self-interest and self-preservation and selfishness.

Man never in his sane mind does anything without a reason. No action is performed without reference to a direct or indirect thought of selfishness. Giving service is indispensable to receiving service. To serve others by financial, mental, or moral help is to find self-satisfaction. Besides, if any one knew beyond doubt that by service to others, his own Soul would be lost, would he serve?

If Jesus know that by sacrificing his life on the altar of ignorance, He would displease God or lose His favor, would He have acted as he did? No, he knew that, although he had to lose the body, he was gaining his Father's favor and his own Soul. Such immortal Sons of God and all the martyrs and Saints, make a good investment - they spend the little mortal body to gain Immortal Life.

RESURRECT YOUR CONSCIOUSNESS

All we have to do is to resurrect our consciousness from the environment of ignorance. Environmental troubles, which we consciously or unconsciously have been creating in the past somewhere, some time, we must blame ourselves for. There must not be an inferiority complex any more than a superiority complex. What are you afraid of? You are not a man or a woman. You are not what you think you are; you are Immortal. Not immortality identified with human habits because habits are your deadliest enemies. At the time of persecution Lord Chaitanya, the Love Incarnate, could forgive and embrace his enemies in the loving name of God and as a result the demon-like persecutors turned great loving devotees of the All-Merciful God. In crucifixion Jesus could keep His love and say: "Father, forgive them, for they know not what they do." So forgive your trials and say: "My Soul is resurrected; my power is greater than all my trials because I am the child of God."

Resurrect your Soul from the dreams of frailties. Resurrect your Soul in eternal wisdom. What is the method? Relaxation; self-control; right diet; right fortitude; undaunted attitude of the mind. Refuse to be defeated. Don't acknowledge defeat. To acknowledge defeat is greater defeat. You have unlimited power; you must cultivate that power, that is all. Meditation is the greatest way of resurrecting your Soul from the bondage of body and all your trials. Meditation! Meditate at the feet of the Infinite. Learn to saturate yourself with Him. Your trials may be heavy, may be great, but the greatest enemy of yourself is yourself. You are Immortal; your trials are mortal; they are changeable; you are unchangeable. You can unleash the eternal powers and shatter your trials.

All those who receive God develop their mental powers by serious application. Your mental powers will expand, your cup of realization will be big enough to hold the ocean of knowledge. Then you have resurrected yourself.

MASTERY OF EGO

Man's attachment to matter keeps the Soul confined to the body prison and prevents it from finding freedom with God In the realm of Eternal Bliss. The Ego attempts to satisfy the Soul's constant, insatiable longing for God through material channels.

Far from accomplishing its objective, it increases man's misery. The Soul's hunger can never be appeased by indulgence of the senses. When man realizes this and masters his Ego, that is, when he achieves self-control, life becomes glorified by Bliss while he is still in the flesh. Then, instead of being the slave of material desires and appetites, his attention is transferred to the heart of Omnipresence, resting there forever with the hidden Joy in everything.

THE APOLOGUE
(For the Entire Family)
THE MAN OF INDIA
WHO WAS THE WORLD'S MOST HUMBLE MAN

Ages ago, Saint Bhrigu of India had a great desire to find the world's most humble man. He wandered all over the Himalayan Mountains and the holy places in search of the man after his own heart. He met many Saints, whom he questioned as to where he could find the world's most humble man. After a strenuous search, he found that all the Saints that he met gave him the names of the same three then-existing prophets, Brahma, Shiva, and Krishna, and assured him that one of them was the world's most humble man.

Saint Bhrigu heard that Prophet Brahma could create anything. Prophet Shiva could absorb anything, and Krishna could preserve anything from annihilation. These three Prophets, in other words, were so Spiritually developed that they could control the creative, destructive, and preservative principles active in all Creation.

Bewildered as to who was the humblest and greatest Prophet of the three, he conceived of a queer plan to test them out. Whistling, he wended his way to the Creative Prophet, Brahma, and without much ceremony of introduction, in a very disrespectful manner and loud voice he began to criticize the Prophet, "Hey, Brahma, what is the matter with you Why don't you stand up and greet me when I come? "

Brahma inwardly was astonished at the audacity of this mortal man and retorted: "Do you know with whom you are talking? " "Yes, Sir," said Bhrigu, "Of course, I know that I am talking with that despicable Prophet who is the creator of vermin, plagues, mosquitoes, diseases, criminals, and all ugly things in Creation, Why don't you reform yourself and create only good things? " Prophet Brahma was beside himself with wrath and threateningly replied: Get out before I convert you into a stone with the gorgon gaze of my will."

Saint Bhrigu laughed at him and left saying: "0, no, you cannot hate me or make me into a stone, for God and I are One. Prophet Brahma suddenly awoke from his error and apologized. Then Bhrigu said: "I forgive you, Brahma, but I am disappointed not to have found in you what I wanted to see."

Then Bhrigu repaired to Shiva, who was seen getting ready to meditate. As soon as Shiva's form met the gaze of Saint Bhrigu, the Saint shouted savagely: "Hey, Shiva, you Grand Cosmic Killer, why don't you stop shattering worlds, murdering innocent babies, and inventing ingenious death-dealing devices Why don't you cease destroying the beautiful and useful things and Beings of the earth and get busy annihilating the wicked things of this very hot place! "

Shiva could not believe his ears, that a mortal man like Saint Bhrigu could be so audacious and free with his speech. Shiva shouted: "Stop your savage voice, or I will reduce you to ashes with the burning magnetism of my Spiritual Eye." Saint Bhrigu derisively retorted: "Fine use you will make of your Spiritual Eye. Go ahead, I dare you to burn up the God in me, you Grand Killer." Shiva remained paralyzed with anger and speechless at the awakening words of Saint Bhrigu, who soon melted away from his sight, saying: "Oh, what a disappointment you are."

91

At last, almost despairing because he could not find the world's most humble man, he skeptically resorted to the third Prophet, Krishna, who controlled the preserving principle of the Cosmos. Saint Bhrigu found Prophet Krishna sound asleep on his wonderful bed. He stood there watching the halo of peace radiating from the prophetic face of Krishna. Then, unable to think of any way to test him, in a fit of emotion Saint Bhrigu kicked Prophet Krishna on the chest, shouting: "You sleeping fool, wake up, see who is here." Krishna awakened with the sweetest, most undismayed, loving voice, and quickly picked up the kicking foot of Saint Bhrigu, and while massaging it, he said: "Ah, my Lord Bhrigu, is your foot hurt?"

Saint Bhrigu, beside himself with simultaneous visitations of remorse and joy, cried out: "I have found Him: I have found Him. O, Prophet Krishna, Thou art the world's most humble Being, even as God is. Thou art, O Krishna, the greatest, the most humble superman of this earth. I accept you as the greatest Guru-Master. Will you accept me?" Krishna accepted him as his disciple.

Now, dear friends, you realize that if you want to know the greatest of all Beings, the wisest in the Cosmos, our God, you must be humble, for the humble man makes a charming altar for God in himself, and establishes His altar of humility in every heart that he meets.

HEALTH CULTURE

CURATIVE FOODS And God said: Behold, I have given you every herb bearing seed, which is upon the face of all the earth, and every tree, in which is the fruit of a tree yielding seed; to you it shall be for meat. And to every beast of the earth, and to every fowl of the air and to everything that creepeth upon the earth, wherein there is life, I have given every green herb for meat; and it was so.

ALFALFA My student, and personal friend, the late Luther Burbank, famous plant wizard, said that alfalfa contained some of the most important nutrition substances known, and would become the future food of Man. The ancient Arabic name for it is "Alfalfa" or, "Father of all foods." It is recorded that hundreds of years before Christ the Persians invaded Greece with the help of horses which had been foraged on alfalfa.

Apparently, the extent of its healing and nourishing value can be accounted for by the fact that it has the longest roots of any plant known, sometimes attaining a growth length of 50 feet. Therefore, it may be readily seen that a root which plows that depth into tile bowels of the earth is bound to absorb powerful magnetic qualities, probably extracting minerals of more concentrated and intensified strength than those nearer the earth's surface.

Until recently, in America, it was used only to feed and fatten pigs, and was found to produce such fine specimen of bone structure, and growth in general, as well as elimination of the usual hog diseases, that some enterprising pioneer figured that what was good for the baby pigs might have the same effect upon human babies, since which time it has earned a reputation as a miraculous healer and builder for mankind.

ALFALFA TEA For each cupful of tea desired, use 1 tablespoonful of alfalfa. Put it into cold water and slowly bring to a boil. Simmer; steep; strain. Honey may be added to taste. Orange Juice squeezed into it gives a delightful aroma and taste.

An inferiority complex is born of contact with weak-minded people and the weak innate subconscious mind. A superiority complex results from false pride and an inflated Ego. Both inferiority and superiority complexes are destructive to self-development. Both are fostered by imagination, ignoring facts, while neither belongs to the true, all-powerful nature of the Soul. Found your self-confidence upon actual achievements, and you will be free from all inferiority and superiority complexes. Conquer pride by humility, wrath by love, excitement by calmness, selfishness by unselfishness, evil by good, ignorance by knowledge, and restlessness by the ineffable peace acquired in the stillness of complete silence. Take pride in being humble.

FORTNIGHTLY AFFIRMATION

"In the stillness of my Soul I humbly bow before Thy Omnipresence, knowing that Thou are over leading me onward and upward on the path of Self-Realization.

NOTES OF VALUE

1.   To assure safe, regular receipt of all mail, please keep the Headquarters informed of your change of address, or of your forwarding address, a week or two in advance.

2.   Be a devoted, faithful Crusader of Truth and Self-Realization. Send in the name of any friend or person whom you think to be sincerely interested in his self-betterment.

3.   Review the Preface to the Fortnightly Praeceptum, in order to firmly establish the method of study in your mind and to make it of practical use.

Resolve to regularly and consistently study your Praecepta, for therein lies the Key to your own Self-Realization. If you are unavoidably "behind" on your studies, resolutely decide today to "catch up" by devoting a little more time and attention to these invaluable teachings.

5. Conscientiously follow the Diet Laws and Principles in order to more harmoniously and more perfectly develop yourself in every respect.

6. But more valuable and more enjoyable and more enlightening than all to you will be the priceless time that you devote to your daily Meditation. Solemnly resolve to bathe your every thought and notion in that Ever-New, Ever-Conscious, Ever-Present Bliss and Joy of Meditation. (The elementary technique of Meditation was presented in Praeceptum No. 1 - The Tunnel to Eternity).

YOGODA SAT-SANGA FORTNIGHTLY INSTRUCTIONS
BY
PARAMHANSA YOGANANDA
(To Be Confidentially reserved FOR MEMBER'S USE ONLY)

I was made for Thee Alone.
I was made for
Dropping flowers of devotion gently at
Thy Feet on the altar of the morning.
My Hands were made to serve Thee willingly;
To remain folded in adoration, waiting for Thy coming; and when
Thou comest to bathe
Thy Feet with my tears.
My voice was made to sing Thy Glory.
My Feet were made to seek Thy Temples everywhere.
My eyes were made a chalice to hold
Thy burning Love and the Wisdom falling from
Thy Nature's hands.
My Ears were made to catch the music of
Thy Footsteps echoing through the halls of space.
And to hear Thy Divine Melodies flowing
Through all heart-tracts of devotion.
My Lips were made to breathe forth Thy praises
And Thy Intoxicating Inspirations.
My Love was made to throw incandescent searchlight
Flames to find Thee hidden in the forest
Of my desires.
My Heart was made to respond to Thy Call alone.
My soul was made to be the channel through which
Thy love might flow uninterruptedly into
All thirsty Souls.

PRAYER TO PRECEDE THE PRAECEPTUM STUDY

"Every sound that I make, let it have the vibration of Thy Voice. Every thought that I think - let it be saturated with the consciousness of Thy presence. Let every feeling that I have glow with Thy Love. Let every will that I will, be impregnated with Thy Divine Vitality. Let every thought, every expression, every ambition, be ornamented by Thee. O Divine sculptor, chisel Thou my life according to Thy Design!"

GOOD AND BAD HABITS

The power of habit The power of habit is all supreme in the life of man. Most people spend their lives just in making good mental resolutions, but never succeed in following what is wholesome. We usually do not do what we wish to do, but only what we are accustomed to do. This is why materially-minded people find it difficult to be Spiritually-minded even when they try hard. So, also, Spiritual people find it difficult to be material even when they associate with materially-minded people. It is difficult for vicious people to be good and it is difficult for noble people to be mean.

Habits are automatic mental machines installed by man to exercise economy in the use of initial will power and effort required in performing actions. Habits make the performance of actions easier. Friendly habits are very helpful in performing difficult good deeds easily. Evil habits, however sympathetic, are deadly, inasmuch as they are die-hards and do not stop disturbing the Mansion of Life even when they strongly will to do so. Bad habits and sin are temporary misery-making grafts on the Soul. They must be thrown out sometime.

Very seldom have you realized that the health, success, and wisdom outlook of your life entirely depends upon the issue of the battle between your good and bad habits. Henceforth, you must not allow your bodily Kingdom to be occupied by bad habits, you must learn to put your bad habits to flight by training all your diverse good habits in the art of victorious psychological warfare.

The soldiers of bad habits and of ill health and negativeness are invigorated by specific bad actions; whereas, the soldiers of good habits become stimulated by specific good actions. Do not feed bad habits with bad actions, starve them out by self-control. Feed good habits with good actions.

Influence of Early Habits

The unwelcome habits that came earliest in your life have kept you quite busy now. and have crowded out many worth-while things of life. The social world moves on the wheels of certain habits. Few realize whither the social machinery is headed - to the chiasm of ignorance or toward the mire of petty engagements, which choke the steady progressive activities of life.

From childhood one should develop the better taste of contacting the superior pleasures of peace, harmony, and so forth, and should form spiritual habits early. We are ruled by habits which form our tendencies, moods, and desires, and if bad habits are in the lead, our moods and actions become evil, so, the precedence of good habits is desirable, as they can guide our actions and moods to a happy goal.

Bad habits promise little temporary happiness and ultimately they invariably cause misery or destroy all happiness, people who yield to bad habits do not know this. They helplessly get so used to drifting with bad habits and their subtle tortures that they became shocked at the thought of forsaking their poisonous comfort. It is, therefore, natural for people used to the darkness of bad habits to hate the light and comfort of good habits.

The world creates in you bad habits, but the world will not stand responsible for your actions springing from those habits. Then why give all the time to the world? Reserve even an hour a day for actual Soul to Soul God-Realization. Doesn't the Giver of the world itself, of your family, money, and everything, deserve one twenty- fourth part of your time?

People of bad habits seek bad company, people of worldly habits seek materially-minded companions. People of meditative, peaceful habits seek the company of Christ-like saints. There is one thing very good about the promises of bad habits - they seldom keep their promises. Bad habits are easily found out to be habitual liars and deceivers.

That is why souls can never remain perpetually in bondage. Never condemn the sinner, for he knows too well the fears and tortures of sin. Do not drown him in your hatred, but give him a chance to have his own knocks, then he will be only too willing to be lifted up. Jesus said that material habits keep millions away from God.

People do not intentionally love to be evil. They are evil because they do not know the greater charm of good habits, and are unable to compare and select the- best. Most people become evil due to the influence of opinion, and most people are unconsciously led to evil. People are evil due to the precedence of evil in their environment in early life, and people are evil because they wrongly think that through evil they will get happiness easily. People love evil because they falsely magnify the dread and torture supposed to be involved in self-control. People are evil because they are compelled to become so by the compelling influence of evil instincts or wrong determinations.

One cause of failure is that you do not weigh your bad habits against the power of your free will required to combat them. Find out through daily introspection whether you are a free man, whether you eat, walk, move, work, and meditate according to the dictates of your will power and wisdom, or whether you are the tool of your bad habits, which make you do miserable things in spite of the protestations of your reason and will.

Do Not Be a Slave to Your Senses

If you are a slave to your senses, you cannot be happy. If you are a master of your desires and appetites, you can be a really happy man. If you eat against your will; if you wish anything contrary to your conscience; if you act wrongly, forced by your senses, against the wish of your Inner Self, then you cannot be happy. People who are slaves to the senses find that their evil habits compel them to do things which will hurt them. Stubborn bad habits bludgeon your will power down every time it tries to take the lead and guide your thoughts to the kingdom of right action. The remedy lies in rescuing your will power from the imprisoning power of the senses.

To yield to bad habits is to make them stronger and to make your will power weaker and weaker. Fight your bad habits of anger, fault- finding, jealousy, fear, inertia, over-eating, or whatever your particular weakness is, by not yielding to temptation against your will. When you determine to do something that you know is absolutely right, go through with it at any cost. This will give your Wisdom- guided will more power over your bad habits. Last year's material failure, Spiritual indifference, mental and moral weaknesses, and halfhearted meditations must be put into the discard by using your will to be prosperous, to be Spiritual, by exercising self-control and by meditating deeply until you actually contact God.

Almost every Soul is a prisoner of the senses, which are entrenched on the surface of the body. The Soul's attention is lured away from its inner kingdom in the medulla, the Spiritual-Eye, and the plexuses, to the outer region of the body, where greed, temptation, and attachment have their strongholds. The devotee, who wants to lead king Soul away from the misery-making slums of the senses, finds that he cannot do so without a severe clash between the soldiers of the senses and the Divine soldiers of the Soul.

Cultivate Spiritual Habits

The power of habits is especially important in the Spiritual path. If one is accustomed to meditating and contacting God, one will like to meditate more and more in order to contact God more frequently. Those who meditate little, and vaguely contact God, find that their desire to meditate and contact God vanishes when they are invaded by their powerful habits of restlessness. Likewise, those who are accustomed to being calm, attract more calmness and serenity, while those who are a little calm find their calmness easily disturbed when restlessness invades. Unspiritual habits entirely destroy the power of weak Spiritual habits.

Habits of thought are mental magnets which draw unto themselves specific objects relative to the kind and quality of their magnetism. Material habits attract material things and spiritual habits attract Spiritual things. Bad habits attract evil things. Good habits attract good things.

Don't let unhealthy materials float down the stream of your habit-forming thoughts. Watch the quality of the books you read. Watch the kind and quality of the people you associate with. Watch the influence upon you of family, country, and immediate daily friends who constantly associate with you. Many people are unsuccessful because their families have infected them and their subconscious minds with habit-forming, progress-paralyzing, discouraging thoughts.

When one meditates more often and cultivates the taste for peace and contentment, and gradually forsakes the indulgence in sense pleasures, he has a better chance for Spiritual emancipation. The best way of all is to cultivate the habit of contacting superior soul pleasures immediately upon awakening. Then, while filled with the superior pleasures of the Soul, one may enjoy such innocent, harmless pleasures of the senses as eating, meeting friends, and so forth, without any sense of attachment. In this way the Soul will find that it will spiritualize or change the quality of all material enjoyments.

No matter how many times a man suffers from very powerful attacks of sense-habits and restlessness-producing material desires, he finds that the meditation-born, occult soldiers of this life and past lives still come to his aid. a man who is always restless and never meditates thinks that he is all right because he has become accustomed to being a slave of restlessness. However, as soon as he tries to meditate and be calm, he finds resistance from the bad habits of mental fickleness. Then, again, when the habits of restlessness try to usurp the throne of the devotee's consciousness, they find the occult soldiers of past lives offering resistance.

THE APOLOGUE
(For the Entire Family)
THE STRANGE MUSICIAN

Nestled in the heart of Calcutta, India, once upon a time there lived an eminent musician. Music-loving students from far and near came to take music lessons from him. This famous man was rather peculiar in his ways. Being a musician, he had a keen perception of the psychology of his students. He treated each student according to his moods, character, and training. Being kind-hearted, he didn't charge the poor but eager students for their lessons, but, being strict, he he could not be induced to teach an unwilling rich student just because he offered to increase the tuition fee.

One day, while the music master was sitting in his studio, two students, John and Jelico, visited him. John was the son of a very rich man, while Jelico come from a comparatively poor family. The master happened to know the financial status of both these students.

After greeting them, he inquired: "John, have you ever studied any music?" "None at all, sir, but I would like to study; pray tell me what the charge would be per lesson," said John, The music master replied; "I accept you as a student at £.3 per lesson."

Then the music master turned to Jelico and asked: "pray tell me, have you ever studied music?" "Yes sir, I have somewhat absent-mindedly and discouragingly dabbled in quite a little music, but I don't seem to get any music selection right. Now I am willing to learn. How much will you charge me, please?"

The master said, after a long period of silence: "All right, I can take you, but I shall have to charge you £.6 per lesson." Saying this, the master remained in a firm, unyielding, unmelting taciturn mood, even though Jelico repeatedly protested against his injustice in charging him more than the rich man's son.

At last, after remaining stubbornly silent for some time, the master musician exclaimed to Jelico: "son, I shall have to charge you £.3 in order to make you first forget the little dangerous musical knowledge that you have now and £.3 more for my usual fee, for teaching you what I know."

HEALTH CULTURE

SEASONAL FOODS

TOMATOES When enjoying a ripe, luscious tomato, it would be difficult to realize that not so difficult to realize that not so very long ago this so-called "love apple" was an unknown quantity in the human dietary. In fact, it was considered poisonous, and tolerated only in the garden for decorative purposes because of its rich red coloring, Today, by dietitians everywhere, it is conceded to be one of the most important vegetables from the standpoint of alkalinity and wealth of important vitamins needed by the body. It is easily digested, attractive to the eye, pleasant to the taste, and highly recommended as a curative food. Also, it is an excellent substitute, periodically, for orange juice.

One of the most interesting laboratories in the world is located right within each individual Body. The liver, incidentally, it is the largest organ, and has a tremendous work to do, as well as an important one. Usually it has been overworked, in which event, like an overworked horse or human being, rebels and lays down on the job. In the liver, (together with the spleen), iron is stored and utilized as it is needed normally, or in emergency when there has been any undue loss of blood. Therefore, it is essential that its needs are considered, overeating is avoided, (which is the chief cause of enlarged liver) and a rest period is permitted it to "sort o' catch up" on its accumulated duties. The latter is best accomplished by a complete fast on high-vibrating fruits or vegetable juices, or both.

Tomatoes vibrate with the Liver. While there are some few foods which contain more iron than do tomatoes there are very few, indeed, that seem to work upon that organ with its efficacy, indeed, tomato is a curative specific for most liver conditions. Lemon is another liver-tonic, but though its antiseptic value is incomparable, it could not be taken in as large quantities as the tomato, for it is not as nutritious and sustaining.

It is one of the few foods that does not lose its mineral properties with cooking or canning. Nevertheless, any food, kept as near its natural state as is possible, is the ideal. Frying, stewing, pickling, peeling, salting, and preserving was never originally intended by Mother Nature, and though canned tomato is certainly recommended during the winter months and in localities where it is not obtainable fresh, there is nothing to quite compare with a ripe Juicy tomato picked right from the vine in its sun-soaked state. To those of my students who have a garden, include this plant in your next crop, and use an abundance of them if your local season has terminated; and to my many students scattered about the four corners of the earth, where only the canned product is obtainable, I advise its frequent use in this form, as it is a splendid substitute, and highly beneficial.

Tomato Juice diets have become very popular, and rightly so. Anyone can stand the "rigours" of a 3-day fast on tomato juice; taking a glassful, say, every 2 hours, followed by a glassful of water. Or, if desired, but three glasses may be taken, namely, morning, noon, and evening. Or, it may augment another cleansing outline such as salads, vegetables slightly steamed, and vegetables broth.

The ways in which this versatile vegetable may be used in the daily diet are innumerable. Cream of tomato soup is delicious in heavy weather when warm broths are desired. Stewed tomatoes, flavoured with minced garlic and sweetened slightly with honey, is another popular dish; or stuffed with vegetables or combined with string beans.

LIVER COCKTAIL TONIC Grind the whole tomato in a food chopper. Drink several times a day between meals. This tones up a sluggish liver, and will give the feeling of renewed energy.

FORTNIGHTLY INSPIRATION
BE THE CREATOR OF GOOD HABITS

You are the sole creator of good or bad habits. Till the soil of your mind with discipline, and sow the seeds of good habits. To thoroughly replenish your mind with good habits, you must be patient in cultivating them, while you continuously keep weeding out the bad habits. The taste for evil habits, like fire, dries up the taste for better Spiritual perceptions.

Distinguish between the Soul's lasting happiness and the temporary pleasures of the senses: touch, taste, smell, sight, and hearing. Strengthen your will power; do not be enslaved by bad habits; be guided by good habits, formed through cultivating good company and practicing meditation. Above all be guided by wisdom; stay away from evil by exercising good judgment and discrimination. Adopt the good in everything, being guided by free choice and not compelled by habits.

FORTNIGHTLY AFFIRMATION
"I form new habits of thinking by seeing the good everywhere and all things as the perfect idea of God made manifest."

YOGODA SAT-SANGA FORTNIGHTLY INSTRUCTIONS
BY
PARAMHANSA YOGANANDA
(To be confidentially Reserved for MEMBER'S USE ONLY)

IN STILLNESS DARK

Hark!
In stillness dark,
When noisy dreams have slept,
The house is gone to rest,
And busy life
Doth cease from strife, —
The Soul in pity soft doth kiss
The Truant flesh to soothe, and speak
With mind-transcending grace
Its soundless voice of peace.

Through transient fissures deep
In walls of sleep
Take thou a gentle peep;
Nor droop, nor stare, But
watch, with care
The sacred glare,
Ablaze and clear
In golden glee
Flash past thee
So nigh.
Ashamed, Apollo droops in dread
To see that luster spread
Through boundless reach of sky.

PRAYER TO PRECEDE THE PRAECEPTUM STUDY

"The dove of my love, whether singing through whirlwinds of destiny, coursing through bursting shells of impediments, or flying across the dense smoke-screens of colossal bewilderment, must ever be attracted toward Thee. 0, North Star of our wisdom-skies, the twinkle of Thy Light called me back to Thy Eternal Shores of Concentration."

THE ART OF CONCENTRATION AND MEDITATION

Concentration is the power to focus the mind on any desired line of thought. Meditation is concentration used only to know God. Every activity requires concentration, and no effective action can be performed without the help of concentration. Hence, business men, artists, students, and Spiritual individuals must know the art of focusing all the powers of attention upon a single point, in order to effectively succeed in their respective vocations. Concentration denotes the art of withdrawing attention from objects of distraction and then placing that recalled attention upon one thing at a time. Therefore, it is evident that the primary factor in concentration consists in withdrawing the attention from all diverting objects.

The consideration of environment is extremely important in gaining the best results in practicing concentration and meditation. There are two kinds of environment (1) inner, and (2) outer. Outer environment consists of the state of the PHYSICAL surroundings, noisy or quiet in which you are, preceding your concentration practices. The INNER environment consists of your mental state preceding meditation.

One can be restless even in a very quiet place and while the body is motionless and relaxed. So, remember, quiet yourself internally first no matter whether you are in a quiet or noisy place. If you are calm inside in spite of surrounding noises and disturbances then that inner mental environment is the best altar for concentration and meditation. Of course, quiet places are conducive to inner calmness. But remember, if you are determined, you can be calm, in spite of all noises. Do not stop meditating because you cannot find a quiet place.

Before lunch, at noon, sit in silence at least 10 minutes and do the same before dinner at night. At the Headquarters of the Self-Realization Fellowship the students usually meditate in the morning and at night, and sit in silence for 10 minutes at the table, before lunch and dinner.

Meditation is the Way to God

The surest sign that God exists is the increasing heart-bursting Joy felt in Meditation. When your mind is free from prejudice, when narrow-mindedness vanishes, when you unreservedly sympathize with everybody, when you hear the Voice of God in the chorus of churches, tabernacles, temples, and mosques, when you realize that life is a joyous battle of duty, and at the same time a passing dream and above all, when you became increasingly intoxicated with the Joy of Meditation, and in the making others happy by giving them God-peace then you will know that God is with you always, and you are in Him.

You can never have a truly inwardly and outwardly happy life unless you use the power of God-given concentration to reclaim, your lost Realization of God, to control destiny and to conquer the mysteries of life. Through the art of Meditation one learns how to actually contact Gad, the Divine Bliss, by faithful application of the science of Spiritual law. The scientist uses God's Law in order to find out the secrets of Nature, and the Spiritual man ought to know how to use his God-given powers of concentration, meditation, and intuition to know Divine Law.

Meditation Plus Activity

It must be remembered that finding God does not imply complete neglect of the various physical and Spiritual battles of life. On the other hand, the climbing Spiritual aspirant must learn to conquer in order to make the Temple of life free from the darkness of ignorance and the weakness of disease, so that God's perfect Presence may be perceived.

As a house full of jewels cannot be seen in the dark, so the presence of God cannot be felt while the darkness of ignorance, overpowering disease, or mental inharmony prevails.

When and How to Meditate

Select a noiseless place. As the drawing room produces conversation consciousness; the bathroom, cleaning consciousness; the bedroom, sleeping consciousness; and. the library, reading consciousness, so also, a little place for meditation produces the silence consciousness. A little room with one or more windows, or a little closet with open door, or a corner screened off, or a mountain top, or a forest in the summer, or an evenly heated room (neither too warm nor too cold) in a quiet place, is very suitable for meditation. Even while riding in an automobile or Pullman car, or lying down in the same bedroom with others, you can pretend to be asleep and can still practice.

In a small room or in a corner of a room screened off, put a small table and a straight armless chair facing the East. Then place a woolen blanket covered with a silk cloth on the chair, covering the back, the seat, and running down your feet - (for European-dressed students). Otherwise, place a woolen blanket 'asana' on a deer skin or on a simple 'kusan-asan' (mat of 'Kusa') grass and sit in lotus or any comfortable posture. The blanket & skin insulate your body and prevent the Life Current and consciousness which is moving toward the spine, the brain, and God, from being held back in the sense centers and drawn into the earth by the earth currents. Be sure to practice meditation in the early morning and before going to bed at night, when the Life Force in the brain can easily be turned off from the sense-nerves to God.

101

Principles and Exercises

It must be especially remembered that in the practice of concentration, the relation between breath and Life Force, mind, and vital fluid (sex energy) must be known by the Spiritual beginner. A balanced control of these four bodily forces brings quick Spiritual results without any downfall or hindrance. Every Spiritual student can attain a concentrated mind by the single separate control of any one of the four bodily factors. By strict celibacy alone, one can gain great mental concentration.

The balanced way to Self-Realization consists in practicing exercises and following principles which simultaneously control and harmonize breath, Life Force, mind and vital power. Therefore, every Spiritual aspirant should practice real breathing exercises, Astral techniques, control of energy flowing in the sensory motor nerves, methods of mental meditation, and principles of calmness-producing celibacy. Students who mediate regularly without calming the restless breath or the Life Force and vital essence, often find insurmountable difficulties in the Spiritual Path.

If one is nervous and keeps his body in constant motion if his Life Force is restless, then his mind is restless, vitality is restless, and breath is restless. But if one controls the life Force by Spiritual exercises and the practice of calmness through meditation, then his mind, breath, and vital power are within his control.

If the breath is restless, as in running, the Life Force, mind, and vital essence will be restless. On the other hand, if breath is made calm and rhythmic by the practice of these Lessons, the Life Force, mind, and character will he under control. Likewise, if the mind is restless the Life Force (through nervousness), and physical life become restless. Mental calmness is usually attended by calm nerves, controlled bodily energy, and a well- regulated moral life. Similarly, loss of vitality, resulting from living too much on the physical plane, produces mental dissatisfaction, melancholia, peevishness, nervousness, lack of energy, and heavy restless breathing.

Don't drug yourself with too much sleep and thus lose your vitality. Six hours of sleep is plenty for most people. Wake up at 5:00 A.M. and meditate. This time is suitable because your home and the neighborhood are usually quiet. Metaphysically this time is suitable because the rays and vibrations of the dawn are- vitalizing and Spiritually uplifting. At night, meditate from 9 to 10 P.M., or 10 to 11 P.M., or 10 to 11:30 P.M. When everybody is asleep and quiet, you remain awake in God.

Remember that the longer you practice with intensity, the nearer you will be to the joyous contact of silent God. Intensity consists in making every today's meditation deeper than the yesterday's; and every tomorrow's meditation deeper than all of yesterday's meditation.

The more sweetening you put in water, the sweeter it becomes. Likewise, the longer you meditate intensely, the greater will be your Spiritual advancement. On Sundays, holidays, and do-nothing-loafing days, meditate in the early morning from 6 to 9 A.M. and at night from 9 to 12 P.M.

By breathing exercises and attaining breath calmness, one can attain great concentration. By control of the Life Force in the sensory motor nerves, (by Pranayama) as taught in the higher Self-Realization Lessons, one can withdraw the currents from the senses and prevent the disturbing sensations from reaching the brain, and thus calm the mind. By mental concentration and self-control, as in meditation, one can find the breath and the Life Force automatically calmed, and the stability of character attained.

The real Spiritual teacher knows that the safest, quickest, and the best Spiritual method for the beginner lies in learning harmonization of these four bodily factors. To approach God by any one path, by the breath way, the energy way, the mind way, or control of Life Force way, is a limited and one-sided method and fraught with many grim difficulties.

Some people perform breathing exercises without realizing their Spiritual significance. They will grow into good athletes with lots of lung power, but that is all. Others try to approach God by the energy way, by controlling the life Force in the body. If they forget the Divine conception of the Astral technique (Pranayama) they satisfy themselves with certain mental and Astral power and forget God entirely. Some people try to know God by mental meditation - by mental imagination only. They see false visions for the most part, or live in the law of subconsciousness and frozen images of imagination.

THE APOLOGUE
(For the Entire Family)
"MONKEY CONSCIOUSNESS"

Tej Bahadur, a young business man in India, took great pains and spent considerable of his hard-earned money in going to London to confirm his business transactions. He had harbored within himself, an extraordinary desire and constant caution, about the art of business economy. No matter how he cut down his overhead, he was never satisfied and constantly thought of numerous fantastic schemes for saving money. Though he was a wealthy business man, he once brooded over the idea of going to London by working his own way as a sailor. Also, he thought of inventing oil-run, inexpensive seaplanes in order to go to London more economically.

Tej Bahadur often indulged in wild fantasies and wondered why God had not made him fast-moving like the electricity which traverses over vast tracts of space during the twinkling of an eye. While he was, in his imagination, bemoaning the fact of not being speedy, like the lightning, a friend of his, who knew all about his strange plans of economy, came scurrying toward him and poured forth a volley of excited words: " Tej Bahadur, come to the banks of the river Ganges. I have found a man who can levitate himself and walk on water, and is willing to teach the method to a worthy student." Listening to this, the wealthy Tej Bahadur was greatly impressed with this new idea and said to himself: "Thank God for sending me a levitating tutor. I guess I will ask him to teach me levitation, and that will save me a lot of money which I annually spend on my European business trips."

Thinking this, he wended his way toward the river-banks, where the Master had temporarily encamped himself. The business man requested the Master to teach him levitation. The Master agreed to do so and started giving him a lesson.

The Saint softly said: "Son, every night, dim the light in your bedroom, lock the doors, and sitting erect on a straight chair, facing the East, with closed eyes, mentally chant the Holy word of the Cosmic Vibration, "Om," for an hour, and then at the end of one month you will be able to race over the waters."

As the business man thanked the Master for the lesson, and was about to return home, inwardly wondering about the extreme simplicity of the lesson, he was gently called back by the Master, who cautioned: "Son, I forgot to tell you something about the technique of levitation. While you are mentally chanting "om" and are concentrating, be sure not to think of a monkey." "That is simple," said the business man, "of course I won't think of a monkey." After duly saluting the Saint, he returned home.

Evening came fast on the wings of time. Tej Bahadur closed the windows and pulled down the shades, and sat in a straight chair in his bedroom to practice the technique of levitation. No sooner had he done so than the first thought that struck him like a thunderbolt was: "I must not think of a monkey."

Two minutes passed and several times he warned himself inwardly: "I must not think of a monkey." Ten minutes passed and he thought of all the different kinds of monkeys in South America, India, Africa, Sumatra, and other places, that he should not think of. He was furious. He willed himself to banish the thoughts of the monkeys which, in a fast moving procession, were leaping through the window of his helpless mind. At the end of an hour he found himself thinking of nothing but monkeys. With each succeeding day he faithfully meditated, but, to his great annoyance, he found that he was frantically trying not to think of millions of mental monkeys which were jumping into his mind.

Beside himself with rage and helpless fury, the business man, after a month's concentration upon the forbidden monkeys, raced back to the Master and loudly exclaimed: "Master, take back your lesson on levitation. I don't want to learn to walk on the water. You have taught me to meditate upon monkeys instead of levitation. You have developed and increased the monkey consciousness in me."

"Ha, ha, ha," merrily laughed the Saint, and gently advised him, in a voice like the soothing dew: "Son, I tried to show you how untrained and slavish your mental state of concentration is. Unless you learn to make your mind obey you, you cannot achieve any success, not to speak of the difficult art of attaining the power of levitation. First learn to attain mental control, and then use that power to achieve small things, and when you are able to do that, try that on bigger and bigger achievements, until your inner power becomes developed enough to levitate you, or to accomplish even greater Spiritual miracles."

FORTNIGHTLY INSPIRATION
OUR CONCEPTION OF GOD

The usual conception of God is that He is superhuman, Infinite, Omnipresent, and Omniscient, but in this general conception there are many variations. Whatever conception we have of God if it does not influence our daily conduct; if our everyday life does not find an inspiration from it, and if it is not found to be universally necessary, then that conception is useless. If God is not conceived in such a way that we cannot do without Him in the satisfaction of a want, in our dealings with people, in earning money, in reading a book, in passing an examination, in the doing of the most trifling or the highest duties, then it is plain that we have not felt any connection between God and Life, intuition is the direct grasp of Truth. It is in this Intuition that Bliss Consciousness, or God Consciousness, is realized. God is Bliss. He is Ever-Existent. When we wish Eternal Bliss, or God, we also wish Eternal, Immortal, Unchangeable, Ever-Conscious Existence.

FORTNIGHTLY AFFIRMATION

"Teach me to find Thy Presence on the Altar of my constant Peace, and the Joy that springs from deep Meditation."

JOY! Peace! Joy!

YOGODA SAT-SANGA FORTNIGHTLY INSTRUCTIONS
BY
PARAMHANSA YOGANANDA

WE ARE ONE

Thy Cosmic Life and I are One.
Thou art the Ocean, and I am the Wave;
We are One.
Thou art the Flame, and I am the Spark;
We are One.
Thou art the Flower, and I am the Fragrance;
We are One.
Thou art the Father, and I am Thy Child;
We are One.
Thou art the beloved, and I am the Lover;
We are One.
Thou art the Lover, and I am the Beloved;
We are One.
Thou art the Song, and I am the Music;
We are One.
Thou art the Spirit, and I am all Nature;
We are One.
Thou art my Friend, I am Thy Friend;
We are One.
Thou art the Master, and I am Thy Servant;
We are One.
Thou art My Mother, I am Thy Son;
We are One.
Thou art my Master, I am Thy Disciple:
We are One.
That is why Thou and I are One.
Thou and I were One, and Thou and I will
Be One Ever Anon.

PRAYER TO PRECEDE THE PRAECEPTUM STUDY

"I wandered through forests of incessant searchings, and arrived at the mystery door of Thy Presence. On the doors of Silence I knocked loudly with my persistent blows of faith, and the doors of space opened. There, on the altar of glorious visions, I beheld Thee, resting.

I stood, with restless eyes, waiting for Thee to speak. I heard not Thy Creation-Making-Voice. At last the spell of stillness stole upon me, and in whispers taught me the language of angels. With the lisping voice of new-born freedom, I tried to speak, and the lights of Thy temple assumed, sudden brilliancy and wrote letters of light."

POPULAR MISCONCEPTION OF CONCENTRATION

There are two ways of typewriting: (1) By the "Hunt and Pick Method," by which the student hunts for every letter: he can never develop speed by this method. (2) But by the "Touch Method" the typist not only types easily and scientifically, but he also develops enough speed. So, also, there are two methods of concentration. (1) The "Hunt" method by diversion of the attention. In this method you try to get your mind off a certain thing, but find yourself, in spite of everything, automatically thinking more and more about it. (2) The scientific method of concentration by which you learn to throw your attention on God, and appeal to Him to recharge your concentration with His super-concentration.

Self-Realization Fellowship Instruction teaches you the scientific method of concentration. When you learn to throw your thought concentratedly on God, and successfully appeal to Him to recharge your concentration with His super-concentration, then, and then only, can you accomplish all things. When the concentration of the Spirit charges the scientifically-acquired human concentration, then it is that one can demonstrate, "O, ye mountains, go into the depth of the Sea," and they shall go.

The popular ineffectual method of concentration may be graphically depicted by Madam Butterfly's useless attempts at concentration, as follows: The scene is the home parlor after lunch, about 2 p.m., on a cold wintry day. Madam Butterfly enters, pulls down the shades, and hurries to sit in a straight-backed chair to concentrate. No sooner has her body touched the chair than she exclaims: "My goodness -this seat is too hard. Let me fetch a pillow." Seated on the pillow with the thought: "All is now ready on the Western Front," she suddenly discovers that the chair is maliciously squeaking, and disturbing the beginnings of her concentration. So she transfers her pillow and her body to another chair.

A moment later she is about to sneeze; a draft is coming from a nearby open window. "Oh, where could I have put my handkerchief?" Looking around, she discovers it beside her former squeaking altar of concentration. Handkerchief reclaimed and used, window closed, radiator shut off, she contentedly now thinks: "Now, at last, everything is hunky-dory - now for a delightful dip into the depths of concentration." Only a moment passes, when just as she is about to plunge within, "Ta, ta, ta, ta, ta, tang, ta, ta," bubbles out the boiling radiator. In disgust, she vexingly refrains from plunging any deeper into her inward concentration, and with rough hands chokes the radiator's voice. In righteous indignation she now increases her determination to dive deep, deep, down into the heart of meditation, stumbling, against the piano stool or her way back to her chair, in the semi-darkened room, inwardly cursing, but still determined to concentrate, she once more begins, like a veteran Yogi, a moment later, "Plung, ploong, ploong-plung" goes the piano in the apartment next door, accompanied by rough laughter and loud talking. Mad by this time, and disgusted, she thinks: "There goes that infernal piano again, just as soon as I sit down to meditate."

Next thing, as her holy wrath begins to calm down in the semi-darkness, she begins to think: "Well, that's really a fairly good piano; it only needs a little tuning." Then the thought of half a dozen different makes of pianos comes to her mind, followed, by the memory of her dear old grandmother's piano in the sweet old days of long ago, when she used to dance accompanied by rustic airs played in the days of her grandmother's youth - her dear grandmother, who always protected her from the harsh discipline of her parents and so on, with loving memory and thoughts of her grandmother.

Suddenly, then, she jerks herself from her sweet reverie, and thinks: "Oh, I must practice silence; I must concentrate." Now she begins to consider herself as the brave martyr in the hands of her rowdy restless thoughts. So once more, with saintly dignity, her spirit rebuked for its restlessness, with rather battered self-control, she once more begins to meditate.

Her eyes have hardly closed again, with this now attempt, when, "Gr Gr Grr Grrrrrrrrrrrrr—" crows out the telephone with impudent, inconsiderate, continuous silence and patience-piercing pertinacity. She breathes to herself, through grinding teeth: "I will not answer. Crow all you like, Mr. Telephone Bell." But "Grrrrrrrrrrrrrr" goes on the impertinent bell with unimaginable bravery.

"Well, maybe it is an important call. "Hello, there! — What is it you want? This is Somerville 2924..." Violently goes the mouthpiece onto the hook, plomp goes the telephone onto the table, as she hears the soul-disgusting answer: "Wrong number."

This terrible ordeal over, she musters up courage enough to again begin to concentrate, while her brain is seething with the thought: "I will break that telephone forever and ever. I will choke its throat. I will cut the cord. It will then disturb me no more." So wrought up is she with the inconsiderate incivility of the telephone bell that she thinks it unwise to take a chance on its incorrigible fickleness, with scissors in hand, she is about to cut the cord, when she thinks of the inconveniences that might follow, she changes her mind and sensibly puts a piece of cardboard between the hammer and the bell on the telephone box.

That accomplished, victorious, she sits once more on her throne of concentration. A few more minutes pass and she is half dozing, her head nodding, due to her successive battles with piano noises, telephoto, and so forth, in her "Hunt" method of concentration. Catching herself sleeping and half ashamed, but yet in self-pity for her exhausted condition, she sits up straight once more to again begin to meditate. Immediately there arises a clamorous and continued deadly patience-breaking ringing of her hoarse- voiced door bell. As before, she thinks: "I will not answer it.

It is only that audacious salesman, who comes most afternoons despite my giving him murderous looks and slamming the door in his face."

The doorbell goes on ringing, with seemingly dogged patience, until she thinks again: "maybe it is something important." At the door, however, she smiles a galvanized smile as she greets her three lady friends, who have all obtained a master's degree in the art of expertly gossiping about everybody but themselves, and she gushes: "How do you do? Come right in, you three dear darlings. I'm awfully delighted that you came in." Inwardly, behind the artificial forced flower of her smile, lies the wasp of extreme disgust, stinging her within with silent whisperings. "Oh, you pests and gossips, when will you go so that I can concentrate?"

Three hours slip away as she merrily laughs at the folly of her three gossiping aged cronies. They talk about the neighbor's quarrels, the city murders, elopements, and so on. They busy themselves raking and prodding in everybody else's mental dirt heaps, though they have plenty of mental dirt to clean from their own homes. At last, the door closes behind the vanishing forms of these incarnate gossips, Much relieved, once more she sits down to concentrate, or at least to seek her lost throne of silence. Her brain and her attention are mobbed by the memories of piano noises, telephone bells, radiators, doorbells, and gossips. She looks at her watch, and with a resigned sigh she says: "I give up, Mr. Concentration. It seems I cannot be with you today. I have to run now to the kitchen to prepare the evening meal."

The above is not exaggeration. It is only a sample of what happens to most housekeepers, church members, and business men whenever they attempt to concentrate.

The business man hurries to his office, rushes in, sits in his chair, and begins to concentrate upon some difficult problem. The din of his secretary's typewriter annoys him. He shouts at her to stop. A moment later, he realizes there is need for hurry on the letter she is typing, so he shouts at her to go on again. Then he begins smoking his after-breakfast cigar. Every day he resolves to quit smoking some time, as he knows that it is a useless, expensive, and unnecessary habit, but he never does quit. After a little more deep thought on the problem, ragged nerves tug at the shirts of his concentration, and finally, hardly able to bear himself any longer, he madly dashes the cigar into the cuspidor, stops the typewriter, and dismisses his secretary because she brought him some bills that needed to be paid. He shouts at the inwardly-laughing, outwardly-respectful secretary, and pleads: "Have pity on me. Be considerate. Don't you see that I am trying to put over a big deal?" He decides to try to concentrate once more, and dozes off in disgust at his inability to work out his problem, and he quietly drifts into deeper slumber, while his secretaries happily and quietly steal off to lunch. He wakes up to find that he has missed his train, lost his appointment, and with it his big deal falls through. This business man does not know the real art of concentration.

"Well," some of you may ask, "How do some business men become successful without the knowledge of how to concentrate properly, as taught in Self-Realization Fellowship Instructions?"

The answer is, that all successful people are men of good concentration powers, but they usually do not realize it. If even they knew the scientific method of Self-Realization concentration they would be still more successful, and would also know how to balance their material success with their Spiritual success. Everyone can reason without learning logic, but the knowledge and study of logic cannot fail to be of great advantage to those who have a natural ability to reason, or who have developed their reasoning faculties by rubbing noses with difficult problems, or who have developed good reasoning as the by- product of the vocation they follow.

The ordinary successful business man uses his powers of concentration only about twenty-five per cent, and even that he uses unconsciously, but the student of Self-Realization can develop his power of concentration one hundred per cent and can use it scientifically to bring him success.

(To be Continued in the Next Praeceptum)

THE APOLOGUE
(For the Entire Family)
WE ARE ALL A LITTLE BIT CRAZY AND DON'T KNOW IT

The iron horse "Chief" was racing over the tracks with its noisy hoofs carrying us off fast in its gorgeous Pullman cars. I was seated on the lower berth of car 17, peering through the window, watching the mountains, trees, and landscapes flit by. Opposite sat an Ego-inflated movie actor, wearing a face painted with sarcasm and pity. He condescended to sit in front of me, a Hindu with long flowing hair, and orange robe. He gave me an indirect look or two of mystic disgust, almost openly signifying that I had no business sitting in front of him in such a strange attire. Due to my clean-shaven face and long flowing hair, he looked as if he thought I was [a] strange woman imported from the Orient. Anyway, his face writhed more and more into a look of agonized disgust when he saw that I was looking at him with an unperturbed gaze.

Suddenly, I pounced a few words upon him even before he could think, and with a calm, firm, but loving kindly face, with soft audacity I demanded: "Mister, will you please tell me why you have assumed such a horrid expression?"

"None of your business," he angrily replied. And he was about to leave when, with the firm hand of a mother's love curbing a wayward child, I caught hold of his hand and commanded him to sit down, saying that I wanted to talk to him, please. He automatically and helplessly sat down, remarking: "You are the most audacious person I have ever met during my travels." Paying no attention to his remarks, I went on and promptly answered his previous question.

"It is none of your business what kind of a face I have," he further remarked.
"Of course it is my business, sir, to tell you about your self-distorted face, as I have to look at it steadily in front of me. Won't you please paint a rosy smile over your dark, gloomy face?"

To this, he smiled from ear to ear, his well-formed, well- polished teeth partially showing. My movie friend, by his smile signified: "Hostilities have ceased, now state your intention in as few words as you can quickly do so."

Finding him in a receptive mood, I started: "Well, my friend, it was an accident that you were born an American and I was born a Hindu, but I know that you and I are both God's children, now and always. Before we leave this earth, we shall have to drop our nationality and all our mortal titles and know ourselves only as God's children."

"Yes, I know all that," was the bland, dry reply.

I, with unabated warm enthusiasm, in spite of the cold blanket of indifference which he cast over me, continued: "Brother, do you know that in this world we are all a little bit crazy and don't know it?"

"Why, what do you mean," replied my movie friend. He apparently did not like (indicated by his silence) to agree that he was crazy too. Paying no attention to his question, I went on: "Do you know why people can't find out their own craziness?"

"Why don't they?" was the child-like inquiry. By this time my movie friend was getting to be receptive to my talk. Then I went on: "Well, you know people don't detect their own craziness because crazy people of the same feather flock together."

"It is true that material business men like other business men, and spiritual monks like their own kind, and so on. If I were a movie actor, then we would have at least tolerated each other, and if I had met another Hindu with my tastes instead of meeting you, then we would perhaps have had a jolly good time. But, you know, I know about your craziness as movie actor, but you don't know anything about my craziness. Well, I promise you, it is a very interesting occasion because you have the chance of a lifetime to know about the truth that, when people differently crazy come together, then they find out about their own craziness."

My movie actor friend came down from his sarcastic pedestal, lost control of his guarded manner, and burst into a long, loud laugh: "Ha, ha, ha; that is well said."

But I wasn't through with him yet. I made him promise to carefully listen to me, saying, "I know about your craziness for movies, but you don't know about my craziness. Here is one chance in Eternity, after finding out about my craziness, to still further find out whether my craziness is better than yours, or vice versa, or whether mine will afford more real happiness than yours."

I warned him against stubborn, wandering arguments by enjoining: "Remember, fools argue, while wise men discuss." I made him feel that he too was as wise as I, so he raised no protest when I asserted: "Mr. Movie Actor, if I can convince you by logic that my God-craziness is better than your movie craziness, then you must follow me, but if you can talk me into believing that yours is better than mine, then I will be a movie actor."

Well, I am not a movie actor yet, for my friend lost out and followed me instead.

The fact is, we must not dislike people because they are different from us, or because they hold different opinions from ours. We are almost crazy to believe in our own pet formed opinions more than the judgment pronounced by the true logic of facts. So, also, others are madly in love with their favorite unformed convictions. Since we of the East and the West don't know about our individual craziness, it is best that we come together and point out to each other our specific craziness.

When the East will talk about the West's craziness for material possessions, and when the West, in a friendly way points out the Spiritual one-sidedness of the East, then they each will remove their one-sidedness and constructively exchange their experiences for a balanced civilization after the pattern of God's Cosmic Plan.

HEALTH CULTURE

PROPERLY COMBINING FOODS To obtain the best results from your food, the matter of properly combining the items used at one meal, reducing them to the very minimum, should be given careful consideration when planning your meals, in order to prevent eventual digestive disturbances. The fewer the items used at one meal, the better. Even when eating fruits, it is well to use but one. In fact, frequent meals composed of only one fruit is an excellent idea. Try eating, for example, all the apples you wish for your noon lunch; nothing else. They are filling, satisfying, and have much food value, as well as being on important source of Sodium, the dissolving and alkalizing chemical. Or, you might try grapes, oranges, or any other fruit you may prefer.

While the body does require various types of food for harmonious balance, it is impossible to handle them all at one sitting. In the beginning, healthy, normal cells have selective intelligence the same as the Composite Man, and possess the faculty of choosing that which they need, attempting, to discard that which they cannot utilize, in most cases, due to misuse, they have lost that power of selection, as have the taste buds in the mouth. All this is the result of years of ignorance and disregard of their normal requirements.

FORTNIGHTLY INSPIRATION
CONCENTRATE FOR HAPPINESS

When the Soul's potential lasting happiness becomes encrusted with the temporary pleasures of the senses, then the golden luster of the Soul becomes obscure. When a man's mind is attentive to jealousy, worry, and so forth, he becomes thoroughly miserable, but when he turns the same attention to love, peace, and harmony, he feels supremely happy. So, also, the Soul becomes happy when it turns from the lesser misery-making pleasures of evil to the superior pleasure-producing Soul qualities. If the Soul becomes completely engrossed in lesser happiness, it fails to be attentive to the investigation of superior lasting happiness. Many persons may reason that renunciation of material pleasures i s almost an impossibility in the world of business existence, but every man is not advised to return to the jungle in order to find peace. He must be in the world and yet not of it. He must not be negative, and should not blind himself with material pleasures, and thus fail to enjoy the vision of superior pleasures.

FORTNIGHTLY AFFIRMATION

"Teach me to open the gate of meditation which leads to Thy blessed Presence. Teach me to behold Thy face in the mirror of my Stillness within."

OM!   PEACE!   Bliss!

YOGODA SAT-SANGA FORTNIGHTLY INSTRUCTIONS
BY
PARAMHANSA YOGANANDA

WHERE I FOUND THEE

I bow to Thee in the Silver Rays;
I drink to Thee in the sunbeams;
I stand in reverence before Thy Mountain Majesty;
I clasp Thy Image reflected in the Lake;
In the voice of the Echo I hear Thy voice;
I embrace Thee in the calm caress of the Breeze;
I bathe in Thy bubbling fountain of my bosom.
The explosions of my passions have died away
And I hear Thy Whispers in the pines and in the
Gentle swish of the laughing waters of the Lake.
I listened to Thy sermons through the voice
Of my reason,
I beheld Thee ploughing the soil
Of my soul with trial,
And sowing the seeds of Thy Wisdom therein.
Every day I watered the seeds sown by Thee,
But it was only when the sunshine
Of Thy Mercy came
That those seeds sprouted, grew, and
Yielded the harvest of contentment.
Suddenly the waters, Nature's green carpets.
The blue vastness overhead, the opaque stones.
And my body became transformed into a vast mirror
By the magic touch of my silence,
And I saw myself reflected in everything.
And when in concentration I looked at myself
I became transparent— and in my transparency
I could not find me — but only Thee, only Thee.

PRAYER TO PRECEDE THE PRAECEPTUM STUDY

"Many doors opened of themselves before me because of Thy Coming. O Lord, everything shone with life when Thou earnest. The temple's marble floor, on which I stood, thrilled me because of Thee. Everywhere dumb-matter spoke, spirit-resurrected by Thy Touch. Everywhere throbbed the incense-breeze of stillness, bearing to me Thy perfume of Bliss. I behold Thy sanctuary, hidden beneath the broken rocks of silence."

PART TWO
THE RIGHT METHOD OF CONCENTRATION

Self-Realization Technique of concentration is different from all other methods of concentration because it is scientific, and because it teaches students how to reinforce the mind with the super-charged Concentration of God.

The constant, blind, dogmatic, and superficial church-goer, or the seat-warming, impractical person who has a mania for attending lectures without discrimination, each goes to the temple of worship and listens half-heartedly, all the time thinking of the chicken dinner which is to follow later in the day. Maybe he is thinking of it even when he is repeating "The Lord's prayer." He mumbles the prayer - a vague, meaningless volley of words. They fall on his ear-telephones, which are busy reporting them to the brain, all intermingled with the noise of the horns of passing automobiles, screeching fire sirens, and so on. Along with these, his tactual telephone keeps reporting to the chamber of silence in his brain all about the discomfort of his new clothes, his pinching shoes, his itchy head, his tickling nose, his tickling ears filled with wax, and the overheated atmosphere. He prays on like a Victrola, which does not know anything of the message it grinds out, while his optic telephone is busy scrutinizing the shabby dresses worn by the women sitting in the bock seats, and the rich dresses and the diamonds worn by the self-satisfied, price-saturated church members sitting in the mammon-reserved exalted pews.

God tries to speak to His children through the voice of silence and peace in response to His children's prayers, but His voice is usually drowned out by the ringing of the telephone, sensations of touch, smell, taste, hearing, and sight, and by the rowdy noises of the sensation-roused thoughts and the memory-roused thoughts. Then, sadly, God's voice turns back from the depths of silence, finding the operator's intelligence too busy with the switchboard of sensations, and His devotee's attention entangled in the hands of the robbers possessed by restlessness. God sadly turns away, finding this His temple of concentration has been made a noisy place for the money-changers of material desires and sensations. The Christ-like Guru-preceptor, Intuition, must come with the whip of self control to drive away the materially busy, restless thoughts, and make the Temple of Silence into a Temple of God.

Everyone needs the scientific Self-Realization method of God-directed, God-charged concentration, including the busy, worry- burdened housewife, the business man of the world at large, the dogmatic, devout, self-deluded, self-sufficient, little-knowing churchman, the restless minded, who are unable to concentrate because of thoughts that make them like jumping jacks, the wise, something-knowing, intelligent churchman, and last, but not least, the real Spiritual aspirant; all these I say, need the scientific Self- Realization method of God-directed, God-charged concentration.

The inequalities of the powers of concentration in people are responsible for the different degrees of their success. Self- Realization Fellowship teaches that the man of concentration will be able to do anything successfully, for God-guided concentration is powerful, and Self-Realization Fellowship also teaches that the same focusing power of detached attention is required in making a success of a home, a business, a church, or a temple of silence established in the soul. To bring equality successfully on earth, one must not use high- powered concentration for self-success at the expense of others, but one must know how to guide and reinforce concentration with the just, unselfish, service-giving, sympathetic, super-concentration of God.

Most rich people are satisfied with using their high-powered minds for gaining material success, but they turn a deaf ear to the cries and misery of others. But the man charged with the super-concentration of God wants success only when making others successful, by spiritualizing the ideal of industry as service, and by finding happiness through making others happy. Self-Realization Fellowship teaches the art of ideal concentration for the good of self and all others.

DEFINITION OF CONCENTRATION

The great Hindu sage, Patanjali, said that union with God is established by neutralizing the restless thought and desire-waves of the consciousness. To illustrate, the image of the moon looks distorted if it is reflected in a stormy lake full of ripples, but if the storm subsides, the waves vanish and the clear, undisturbed reflection of the moon is seen. Likewise, the Absolute spirit is reflected in the lakes of myriads of human Souls, just as the one moon maybe reflected in a million lakes. But the lakes of human attention are rippling with sensations and thoughts caused by the storm of breath and of restlessness.

By Self-Realization concentration, by the Christ command of calmness, when these waves of breath cease, due to the restfulness of the heart, then the ripples of sensations and restless thoughts vanish from the lakes of human attention, and the undisturbed reflections of the Soul are seen. Patanjali emphasizes the negative side of concentration; that is, as soon as the attention is free from the objects of distraction, it can reveal the Soul, just as the removal of the hand from in front of the lens of a flashlight would reveal the things in front of it in the dark.

Jesus said; "if thy right eye offend thee, pluck it out, and cast it from thee: for it is profitable for thee that one of thy members should perish, and not that thy whole body should be cast into hell."

By this He means that every devotee must know how to concentrate and do away with all distractions of sensations in the hands or the eyes. He must know how to calm the senses, or take consciousness away from them and withdraw the Life Force from the sensory motor nerves, which are the conductors of disturbing sensations, and thus he will know how to enter the eternal life. The Life Force in the nerves keeps the soul entangled with the messages of the sensations in the eyes, ears, hands, and so forth, and when the Life Force is plucked from the eyes and cut off from the hands and the consciousness of the body through the Soul being free from the messages of the senses becomes cognizant of its Divine self and its Divine Kingdom - then only is a state of concentration reached. This is the Biblical definition of concentration interpreted.

Now comes the psycho-physical scientific definition of concentration; namely, that concentration is the power by which one can negatively free one's attention from its objects of distraction, and positively place one's attention upon only one thing at a time. When the attention is free from minor distractions, then it is free to act positively by throwing its rays upon business problems, upon matrimonial problems, or upon God. You can say: "He is concentrating upon business, or upon God," but you cannot say: "He is meditating upon money," because meditation is that specific form of concentration which is only applied [to] knowing God.

Most church members ineffectively try to meditate; that is, they try to think about God, but they do not forget all about being hypnotized by restlessness, in order that such members nay get results, the minister must know how to teach them the way to detach their attention from distracting thoughts and sensations and apply their attention to God. No meditation is possible without knowing the art of concentration, which consists in forcing the attention from the reports of the senses, and so forth, and placing it upon only one thing at a time, prayer, chanting, and singing all become a mockery without the knowledge of the positive and negative factors of concentration and meditation.

Everyone, including business men, housekeepers, healers, doctors, osteopaths, chiropractors, artists, philosophers, moralists, devotees, and yogis - ALL need to know the art of concentration in order to be a real success, each in his own respective path. No one can concentrate upon art, business, or God, or anything else deeply, without first disengaging the attention from the objects of distraction. Hence, scientifically freeing one's attention from the objects of distraction is the only way to get results. It has often been seen how difficult and how hopeless it is either for the house-keeper, or for the business man, or for the Spiritual aspirant, to concentrate by adopting the popular common way of mental diversion. Hence, it must first be learned what the objects of distraction are, and how they can be scientifically switched off from the conscious attention.

Men and women in most churches do not know anything about the laws of prayer. They try to contact God ineffectively and unscientifically, either by blind devotion or by intellectuality. Of course, if the prayer is intense, the attention automatically disengages itself from objects of distraction and focuses itself upon God. But the program of worship in the churches usually consists of a variety of physical ceremonies, such as singing and talks, which do not give the attention the opportunity to go deep into God-Consciousness. This method of diverting the mind from all distractions, and thus concentrating upon God, is the most effective, as has been shown before. God does not reveal Himself to the intellectually wise, nor emotionally intoxicated, but unto the babes of sincere worship He says:

> "A humble magnet call - a whisper by the brook
>   on grassy altar small,
> There I have my nook.
> A tattered temple shrine, a little place
> Unwatched, unseen, is where I humbly rest or lean."

But He will come into the big churches too, if the doors of the hearts of the people are open, and if a genuine concentration of soul gives Him a welcome. God can never be bribed by the following of a church, or by its wealth, or by well-planned sermons. God visits only altars of hearts which are washed by tears of repentance and soul-stirring love.

(To Be Continued in the Next Praeceptum.)

THE APOLOGUE
(For the Entire Family)
"THE HUNTER WHO BECAME A SAINT"

A cruel hunter marauded the jungles of Bengal, India, ruthlessly killing birds just for the fun of killing, since there were no hunting restrictions in those days as to how many birds one might kill, this hunter, Mr. Nishada, littered the forest with dying and dead birds.

Due to his unscrupulous wholesale murder of the birds, those that were left, having eluded the gorgon gaze of his evil-eyed guns, became so intuitively wise that they flew away at even the faintest noisy approach of the stealthy hunter seeking to kill them. The hunter became beside himself with wrath, when he found that he had so scared the birds that he could not even approach them, he began shooting at random through the thick foliage of the dark jungle.

At last, with his wrath spent, and completely dejected, and after the loss of many cartridges, he walked for a long time and finally emerged from the jungle. He was stupefied at the spectacle which greeted his vision, which stirred fresh hope in his breast. To his amazement, he saw an orange-robed Saint standing knee-deep in the nearby lake on the outskirts of the jungle, with all kinds of game birds trustingly perching on his head, shoulders, and hands, and peacefully floating in a circle around him.

A sudden idea flashed across the mind of the hunter: "If I put on an orange robe every day and pose us a harmless saint, then I can create enough trust in the birds so that they will perch on me and swarm all around me. And then, at my convenience, I can club to death quite a few. In that way I can get even with the birds for flying away at sight of me.

The hunter watched motionless from behind a tree to see how the Saint, like St. Francis of Assisi of yore, fed and sang a sermon to the birds, and then, after finishing his bath in the lake, with difficulty he got away from the birds, who kept flying after him as he retired.

The next day the hunter concealed several clubs, knives, and daggers on his body, and dressing in an orange robe, as is customary among the saints of India, he calmly walked into the selfsame lake. To his great glee, scarcely believing his eyes, the very same game birds who used to fly away at sight of him, now trustingly, like little children, perched all over his body and swarmed around him.

He was happy beyond dreams, but as often as he made up his mind to suddenly pounce upon the birds and choke them to death, he found his hands frozen upon him. He could not do it. He did not have the heart to betray the innocent eyes of the birds who so trustingly found shelter with him.

Then he began to sermonize within himself: "I have been a hateful hunter, whose very sight is shunned by the birds, but behold, the magic of even an outward orange robe of a saint, though it covers a wolf in sheep's clothing, still has led the birds to trust even my very hateful self. "I wonder, the hunter thought, "if simply the outward garb of a saint can create so much trust and confidence in even dumb animals, how much wholesome influence and trust a real saint, plus the orange robe, could exert and create in all people. Thinking this, the hunter, threw his clubs, knives, and guns into the water, and walked away, determined to become a real, full-fledged saint, amidst the clamor of the trusting birds, who followed him as long as they could, and finally reluctantly parted from him.

This hunter-saint was known to wade daily into the lake and feed the birds and sing to them, and he made so many bird friends that all the watery seats of the lake used to be occupied by all kinds of feathery for an audience.

After delivering his sermons of peace, he was happy to see the difference between the life of a hunter and that of a saint. As a hunter, lie repulsed all the peace-loving birds, but as a saint he gathered together all the love of the birds. After making friends with the birds he became a great teacher, who attracted all kinds of human friends, whom he served with the song of Truth from the core of his heart.

Now we find that the hunter, even by imitating the garb of goodness, ultimately became good, do not forget that even though you cannot overcome your inner weakness all at once, it is all right for you to wear the garb of goodness if you really are sincerely trying to be good. It is better even to imitate goodness than to imitate wickedness. One who imitates good actions, even outwardly, gets a chance to smell the alluring fragrance of goodness, whereas, one who even hypocritically imitates evil, contacts the odor of the polecat of evil.

Of course, to deliberately use goodness to deceive people is the greatest blasphemy against God and yourself, but do not care if people call you a hypocrite on account of a few of your discovered failings if you are sincerely trying to be really good.

We should not expect too much goodness from anyone who is trying to be good, nor should we expect nothing but goodness from one who has done his best to be good. Even if one falls down from the grace of goodness, he is safe if he tries his utmost to become good again, such people are far better than those who use goodness outwardly to deceive people. Why should those who are trying to be good, once they are discovered doing wrong, be labeled as hypocrites

"Judge not, that ye be not judged," because to label anybody as bad or as a hypocrite, when he is really trying to be good, in spite of his failings, is the greatest blasphemy against God and all His children, Naughty or good - all are equally loved by God. God not only rejoices when His good children come back to His home of wisdom, but it gladdens Him most when He finds His naughty, prodigal children returning home from their truant wanderings.

HEALTH CULTURE

HYDROGEN Foods, too, are subject to the law of Vibration, and it is incumbent upon us, as students of Self-Realization, to cultivate the quality of discrimination in our choice from among those having the highest rate of vibration, thus taking our fate out of the hands of Chance. Tree foods are the highest vibrating and most spiritual of all.

However, we cannot all live upon them exclusively (though 60 per cent of our dietary should consist of fruits and vegetables) for we are still of the Earth, and must "Watch our next step even while hitching our wagon to a star."
Hydrogen, the most radiant and high-vibrating of all the organic chemicals, giving us power to live on the higher planes, is found in lemons, limes, oranges, grapefruits (known as the super-hydrogen fruits) and pineapples, peaches, melons, as well as the succulent vegetables such as tomatoes, which contain a great deal of liquid (Nature's distilled water.)

FORTNIGHTLY INSPIRATION
INTERIORIZE YOUR ATTENTION
The joyous rays on the Soul can be perceived if you interiorize your attention. This can be done by using the archive of your mind to enjoy the beautiful scenery of thoughts in the invisible, tangible Kingdom within you. Do not search for happiness only in beautiful clothes, clean houses, delicious dinners and soft cushions and chairs. These will imprison your happiness behind the bars of externality or Outwardness. Rather, in the airplane of your visualization, glide over the vast tracts of Fancy, beholding the limitless empire of thoughts. There behold the mountain ranges of unbroken, lofty, spiritual aspiration, for improving yourself and others. If you have made up your mind to find joy within yourself, sooner or later you will find it.

FORTNIGHTLY AFFIRMATION
"I shall seek Thee as the ever-increasing Bliss of Meditation. I shall feel Thee as the boundless Joy, throbbing in ray heart. I shall seek to know Thee first, last, and all the time. Finding Thee first, I shall find things I crave through Thee."

OM PEACE

YOGODA SAT-SANGA Fortnightly Instructions
BY
PARAMHANSA YOGANANDA
(To Be Confidentially Reserved FOR MEMBER'S USE ONLY)

I SHALL CATCH THEE

I cast my Net of Devotion in the vast sea
Of my mind.
Thou hast fled from me many times.
Diving deeper in the farthest depths
Of my peace.
I am unceasingly casting bigger
Nets Of Devotion,
Everywhere - over the Surf, on the
Wavelets Of Life, over the waves of stars,
And all over the billows of Souls,
With the conviction that some time
Thou wilt be caught in the deep
Net Of my Adoration.
All I know is that I am a fisherman.
And I must keep fishing for Thee
Until I find Thee.
Storms and gales of trials rock my boat
Of unceasing effort.
I am being tossed, but I shall keep casting My
Net of Love until Thou dost get
Entangled in it, and, unable to escape again,
Thou wilt surrender Thyself unto me.
I knew that some time I shall catch
Thee In the Net of my Devotion.

PRAYER TO PRECEDE THE PRAECEPTUM STUDY

"I come to Thee with the song of my smiles. Whatever treasures lie in the secret safe of my Soul, I have brought eagerly to Thee. I have brought all the honey from the hive of my heart. Whatsoever is mine, that also is Thine. The taper of my happiness will merge with Thy Blaze of Bliss. The aroma of Thy scented Flame and its murmuring joyous waves come floating to me. In Thy enchanting Light I will swim forever. Teach me to drown in Thy Divine Light and live, rather than live in a mirage-paradise of earthliness and die."

PART THREE
THE ART OF CONCENTRATION
DISTRACTIONS WHICH INVADE SILENCE

There was a great exodus from the churches when some reformers offered healings of the body, and when they over-emphasized prosperity, but people are restless just the same. Their Souls' hunger can never be satisfied

117

by false substitutes and artificial, malnutritious, theological chaff.

Some modern denominations and religious movements are adopting "Going into the Silence" in their program of Sunday worship. But their "Going into the Silence," though it brings some peace, does not teach the groping, Spiritual aspirant how to contact God. This "Going into the silence" is a glorified method of reaching God by diverting and silencing thoughts. This is the negative factor of concentration only.

The difference between loud prayers and silence is considerable. In loud prayers the mini is busy with loud sounds and bodily motions, as well as with restless thoughts. In ordinary silence, the mind is kept somewhat still by keeping the body still and the optic telephone is closed by the closing of the eyes, but the thoughts within run just as wild as over. Some people succeed in silencing their thoughts for a moment or two, and get a little glimpse of the peaceful face of God through this momentary crack in their wall of restlessness, but when the real seeker confronts a perpetual darkness, with only an occasional glimpse of peace in the Silence, always broken into by the disturbances of restless thoughts, he begins to wonder: "Is this all there is to God and His inspiration?"

When he opens his eyes and gets out of this state of negative silence, he wonders at the glory and immensity of the sunlight, and the electricity which races the trolley-cars here and yonder, at the sky scrapers, at the lightning searing the sky, and again he wonders in the evening at the power of the light of the moon, and many more of Nature's wonders. The man who has the experience of only a little peace in the Silence finds a bitter consolation in the powers and manifestations of Nature, and he begins to belittle his strivings for more spirituality and his inner experiences in his states of silence.

But Self-Realization Instructions teach that there are higher states of concentration, and that as you ascend them, one by one, you come into higher and higher spheres of indescribable joys and experiences and visions, feeling and beholding which the student can say: "He whom I was seeking in the clouds, in the forest of the blue - He is with me, within me."

Then he says: "Him whom I sought as power without, I find Him as the fountain of all Nature's forces, existing within me, just behind the walls of darkness I perceive Him in the silence."

The Light, or Cosmic Energy, the creator of all forces, hides behind the darkness perceived in Silence, but those who are in the darkness of negative Silence do not comprehend that. Thus, you see that Self-Realization Instructions teach what should be done positively in the Silence, and how to produce Silence negatively and scientifically, and thus silence all thoughts and sensations.

Now, after describing how the temples, churches, business concerns, and homes need to learn the scientific and positive and negative factors of silence, I shall proceed to describe these. First of all, we should find the distractions that are the definite psycho-physical elements which invade Silence as it tries to march toward a mental object.

They are three-fold: (1) Sensations; (2) Thoughts roused by sensations; and (3) past memory thoughts, roused by sensation-born thoughts. SENSATIONS As soon as you sit to concentrate upon your business in your office, or upon God in the church, your attention is busy with the noise of typewriters, and other office noises, or with the noise of street cars and automobiles in the street outside, coming through your auditory nerve wires, or with the touch sensations of comfort (pleasurable feelings of the flesh, such as after-dinner drowsiness, low vitality, and so forth,) or of discomforts of the body (disagreeable feelings like itches, aches, tight clothing, sweat, heat, cold, hunger, weariness, and so forth,) - all pouring into the brain through the tactual nerve wires. Or your attention may be busy with odors of nearby bodies, or with the fragrance of flowers in the room, or with the perfume of ladies' dresses, which keep pouring into your brain through your olfactory, telephonic nerve wires.

Or again, your attention may be busy with visual sensations, caused by the sight of the decorations of your office, or the church auditorium, or the dresses of the people, coming into your brain through your optic nerve telephones. Or your attention may be busy with the pleasant, or unpleasant sensations on your palate, from the taste of peppermint candy, or chewing gum, or an after- smoking taste, or the after-sensation of the cool taste of cold water, which you may have drunk not long before. So you see that your attention meets with many distractions from the sensations of sight, hearing, taste, touch, and smell, the very minute it wants to concentrate upon any problem, upon business, or upon God.

THOUGHTS EVOKED BY SENSATIONS But the above-mentioned five kinds of distractions are not the only kinds which distract your attention, for these sensations give rise to thoughts.

For instance, when you hear the noisy automobile outside the room in which you are sitting, trying to concentrate, you perhaps begin to have thoughts about different makes of cars; the chewing gum taste in your mouth may make you think about the many kinds and flavors of chewing gum. The fragrance of the few flowers in the room may make you think of the florist's shop, or your grandmother's delightful garden in the days of long ago; the sight of your business office may make you think of the nicer business offices you have been in, and the sight of the dresses of the people around you may make you think of all the lovely dresses you would like to own.

PAST THOUGHTS ROUSED BY PRESENT THOUGHTS So you see that sensations give rise to thoughts. Then fresh thoughts, arising from sensations, rouse the sleeping thoughts in your subconscious memory; for instance, the sound of automobiles around your place not only rouses many thoughts about other models of automobiles, but these, in their turn, may rouse in your consciousness sleeping thoughts of how you have driven many models of both slower and faster cars, or may remind you of the bad accident you had with that very powerful car. So you see, your attention generally meets with sensations, then it meets new crowds of thoughts waking from their subconscious slumber.

The three-fold distractions or enemies of attention are (1) sensations; (2) Thoughts roused by sensations; (3) Past memory- thoughts roused by present thoughts. The minute your attention wishes to march along [a] pathway of concentration toward a definite goal, it is waylaid by the three above-mentioned inner bandits of distractions.

THE POPULAR WAY OF CONCENTRATION IS BY DIVERSION
Q. What is the scientific way of freeing the attention from the above-mentioned distractions?
A. If you should ask why you cannot succeed when trying to concentrate upon a problem, or upon the Sunday sermon,

most religious dignitaries would tell you to divert your mind from the objects of your distraction. But this seldom works successfully, for your mind dwells more upon a thing, or upon a subject, whenever you try hard not to think about it.

We have described before how the business man in India fruitlessly tried to divert his mind from the thought of a monkey, after he was asked not to think about monkeys whenever he tried to concentrate. Likewise, it is almost futile to try to divert your mind from a constantly ringing telephone bell when you are trying to concentrate. This is because, when the bell rings, the report of the sound is carried to the brain by the Life Force in the auditory nerves. Whether you wish to hear, or not, the bell sound floating through your auditory nerves, it is bound to register in the brain.

The popular method of diverting the attention from the sound of the bell, during the attempt at concentration, is unscientific. Of course, a man of very deep concentration habits may so turn his mind within himself as not to hear the ringing of the telephone bell. The question then arises; "What happens in him?" What physiological changes occur in this man of such deep concentration, so that he really does not hear the sound of the telephone bell, although that sound strikes on the tympanum -drum- of his ears?

The only logical conclusion that can be drawn here is that there is an inseparable connection between the Operator of intelligence and the Life Force flowing in the auditory nerves. When the operator of the sense-telephones, this Intelligence, chooses, he can make or manage so that by diversion, or by scientific relaxation, (as taught in Self-Realization Instructions), the sound of the telephone bell will not disturb him. a regular telephone operator, working at a switchboard, can do two things to be free from the disturbance of a ringing bell.

(1) She can fall asleep before the switchboard, and then she Will not hear the sound of the bell through the wires; or (2) by the scientific method she consciously or unconsciously might switch off the current from the wires during her spell of sleep, and thus prevent the sending of the sound of the bell through the wires.

Likewise, a man may do three things to stop himself from hearing the sound of a telephone bell. (1) diversion, he may disengage the attention of his intelligence, operating the switchboard of his auditory sense telephone, in this case, the careless operator is so busy mentally doing something else that he does not listen to the telephonic sound, though it rings in his brain, for it is transmitted through his auditory nerve wires. By this method, he does not remove the real cause, through which the disturbing bell sound reaches his brain. (2) Sleep, or unconscious, sensory, muscular relaxation, is another passive, unconscious method by which he can stop the entry of the bell sound into the brain. In sleep, the Life Force is relaxed from the muscles, and from the five telephone wires of the sense of touch, smell, taste, sight, and hearing.

(To Be Continued in the Next Praeceptum.)

THE APOLOGUE
(For the Entire Family)
THE ALASKAN SOURDOUGH

Sourdough is very precious to the prospector in the hills of Alaska. He carries a knapsack containing flour and a piece of sour dough to make bread with. The gold seekers disappear for months in the jungly hills searching for nuggets of gold. The prospector's life depends upon the chance caribou meat which he gets by hunting and upon the sourdough which creates leavened bread for him. In fact, these prospectors are called "sourdoughs" because they are so noted for their unquenchable pursuit of gold and their tenacity in saving sourdough for making bread.

While in Alaska, I heard of nothing but elusive gold dust trickling down the mountain streams, and gold nuggets and sourdough until I began to see the hills and streets of Alaskan cities paved with gold nuggets and plastered with sourdough. Everyone I met was, to me, a "sourdough." It is said that one of these sourdoughs, by a stroke of luck, (good Karma) chanced to slip into Heaven. When he got there, he created untold music of mischief for the gods. The Heavenly Deities, with their gold Rolls Royces and Packards, had a hard time bumping over the former gold-paved streets of Elysium, because the sourdough had rutted all the streets by digging for gold. All the celestial members complained to St. Peter about this gold-greedy sourdough's persistent and ceaseless gold digging on the highways and byways of Heaven. But St. Peter only remarked: "According to the laws of Heaven, all people can come here who come willingly, and they can never be ejected, except when they want to relinquish the peace of Heaven of their own accord. But, dear Heavenly Hosts, do not worry, when the sourdough has had enough gold, he will, of his own accord, leave the Divine Kingdom for his family on earth. Something may turn up to save you all from this mischief-making sourdough. Mischievousness and inharmony cannot exist long, you know, in Heaven."

The sourdough had dug up cartloads of gold from the streets of Heaven, which made the streets look like volcanic craters. The gods had to take to walking, since the roads were declared impassible by the Heavenly policeman.

One day, St. Peter was standing pensively by the Pearly Gate, brooding over some way of getting rid of the very troublesome sourdough, when another rusty-looking, shabby man arrived outside the Pearly Gates. St. Peter challenged; "Hey, who are you?" "Let me in; I am a sourdough," replied the old august prospector, but St. Peter shouted; "Nothing doing; get out, we are having a merry time with one sourdough who has marred all the streets of Heaven."

But the sourdough was insistent and appealed: "Mr. St. Peter, I promise you that I will not dig up the gold streets of Heaven, and I will vouch for the ejection of the other sourdough if you let me in."

St. Peter finally yielded and the august sourdough requested; "Honored sir, before I receive your hospitality in Heaven, I wish to state that I mean business, and I shall forthwith show you that I intend to fulfill my promises. So, while I am yet on the outer wall of Heaven, please call the mischief-making, gold-digging sourdough. I want to talk to him."

In due time the havoc-making sourdough appeared at the inner wall of Heaven and the newly arrived sourdough whispered something to him over the outer wall of Heaven. No sooner had the gold-digging sourdough heard the whispered counsel of the second prospector than he leaped into Hades.

St. Peter, wondering at this miracle, which all the counsel of the gods had failed to accomplish, welcomed the august, triumphant sour dough within the walls of Heaven, and with great curiosity inquired: "What did you tell him, that he left all his accumulated gold and willingly jumped into Limbo?"

The second sourdough laughingly replied: "Well, sir, St. Peter, I told him that he was foolish to waste his time digging gold in Heaven when he could get more precious platinum, all he wanted, from the unrestricted streets of Hades."

The above story carries the moral that men are persistently seeking happiness everywhere in Heavenly surroundings by wrong methods, or in Hades, by evil actions. Evil deeds sometimes seem to promise more precious platinum-like happiness than the golden happiness of Heavenly deeds. There are people who do not hesitate to jump from the pursuit of happiness in good to the elusive happiness in evil.

Heavenly peace can be found in the willing cultivation of good, and once formed, no one can take it away, not even the gods, unless man of his own accord, chooses to relinquish it. We should never be like the first sourdough and give up the peace and prosperity which is within our reach for the uncertain, more glaring prosperity and comfort which evil, hellish deeds may promise.

HEALTH CULTURE

PART II HYDROGEN (The following natural remedies have been tested, proven efficacious, and advocated by various leading Nature healers of the day, among the bio-chemists, naturopaths, osteopaths, and chiropractors.)

Some authorities advise laying a slice of lemon against the sore spot when you have a toothache; hard city water can be softened by the addition of a little lemon juice; a bilious attack will often respond quickly to a sour lemonade; lemon packs have given wonderful results in cases of necrosion of the bone, also appendicitis attacks; put a felon* into lemon; when there is a wound, use lemon water, applying olive oil first if the skin is broken, the strength of the lemon solution to vary with the degree of injury and the fortitude of the patient. [*Editor's note: I've heard of putting felons in jail but never into lemon; the manuscript is quite undecipherable at this point; I've found nothing in naturopathic literature to clarify.]

Burns should first have thick applications of olive oil, then a little strained lemon juice. Cataracts will respond to lemon packs over the eyes: 1/2 lemon juice and 1/2 distilled water (with olive oil smeared over the skin first). In this condition, the lemon packs should be alternated with Epsom-salt solution packs. In the kitchen, lemon should be always substituted for vinegar, as the latter dries up the red corpuscles.

By the token that all things are good in their place, there are, of course, occasions when much citrus fruits are contra- indicated, temporarily at least. Especially is this so of the lemon, which thins the blood. In the case of the anemic, the very thin person, the aged, or wherever there is a tendency to profuse bleeding, or ulcerated stomach, in these, and a few other conditions, it should be used with discretion, and then only under capable guidance.

When considerable citrus fruit is taken, as in an eliminative diet or fasts where it is the only food taken, we have found it advisable to take 1 to 3 glasses of salt water per day in order to prevent soreness within. Normally, the stomachs business is to manufacture hydrochloric acid, but often this power has been diminished through years of wrong living, and the salt and fruit acid, taken at intervals.

will neutralize the poisons stirred-up; for that is the power of hydrogen, to penetrate and stir up.

(To Be Concluded in the Next Praeceptum)

FORTNIGHTLY INSPIRATION
THE MIRROR OF SILENCE

When you find that your Soul, your heart, every wisp of inspiration, every speck of the vast blue sky, every shining blossom of the sky, the mountains, the earth, the whippoorwill, and the bluebells are all tied with one cord of Rhythm, one cord of joy, one cord of unity, and one cord of Spirit, then you know that nothing exists but the waves of His Cosmic sea. Like a silent, invisible river flowing beneath the sands, flows the vast dimensionless river of spirit through the sands of time, through the sands of all Living Atoms, and through the sands of all space. He is the fountain of wisdom, and radiant inspiration flowing through all Souls. He is a garden of celestial blossoms and bright thought-flowers. He is the Love which inspired our love dreams. He is the eternal motion of Joy. He is the mirror of Silence, in which all Creation is reflected.

NIGHTLY AFFIRMATION

"Every star, every pure thought, each good act will be my window through which I shall behold the Father."

YOGODA SAT-SANGA FORTNIGHTLY INSTRUCTIONS
By
PARAMHANSA YOGANANDA
(To Be Confidentially Reserved FOR MEMBER'S USE ONLY)

DIVINE JOY

Bless us with Thy intoxicating, ever-new,
Joyous, supremely satisfying Contact.
Teach us to drink Thee, that every blood cell,
Every thought, and every feeling may become
Saturated with Thy joy and have their pleasure
Thirst quenched forever.
After we are sure of Thy most tempting,
Everlasting gift of Thyself, then test us
With all Thy temptations if Thou wilt.
Bless us first with the light of Godly habits, so that
Whenever the darkness
Of bad habits approaches.
It will be spontaneously driven away.
Teach us to be so attached to Thee that we can
Not be at all attracted to material pleasures.
Teach us by Thy Love to conquer all loves
For worldly life.
Millions do not love Thee because they know
Not of Thy alluring Love.
Millions love matter because they meet it first.
Divine Beloved, why dost Thou not come first
In human life?
Oh, Father, how canst Thou expect frail Souls,
Ignorant of Thee and burdened with bad habits.
To know Thy all-healing Joy?
Of all Thy punishments, forgetfulness
Of These is greatest.

PRAYER TO PRECEDE THE PRAECEPTUM STUDY

"Bless me, that I may behold nothing but that which is good. Teach me, that I may touch nothing but purity. Train me, that I listen only to Thy Voice in all good speech and in the beauty of songs.

Direct me to inhale only the breath of purity-exuding perfumes from the flowers of the Spirit, invite me to indulge in wholesome tastes of soul-nourishing food. Teach me to touch that which reminds me of Thy Touch."

PART FOUR

FURTHER INSTRUCTIONS ON CONCENTRATION

During slumber, the Life Force is switched off from the sensation-receivers of the eyes, palate, olfactory nerves, tactual centers, and auditory centers. Hence the bell sound cannot reach the brain.

This shows that the operator, intelligence, unconsciously switches off the auditory nerve telephone, with the others, and so the man who is asleep does not hear the telephone sound in his brain. Though sleep is a good, scientific method of getting away from the constant sound of noises passing through the auditory nerves, still it is an unconscious passive method. If one can sleep at will, then he can produce unconscious sensory relaxation, or the switching of the Life Force off from the sense telephones at will, and thus he can prevent the noises from entering his brain. But one does not wish to sleep every time he wishes to become really quiet.

Self-Realization Instructions teach the third method of consciously switching off the Life Current from the nerve-wires of touch, smell, taste, sight, and hearing. This is the easiest and greatest scientific conscious method of disconnecting the Life Force from all the five sense-telephones, so that the optical, gustatory, olfactory, tactual, and auditory stimuli, and their resulting sensations, may not reach the brain at all. This scientific method demonstrates that, if you learn to switch off at will consciously the Life Force from the five sense-telephones, with which your operator, Intelligence, is working, then you can really remove the disturbing medium, which is directly responsible for allowing the stimuli of touch, smell, taste, sight, and hearing, to flow through it into the brain.

Each human being is the owner of a bodily house, into which is fitted two distinct sets of telephones, His home telephone wires receive and transmit messages, both directions, along the same wire. But the bodily house has two sets quite separate from each other in their function. Through the five sensory, receiving telephones of taste, touch, smell, hearing, and sight, the stimuli of tactual, gustatory, auditory, and optical sensations are received into the brain by the operator, Intelligence. Then another operator, Will Power, transmits messages of eye movement, nostril inflation, ear movement, or the movements of the tongue, or of any muscles of the limbs, through another set of nerves called the "Motor" nerves.

By stillness, by complete relaxation, or by lying down without tension of muscles, one can remove the life energy from the motor nerves and their connecting muscles. But this withdrawal of Life Force from the muscles and motor nerves is not complete sensory relaxation, for the five sense-telephones are not shut off; one can still see, taste, hear, smell, and touch, even when one is relaxed in the muscles. In sleep, the energy is switched off unconsciously from the five sensory-telephones; this Lesson teaches the method by which one, by proper practice, may be able to withdraw consciously and scientifically the Life Force from the five sensory nerve-telephones, and thus prevent the stimuli from reaching the brain and disturbing the attention with sensations, thoughts roused by sensations, and past thoughts roused by these new-born thoughts.

Q. Is it possible to switch off the Life Force from the five nerve-telephones, scientifically and consciously?

A. Yes, by quieting the dynamo of the heart, which controls the Life Force in the sense-telephones. In sleep, your heart action slows down, and this helps to withdraw the Life Force from the five sense-telephones, and also from the motor nerves. When the heart

125

stops, one dies, because the heart is the dynamo, or the life, of the muscles, cells, and the five sense-telephones.

The yogis of India say, with St. Paul, (1st Corinthians 15:31) "I protest by the rejoicing which I have in Consciousness (Christ), I die daily." (Withdraw daily the Life Force from the heart, or die and live again at will.)

When the heart stops beating suddenly, one dies, but when one can, by calmness, and at will, switch off the energy from the heart, then one can die or live at will, and conquer death. Mortals die once, and stay dead, but St. Paul, like the Hindu Yogis, says that by learning to control the heart one can die daily. In order to die daily, one has to live daily. When one learns to live and die at will, he becomes free from the flesh.

The main purpose of this instruction is to quiet the heart by giving up worries and fears, and thereby controlling the Life Force, which works in five sense-telephones. The heart of a mouse in a mousetrap beats 200 times more quickly than usual, because of its intense fear. The hearts of the calm Napoleon and the Duke of Wellington beat only 50 beats per minute. Children's heart-beats are much faster than those of grown people. Their restlessness is the cause. There sense telephones are always busy with outward stimuli. Children find it hard to quiet themselves, but when the child grows to be a man, he becomes calmer, and therefore his heart beats less frequently.

Normally, the heart pumps 10 tons of blood a day. If you worry, you trouble the heart, and its beats become faster. In 365 days, the heart pumps 365 times 18 tons, or 6,570 tons of blood. Just imagine the poor little overworked heart! This poor little heart cannot even rest while its owner sleeps or dreams. It is a much-abused slave. Therefore, when it has done enough, it says: "You have been a bad master, a hard task-master, now I will quit my job." And then, just because the spark-plug of life, your heart, refuses to work, you have to do without the whole machinery of your body.

Do not be frightened and superstitious, ignorantly thinking that you are going to stop your heart beat when you practice this instruction, and that you are going to die right away. This Instruction was not devised to stop the heart beating by force, nor to stop it so that It will not beat again. If anyone wishes to stop the heart, and not revive it, he does not need to bother to study these instructions, for he can very easily jump into a river, or get himself chloroformed for good. In such a case, his heart would surely stop, never to beat again.

Self-Realization Instructions teach that a state of unconsciousness, or passive subconsciousness, should be psychologically avoided during the practice of this instruction. Also, physiologically, no strenuous method of holding the breath should be used, thereby trying unnaturally to stop the heartbeat. It is absolutely impossible to stop the heart beat that way. But, by the practice of the method shown in this Instruction, the heart becomes so restful, and the lungs become so free from venous blood, that it is unnecessary for the heart to work. When the heart rests because of calmness, and because one eats more fruits and less carbonized foods, then the Life Force in the five sense-telephones can gradually be brought under control.

Concentrate [On] These Truths

The soul, being Individualized spirit, if given a chance to unfold, can manifest all the fulfillment and satisfaction of the spirit. It is through long-continued contact with changeable matter that material desires are developed. Desire is an imposter which hampers and encroaches upon your ever-joyous soul and lures your Ego to dance upon the crests of the four fluctuating, short-lived psychological states.

The mind must be protected from the four alternating psychological states of sorrow, false happiness, indifference, and a deceptive, passive peace which claims the Ego for brief intervals, whenever it manages to shake off the other three. Look at any face, and you will be able to tell whether its owner is at the mercy of any one of these.

It is very rarely that people's faces remain calm while they are in the grip of the four unstable mental states. Learn to swim in the calm sea of unchanging Bliss before you attempt to plunge into the maelstrom of material life, which is the realm of sorrow, pleasure, indifference, and a deceptive, temporary peace.

Protect the soul from the disturbance created within your mind by the mad dance of sorrow-producing desire. Learn to overcome wild, wicked desire. Realize that you do not need the things which create misery, for if you search within your soul you will find there true happiness and lasting peace, or Bliss. Thus you will become a "Bliss Billionaire."

When the Ego is not buffeted around by sorrow or happiness, it sinks into the state of indifference. You can look around you and find the faces of many people registering this state of boredom. You ask a person engrossed in indifference: "Are you sad?"

"Oh, no," he replies.
Then you ask him: "Are you happy?"
"Oh no," he drawls.
"Well then," you ask, "what is the matter with you?" "Oh," he cries, "I am just bored."

Day by day, as you offer mental whispers, a new awakening will come. A new living relation with God will be established. The mist of silence and mystery, which hangs over everything, will slowly vanish before the dawning light of your mental whispers for God. The blue sky will speak, saying: "Look! Here He is, spread all over my bosom." The flowers will say: Behold His smile in us." The dumb stones will declare: "See! He is sleeping in us." The trees will whisper; "He is dreaming in us." The birds will sing: "He is awake and singing in us." Your soul will, say: "He is throbbing in me." Your hitherto unmindful, unconscious thoughts will say: "He is awake in thee now, awakened by thy inner whispers. Listen! Through thy soul-stirring whispers, He is whispering songs of His love unto thee everywhere."

When your unceasing whispers shall at last dig deep into the soil of Omnipresent Silence, the fountains of His answering whispers will gush forth from your soul, and with their life-giving waters will refresh thirsting hearts everywhere.

(To Be Continued in the Next Praeceptum.)

THE APOLOGUE
(For the Entire Family)
THE LION WHO BECAME A SHEEP

A huge decrepit lioness carried an unborn baby lion in her body. As the days passed and the baby lion grew heavier within her body, she had a hard time carrying herself around inquest of prey. No sooner would she waddle toward the small animals for food, than they would slink away. Even if the lioness tried to catch her prey in stealth, she wasn't quick enough in movement, and every time she tried to catch some prey, she failed.

Roaring with sadness, heavy with the baby lion, and pining with hunger, the lioness stalked through the forest and fell asleep beneath the shade of a grove of trees near a sheep pasture. As she was dozing, she dreamt that she saw a flock of sheep grazing, and as she tried to pounce upon one of the dream sheep, she jerked herself and woke up. So, her dream came true, for she beheld a large flock of sheep grazing right near her.

Beside herself with joy, forgetful of the baby lion she was carrying within her body, and impelled by the madness of unappeased hunger, the lioness pounced upon the flock, took hold of a young lamb, and disappeared into the depths of the jungle. The lioness did not realize that during her mad leap at the flock of sheep, due to severe exertion, she had given birth to a young baby lion.

The flock of sheep were so paralyzed with fear at the attack of the lioness that most of them had become unconscious or stupefied, and thus couldn't run away. When the lioness departed and the panic was over, the sheep woke up from their stupor and began lamenting the loss of their comrade. As the sheep were bleating out their lamentations in sheep language, they discovered to their great astonishment, the helpless baby lion crooning in their midst. One of the mother sheep of the flock took pity on the baby lion and adopted it as her own.

The young lion grew up amidst the flock of sheep. Several years passed, and lo, there, with a flock of sheep, roamed a huge lion with long mane and tail, behaving exactly like a sheep. The sheep-lion bloated instead of roaring and ate grass instead of meat. This strictly vegetarian lion had perfected himself in all the details of the weak- ness and meekness of a lamb.

Once, it so happened that another great, hungry lion strolled out of the nearby forest which opened into the green pasture, and, to his great delight, beheld the above-mentioned flock of sheep. Thrilled with joy, and whipped by hunger, the great lion pursued the fleeing flock of sheep, when, to his great amazement, he saw a huge, husky lion, with tail high up in the air, also fleeing at top speed ahead of the sheep.

The lion paused for a moment, scratched his head, and pondered within himself: "I can understand the sheep flying away from me, but I cannot imagine why this stalwart lion should run at sight of me. Well, this runaway lion interests me." And so, armed with determination to get to the fleeing lion, he raced hard and pounced upon the escaping lion. This sheep-lion fainted with fear. The big lion was puzzled more than ever, and then slapped the sheep-lion out of his swoon. In a hoarse voice he rebuked: "Hey, wake up. What's the matter with you? Why do you, being a brother, fly away from me?"

The sheep-lion closed his eyes and bleated out in sheep language: "please let me go. Don't kill me. I am just a sheep brought up with yonder flock of sheep that fled away and left me."

"Ah, ha, now I see why you are bleating," and so saying, the big lion pondered a moment and a great idea flashed upon him. Then, without delay, this lion caught the sheep-lion by the mane with his mighty jaws and dragged him toward a lake at the end of the pasture land, where many animals came to quench their thirst, when the big lion reached the shore of the lake, he pushed the sheep-lion's head over the water so that it was reflected there, and began to give a violent shaking to the sheep-lion, who still had his eyes tightly closed saying; "What's the matter with you; open your eyes and behold that you are not a sheep."

"Bleat, bleat, bleat. Please don't kill me. Let me go. I am not a lion, but only a poor meek sheep," wailed the sheep-lion.

The new big lion, beside himself with wrath, gave the sheep-lion a terrible shake, and under the impact the sheep-lion opened his eyes, and was astonished to find the reflection of his head, not a sheep head as he expected, but a lion's head, like that of the one who was shaking him with his paw. Then the big lion said in lion language: "Look at my face and your face reflected in the water. They are the same, and look here, this face of mine roars instead of bleating. My face roars; now you must produce roars instead of bleatings."

The sheep-lion, convinced, tried to roar, but succeeded only in producing bleat-mingled roars. But under the slapping paws and exhortation of the new lion, the sheep-lion at last succeeded roaring. Then both of the lions leaped across the pasture fields, and together they pursued the flock of sheep, and finally returned to live in the den of lions.

The above story very fittingly illustrates how most of us, though made in the all-powerful image of the Divine Lion of the universe, yet being born and brought up in the sheep fold of mortal weakness we bleat with sickness, lack, disease, and death, instead of roaring with immortality and power, and preying on wisdom and unlimited prosperity.

The Self -Realization Teaching is the new lion who will drag you to the crystal pool of meditation and give you such a hard shaking that you will open the closed eyes of your wisdom and behold yourself as the Lion of Divinity, made in the image of the Cosmic Lion. Those of you who keep trying continuously will forget your mortal bleatings of weakness and sickness and death and will learn to roar with the power of almighty immortality.

HEALTH CULTURE

We would suggest that, vegetables in large quantities be taken to prepare the body for the eventual use of fruits. Vegetables may be taken in raw juices, broths, salads, and stewed form. The ideal fruit diet is to make a meal upon one fruit, the orange, for instance, eating, even a little of the peel, which possesses a volatile oil that is beneficial in small amounts.

LIMES are an antidote for brain-fag and inflammation of the brain. Serve limeade occasionally, sweetened with a little honey; they are a powerful cleanser.

ORANGES contain calcium; also, because of their sugar content, they should be used by thin persons rather than the other citrus fruits. Orange juice is wonderful in the treatment of all nervous conditions; it gives one courage, and assists in taking away inflammation from the brain. Whenever you have a lot of work to do, drink a lot of orange juice.

PINEAPPLES have the same vibration as the heart. They do not contain as high an acid as lemons and oranges, limes, or grapefruit, but have many marvelous attributes: having iodine, they nourish the glands; they are a natural anti-septic for the bowels, sore throat, sore tonsils,

and fever. The pineapple contains some chlorine, therefore, has great cleansing qualities. Its dissolving properties enhances its value as a reducing food. It is now obtainable, canned also, without sugar.

GRAPEFRUITS are a combination of lemon and orange, and contain natural quinine.

FORTNIGHTLY INSPIRATION

An unceasing demand for anything, mentally whispered with unflinching zeal and unflagging courage and faith, develops into a dynamic power which so influences the entire behavior of the conscious, subconscious, and superconscious powers of man, that the desired object is gained, a mental whisper, to achieve its object, must be undaunted by reverses and unceasing in its inner performance. Then it will materialize. Seek the contact of the all-satisfying, all desire-quenching God-Bliss.

FORTNIGHTLY AFFIRMATION

"Bless me, that I may find Thee in the temple of each thought and activity. Finding Thee within, I may find Thee without, in all people and all conditions."

PEACE! BLISS! PEACE!

YOGODA SAT-SANGA FORTNIGHTLY INSTRUCTIONS
BY
PARAMHANSA YOGANANDA
To Be Confidentially Reserved FOR MEMBER'S USE ONLY)

ROCK ME TO SLEEP ON THY BOSOM OF PEACE
Thou has[t] come into my temple at last.
The doors of my senses are open wide.
The bird of darkness has taken wing.
I am tuning the harp-strings of my heart
To sing an old song newly - the song
Of my age-old love.
I shall sing unto Thee a song newly costumed
With the fresh notes of my Soul.
The waves of my song will dance on
Thy Ocean of Cosmic Rhythm
And float me on billows of devotion
To Thy Shores.
0 Lullaby of song-waves, sing to me the song
Of my beloved Mother Eternity.
0 Fairy Song of God's Love,
Rock me in your Cradle of Melody
And bring me sleep on His Bosom of Peace.

PRAECEPTUM PRAYER
"0 Fountain of Love, make us feel that our hearts are all flooded by Thy Omnipresent Love. 0 Great Source of the river of all desires, teach us not to run ourselves dry, or lose ourselves in the sands of short-lived, sense satisfaction. Bless us, that the rivulets of all our sympathy, affection, and love lose not themselves in the drought of dreary selfishness."

PART FIVE
THE TECHNIQUE OF CONCENTRATION
Very few people realize the necessity of keeping the attention free from distraction during the practice of the technique of concentration. Most people do not really concentrate, even when they think they are practicing the art of concentration. They try to concentrate upon one thing at a time but they usually forgot about that thing and concentrate upon everything else. Very few people understand that their attention is unconsciously enslaved by objects of distraction, and that is why they are bewildered when they find that the efforts of their slavish attention bear no fruit.

Breath and Life Force
This Lesson teaches the approach to God especially by harmonizing breath, Life Force, and mind. It also teaches that a balanced character is helpful in knowing God and in getting the best results from the practice of Spiritual exercises.

The breath is not life, but it is necessary to life because the red blood needs it and the dark blood has to be purified. Breath is the cord which ties the Soul to the physical body. One who can live without breath, as Jesus did in the tomb, can separate his Soul from breath slavery and body slavery.

131

The function of Life Force is to directly supply energy through the medulla and to store it up in the brain, and from there directly to give power to the heart, lungs, and diaphragm, and to every cell in the body. It is direct electric power in the cells which keeps them energized, working and functioning in a living way. The Life Force Is the electricity of each body cell-battery, and breath, food, sunshine, and so on, are the distilled water of the cell-battery. Food and oxygen stuffed in a dead body cannot bring back life. Yet, in the state of suspended animation, the body can be kept alive indefinitely by spinal and mental energy only, without food and oxygen. Hindu saints have been buried alive beneath the ground for several months and have lived without food or oxygen, and after disinterment have regained consciousness and lived again.

The Life Force is the direct power which changes oxygen into Life Energy, but as dry batteries do not require electricity and distilled water, so by higher training the body is known to have been-sustained by Life Force only (as in suspended animation.) But, because the Life Force, instead of drawing from its source in Cosmic Energy flowing through the medulla, draws energy from food, in mortal life it becomes sustained by food. Food is not the cause of the Life Force in the body, but it is one of the conditions by which life exists. In the same way, light helps in the reading of a book, and without light, reading is impossible, but the reading matter is not caused by the light. Likewise, without food it is hard to exist, yet food is not the cause which creates life. Through habit, the body becomes used to depending upon food and breath. The more the body lives by Life Force, the less it needs to depend upon food and oxygen.

Breath Calmness Is Necessary For Perfect Concentration

The function of breath is to supply oxygen in the body and to change the venous, or dark waste blood, into vitalizing red blood. It indirectly supplied energy to the body by the explosion of oxygen into atoms of Life Force. The Great Hindu Masters signify that Pranayam (life- controlling exercise) does not consist in holding the breath in the lungs indefinitely, but in controlling the Life Force which controls the heart, sensory motor nerves, and all other functions of the body.

If one can stop the accumulation of venous blood by eating loss carbonized food and by higher methods of calming himself, he can make the function of the heart useless, for without venous blood the heart does not have to clean the carbon in the blood nor send red blood and oxygen to tissues which do not decay. If one can prevent decay in the tissue, he can calm the heart. When the heart is completely calm, due to a lack of venous blood and due to the cessation of decay in the body, there is no venous blood to be pumped into the lungs; hence breathing, is unnecessary because of the lack of venous blood in the lungs and because of the suspended state of the body tissues, which makes the absorption of oxygen unnecessary.

The ratio between breath and impure venous blood is: The greater the amount of dark blood, the greater the necessity for breath. If there is no dark blood in the body through the prevention of the waste of bodily tissues, as in suspended animation by conscious rest given to the bodily cells, then there is no necessity for breathing.

For this reason the Hindu Masters taught how to control the Life Force in the heart by stopping decay in the body and producing the resultant breathless state, and not to hold the breath in the lungs indefinitely. Controlling the Life Force in the body enables one to switch off the current from the nerve sense-telephones, thus making it impossible for disturbing sensations to reach the brain and to distract the attention from marching toward its Maker, or toward the Divine Goal. The mortal breath, which binds the Soul to the body, cannot be done away with by forcibly holding it in the lungs, but only by stopping decay in the system through developing calmness and practicing Spiritual exercise.

Without properly regulating the breath and solving its mystery by doing away with it, one cannot reach high Self-Realization. If you can do without breath, you can control bodily life, prolong it, and rise beyond it - to Soul, while living. To do without breath is not to force or suppress it in the lungs. To watch the breath is the preliminary step in controlling it, because then the consciousness of man separates itself from the involuntary bodily function of breathing, and gradually realizes itself as distinct from it. Man's Consciousness is the only thing that is real to him, and by training his consciousness by the method described in this Lesson, the student begins to realize that his life is not identified with, nor dependent upon bodily functions, and that his real nature is Spiritual and Immortal.

"Man (man's body battery) shall not live (cannot be sustained) by bread alone (by solid and liquid food and oxygen only), but by every word (unit of Life Energy) that proceedeth out of (pours forth from) the Mouth of God" (the medulla oblongata in the head, through which Cosmic Energy descends into the body). (Matthew 4:4) (The LIFE ENERGY which transforms food into energy is the real sustainer of life. According to the Hindu Scriptures, the food of the future Super Man will be almost solely this Life Energy from the Cosmos. When man's body, mind, and Soul batteries run down, they will be recharged through Cosmic- Energy).

By breathlessness:- (a) The Soul is released from bodily bondage and breath slavery. (b) The supreme noise of the body is stopped. (c) The decay of the internal organs is stopped. (d) One realizes that the body lives by Cosmic Energy coming through the medulla. (e) The heart calms down and switches off energy from the five sense-telephones, thus helping concentration. (f) One learns to live by Cosmic Consciousness and not by bread or breath alone.

THE "HONG-SAU" TECHNIQUE OF CONCENTRATION

This Lesson teaches you how to switch on or off the Life Current from the bulb of the body (muscles, senses, heart, spine, and so forth) at will, and how to bring about perfect relaxation. Inattention during the practice of this Lesson produces sleep. Concentrated attention will bring a tingling sense of Divine Life to every body cell.

Sit erect wherever you are with the spine straight, and relax. Close your eyes (or concentrate the gaze of your half-opened eyes upon the point between the eyebrows). Then, with the GREATEST CALMNESS, feel your breath as NATURALLY going in and coming out. As the breath comes in, move the index finger of your right hand toward the palm and MENTALLY chant "HONG" (as in "song") without moving your tongue. As the breath goes out, move the index finger away from the palm and mentally chant "SAU" (as in "saw".) (The movement of the index finger is only to differentiate inhalation from exhalation. When you can mentally differentiate inhalation from exhalation, then the movement of the index finger is unnecessary.) DO NOT IN ANY WAY USE MENTAL WILLINGNESS OR FORCE to let your breath in or out. While practicing, take the calm attitude that you are a silent observer of your natural breath coming in and going out, of which you are generally not conscious. You can practice this Lesson anywhere, anytime, day or night, in leisure time. By continued proper practice, you will feel a great calmness in you, and by and by you will realize yourself as Soul, superior to, and existing independently of, this material body.

"HONG" and "SAU" are two sacred Sanskrit chant words with vibratory connections with the incoming and outgoing breath. All sounds of the Universe have a different mental effect and mental correspondence. The mental repetition of "Hong-Sau" has a great calming mental effect and helps the student in this exercise of watching the incoming and outgoing breath.

The more effective way to practice this technique of concentration is to sit on a straight chair with a woolen blanket placed over it and running down under your feet to insulate your body from earthly magnetic influences and disturbances. Or simply sit on a woolen blanket spread on flat ground. Face the East and sit erect, without touching your spine to the back of the chair (if sitting in a chair). This exercise ought to be practiced during your leisure periods, either when you are on the bus or trolley car, or when sitting anywhere doing nothing. Just watch the breath and mentally chant "Hong-Sau" without moving the finger or closing the eyes, or fixing the gaze between the eyebrows, which might attract the attention of people around you. Just keep your eyes open without winking, looking straight ahead on some particular point. Keep the spine and head always in a straight line during practice.

The purpose of this Lesson is Conscious Passivity. It teaches one how to free his attention from sense entanglements. Breath is the cord that binds the Soul to the body. Man lives in and requires the atmosphere of air just as a fish needs water. When he learns to rise above breath, man ascends into the celestial realms of the angels. By watching the course of the incoming and outgoing breath, the breath naturally slows down and calms the violent action of the heart, lungs, and diaphragm. The heart pumps about 17 tons of blood a day and gets no rest at night (as the other organs do. Hence the most overworked organ in the body is the heart, and this Lesson teaches the scientific method of how to rest the heart, thus increasing longevity and liberating a tremendous amount of Life Current, which is then distributed over the body, recharging, revitalizing, and renewing all body cells, preventing their decay.

This marvelous "Hong-Sau" exercise is one of the greatest contributions of India's Spiritual science to the world, as it teaches one how to lengthen the span of his life, and shows the practical method to rise above the body-consciousness and realize one's self as Immortal Spirit.

In sleep, we experience sensory relaxation. In death, complete relaxation involuntarily takes place, due to the stopping of the heart's action. If one can learn to control the heartbeat, he can experience the conscious death, leaving and re-entering the body at will; as Saint Shankara did on one occasion, entering the body of a dead king; he can "die daily", like St. Paul, and like many Yogis of India, who have practiced this "Hong-Sau" exercise and have, through it, achieved mastery over the action of the heart. Such Yogis have learned to leave the body voluntarily, honorably, and gladly, and are not thrown out roughly, or taken by surprise by death, when their lease on their body-temples expires.

Best Time to Concentrate

The four times of change during the day correspond to the four seasons. Noon is summer; 6 P.M. is the rainy season, or fall; midnight is the winter; early morning is the spring. There are four changes which invade the body during those four magnetic seasons of the day. The purpose of this Lesson is to realize the changeless in the four changing periods of the body, by vitalizing and magnetizing it with Life Currents and Cosmic Consciousness. These Currents arrest change and suspend the decay in the cells. Therefore, it is best to practice the changeless-producing Lessons four times a day for sure scientific results. Meditate between 5 and 6 A.M.; 11 and 12 A.M.; 5 and 6 P.M.; 10 and 12 P.M.; or 11 and 12 P.M.

THE APOLOGUE
(For the Entire Family)
THE WOMAN WHO LOVED GOD AS HER SON

Many are the astounding stories told about Krishna, the Christ of India. He lived several centuries before the Christian Era. Around His life clusters many stories parallel to the life of Jesus. Krishna's parents were persecuted by King Kangsa, and King Herod caused trouble for the parents of Jesus. The Christ and Krishna stories have a great deal of similarity. Jadava, the Krishna, and Jesus, the Christ, have great Spiritual concomitance.

Jadava, the Krishna, signifies Jadava, the man, who could project his consciousness into all the Cosmos. Jesus, the Christ, signifies also that Jesus had expanded his consciousness into Cosmic Consciousness. Jesus was born of devout parents, so, also Krishna was born of God-fearing parents. Jesus conquered Satan; Krishna conquered the demon Kaleo (Ignorance), which was destroying people by its venom. Jesus stopped the storm; Krishna lifted a hill over a village like an umbrella and prevented it from being flooded to destruction.

Jesus was called "King of the Jews;" Krishna was a real king of the high caste Brahmins and a large earthly kingdom. Jesus and Krishna both were great personalities. Jesus had his women devotees, Mary and Martha; Krishna had Radha and the Gopis. Krishna taught one of the greatest philosophies of India in the Bhagavad Gita; Jesus taught one of the greatest Western philosophies in the Christian Bible. Jesus was crucified by being nailed to the cross; Krishna was shot to death by an arrow. Jesus and Krishna both performed miracles and both are recognized as the greatest incarnations of God. The word "Christ" was used in India in connection with those who had attained Cosmic Consciousness long before Jesus was born and designated as the "Christ". So, Jesus, being an Oriental born after the time of Krishna, also got the same epithet.

(To Be Continued)

HEALTH CULTURE
(The following is taken from the works of prominent Drugless Healers).

YOUR HEART All about us we hear the expression "Heart Trouble." The poor, dear, much imposed upon heart is, in truth, the last thing to give up, after all the accusative "slings of outrageous fortune" have been flung at its exquisitely organized mechanism. At the Rockefeller Institute in New York a portion of chicken's heart has been kept alive in a certain solution since 1913.

In ancient Esoteric Astrological lore, the heart is designated as the symbol of vitality, the Sun, ruling the fifth house of the Zodiac, presided over by Leo, the lion, King of Beasts, and is known as the most powerful of all the twelve signs. The heart is indeed king -king of the muscular kingdom, and as such demands its proper quality and quantity of nourishment and relaxation, neither of which it receives when it gives evidences of abnormality. Seldom are we born with a weak heart.

The truth is, you can never have heart trouble without a had stomach, faulty kidney elimination, or clogged intestines. The main cause of heart trouble is gas pressure, the result of incompatible mixtures of food, bits of which accumulate through the years and from hardened crusts of mucous in the ridges of the intestines. The large bowel (usually prolapsed, constipated, and filled with aged filth) coming up from the right side and progressing to the left, way up under the ribs, at the vicinity of the heart, turns downward into what is known as the descending colon. Many persons who believe that they

135

have "heart trouble" are merely suffering from pressure from below.

Cardiac affliction is often accompanied by puffiness in the foot; when the heart leaks, the feet and ankles swell; a mucous condition is the cause, mucous that should have been removed by the liver. Kidney and heart troubles are closely associated; when the kidneys fail to eliminate properly, the heart has added burdens saddled upon its normal duties. When red corpuscles are lacking to keep the heart filled, the heart becomes dry, shrivels up, and the blood leaks through its valves.

(To Be Continued)

FORTNIGHTLY INSPIRATION

THE POUR STATES OF CONSCIOUSNESS

The material state of consciousness is marked by the complete identification of consciousness with material struggles and acquirement of material things. This is the state of the gross business man, who never tries to understand the power behind his brain, without which no business man can succeed.

In the second state, the devotee, by concentration, tries once in a while to get away from the senses.

In the third state, the Yogi, by concentration, reaches the middle point, where he finds, in glimpses of Bliss, his good and evil tendencies evenly matched. This is the result of steady concentration and the proper schooling given to the habits of silent concentration.

In the fourth state, when consciousness becomes completely one with the only good, or God, the devotee goes beyond the opposites of good and evil. When awakening in God, the dualities of dreams of good and evil vanish, as do the sorrowful and joyous experiences of disease and health. Death and life in a dream vanish upon awakening from sleep.

FORTNIGHTLY AFFIRMATION

"Teach me to know that Thou art the power that keeps me healthy, prosperous, and seeking Spiritual Truth."

PEACE! BLISS! PEACE!

YOGODA SAT-SANGA FORTNIGHTLY INSTRUCTIONS
BY
PARAMHANSA YOGANANDA
(To Be Confidentially Reserved For MEMBER'S USE ONLY)

Thy mansion of the Heavens is lit by perennial
Auroral displays of mystic light.
The stellar system swings across the endless
Dark Highways of Eternity which lead
To Thy mystic home.
The comet-peacocks spread their plumes of rays,
And dance in wild delight in
Thy garden Of many moons.
I sit on a little patch of the Milky Way
And watch the glory of Thy kingdom spread
Endless everywhere.
The festivities of the Heavens are dazzling
With the fireworks of meteors and meteorites.
Shooting stars are hurled across the blue vaults
By Thy unseen band of obedient, devoted forces.
Everybody, everything, every atom, rejoices
During Thy Coronation as the uncrowned King
Of the Universes.
Every day the trees drop flowers in Thy Honor,
And the skiey Vase sends wisps
Of fire-mist incense to Thee.
Candlesticks of heavenly powers hold the
burning Stars to light Thy temple.
The planetary dance glides in stately rhythm
Awaiting Thy Home-Coming.
Heavenly lights have opened their gates.
Bonfires Of nebulous mists are heralding
Thy approach.
The speedy sentinel of sun and moon patiently
Are waiting for Thy Home-Coming.
And I am running wild, dancing in my little body
On my little earth, or skimming over the
Milky Way, coaxing everything, every atom of
space. Every speck of consciousness, to open its
Gates and let Thy Light shine through completely
And drive darkness evermore from the lonesome
Wilderness of matter.

PRAYER TO PRECEDE THE PRAECEPTUM STUDY

"Teach me to behold myself in others. As I love to forgive myself and correct my own faults; so do Thou teach me to forgive others, and help them to correct their faults. Through the kindly strength, of tolerance, let me lead all stumbling brothers to Thee. Teach me to see that Light shines equally on good diamond-bright souls and bad, coal-black beings. Guide Thou my understanding and powers, so that I may turn dark minds into sparkling seers - that they may reflect Thy impartial Wisdom-rays."

PART SIX
ROUTINE OF CONCENTRATION

LIFE FORCE AND VITAL POWER Life Force is the electric power in the sensory motor nerve-telephones which makes it possible for the Ego and the Intelligence to receive the sensations of sight, sound, touch, taste, and smell through the sensory nerves and to transmit impulses through the motor nerves. Control of the Life Force helps the Ego to switch the electric energy from the nerve-telephones, and thus prevent the invasions of restlessness-creating, attention- enslaving sensations. Control of the Life Force in the five sense- telephones teaches one to practice concentration scientifically. When energy is switched off from the nerve-telephones, sensations are unable to snatch the attention away from concentrating upon its goal.

The vital essence of the body is formed of the most precious tissue and energy of the body, Every drop of creative chemical fluid is said to contain eight drops of blood and the electric energy contained in those thousands of blood corpuscles. Each cell of the creative fluid is a condensed electric battery of microscopic mental brain. Foolishly, to dislodge these mental and Astral storage batteries from the body weakens the vitality of the body and the mind, and makes the breath extremely restless. Myriads of life atoms and atoms of intelligence, like soldiers, remain lodged in the creative chemical compound. To drive them out of the body through being lured by the enemy of temptation is to lose the soldiers of energy and mental power and to become a victim of the army of darkness, disease, weakness, fear, worry, dissatisfaction, melancholia, and premature death.

The mind is the operator which controls the breath, the Life Force, the vital power, and all the functions of the body. Without its guiding power, all functions of the body cease to operate. If consciousness completely departs from the body - from the brain and spine -all functions of the body will cease to operate. Mind control leads to control of all the functions of the body, but mind control cannot control all of the functions of the body until it knows its own powers and the relative powers of breath, Life Force, and vitality in connection with itself. The person who tries to attain mind control by harmonizing breath, Life Force, and vital essence, finds quicker freedom than the person who tries to attain mental control without the aid of controlled breath, energy, and vitality.

PREPARATION AND POSTURE

1. Sit erect on edge of bed with feet on floor, or sit on a cushioned chair, or sit on a bed with your legs crossed, facing East, with spine straight, chest out, abdomen in, shoulder blades together, chin parallel to the ground, and up-turned, cup-shaped palms resting at the junction of the abdomen and thighs. This posture is suggested for those who find it inconvenient to sit on a blanket spread on the ground following padmasan posture.

2. Then precede the actual practice of the "Hong-Sau" Technique with an awakening prayer, which coincides with your desire or purpose of concentration; as, for example, for Wisdom, Peace and contentment, repeat the following prayer:

"Heavenly Father, saints of all religions, the Spirit in my body temple, Supreme Master Minds of India, Supreme Master Babaji, Great Master Lahiri Mahasaya, Master Swami Sriyukteswar Giriji, and Guru-Preceptor, I bow to you all. Lead me from ignorance to wisdom; from restlessness to peace; from desires to contentment."

3. Inhale slowly, counting 1 to 20. Hold the breath, counting 1 to 20. Then exhale slowly, counting 1 to 20. Repeat this 6 to 12 times. Tense the whole body, clenching the fists. Relax the whole body, throwing the breath out. Repeat 6 times.

4. Then exhale quickly, and remain without breath as long as it will stay out without discomfort, and mentally wait for the breath to come in. When the breath comes in of itself, mentally say "Hong," and when the breath goes out of itself, mentally say, "Sau." Keep the eyes closed or open without winking or gazing, and gently fixed upward on the point between the eyebrows.

    5. After practicing this Technique deeply for ten minutes to one-half an hour, exhale slowly and completely. Blow all the breath out of the lungs which you possibly can, and enjoy the breathless state as long as you can without discomfort. Repeat three times. Then forget the breath and pray, or sit in Silence.

FOLLOW THESE INSTRUCTIONS Long concentration must be preceded by 15 minutes' practice of Exercise 1 of the Technique of Rejuvenation, as given in Praeceptum 8. By keeping in touch with the Self-Realization Fellowship Headquarters at Dakshineswar, and with the Preceptor-Guru, and by faithfully practicing this Technique, along with more-advanced exercises that will be taught in future Praecepta, longer in the morning and at night, and once a week, on any day suitable to you, three hours, both morning and night, you will find that in a reasonable length of time you will be well advanced in the Spiritual path - ready to move on the way to becoming an adept.

    In the morning, this Lesson should be practiced after the Rejuvenating and Recharging Exercise as taught in Praeceptum No. 8. you must get used to the practicing of this Technique with your eyes gently concentrated upon the point between the eyebrows. Do not strain the eyes. However, if you are not used to holding the eyes in this position, practice some of the time with your eyes half open, but most of the time with eyes closed. You can practice with eyes closed, and in leisure hours lie down on your buck and watch the breath, mentally chanting "HONG-SAU ." The more your practice in your leisure hours, the greater will be the results. Work overtime and you will gain still better results.

    When you consciously watch the breath, what happens? The heart, the lungs, and the diaphragm gradually calm down and their muscles ultimately, during a long deep silence, refrain from constant motion.

    Thus, decay is stopped throughout the system, and then no more venous blood has to be pumped by the heart into the lungs. When the heart does not pump blood, the lungs do not expand any more to receive more oxygen; then you do not breathe any more. When this happens, decay is stopped entirely. When decay is stopped, you no longer are in need of new, red blood, oxygen, nor food - but can live directly from Cosmic Energy running through the medulla, and not by the energy distilled from food only.

    It is always a good plan to exhale and drive away the poisons before beginning deep breathing. By practicing the inhalation and exhalation exercises, the carbon in the venous blood is burned out and partial decay is stopped in the body. You will notice that when you throw the breath out after practicing this Technique for a long time and deeply, that you have no desire to breathe for a long time. You can remain longer in the breathless state than if you tried breathlessness immediately after restlessness.

THE   ATTENTION   BECOMES   FREE   Death   is   nothing   but   involuntary   complete relaxation. The heart is controlled by the medulla, which is the only part of the human body which cannot be operated upon. The tiniest pin-prick in it will cause instant death. The heart, in turn, is the switch which controls all the five sense-telephones of sight, hearing, touch, taste, and smell. Sensations cannot reach the brain of their own accord, but the messages of sensations in the eyes, ears, nose, skin, and tongue are carried to the brain by the telephone wires of sensory nerves. When the sensations are quieted, thoughts do not arise, and when thoughts do not arise, associated memory-thoughts do not bother the brain. Thus, in practicing this Lesson, when you sit upright, relaxed in the meditation posture, the production of decay and waste is slowed up in the outer muscles and limbs.

As soon as, by the practice of this Lesson, energy is withdrawn from the sensory motor nerves, muscles, limbs, and the heart, no sensations can register on the switchboard of the brain to disturb the operators attention and coax it to rouse thoughts. This is the time your attention is free to be concentrated, upon any problem or idea, or upon God.

After scientifically freeing; the attention from objects of distraction, learn to concentrate 1 upon any one thing or upon God. That form of concentration in which you disengage your attention from the sense-telephones and apply it upon God, is called meditation, you can concentrate upon money or upon God, but you never meditate upon money. Meditation is only upon God. What meditation is, and how to meditate upon an unknown God, will be explained in future Praecepta.

THE APOLOGUE
(For the Entire Family)

THE WOMAN WHO LOVED GOD AS HER SON
(Conclusion)

There are many ways in which a devotee can worship God. In the Western World, the Father and Son relationship between God and the worshiper is prevalent. In India, the Mother and son relationship between God and the devotee is preferred because the father's love is conditioned by reason, whereas mother's love is not conditioned by anything.

The greatest sinner is still a son, to his mother. When God is invoked as a Divine Mother, the devotee removes all diffidence born of the consciousness of sin and thinks: "Well, Divine Mother, naughty or good, I am Thy child, and as such must find forgiveness under all circumstances, no matter what I have done."

There are other unusual relationships in which God can be known, and these are described in the Hindu Scriptures. God can be worshiped as a lover, as beloved, as a friend, as a Divine servant, as a Master, or as a son.

It is said that the great woman devotee, Jasoda, wanted to look upon God as her Son, so she in time came to adopt Christna (Krishna), the great incarnation of God. Baby Krishna was full of childish pranks, yet he was the "apple of the eye" of the milkmaids and the people who lived with him in the sacred village of Brindaban.

One of Krishna's favorite pastimes was to push the milkmaids, who carried the milk in large goblets on top of their heads, so that the milk pots slanted and poured milk like young Niagara Falls into the open mouth of the waiting Krishna below. The milkmaids never complained but loved to be taken by surprise by Krishna, so that he might have the milk.

Young Krishna used to be very fond of cheese, so one day he secretly took an unusually large piece of cheese and began to run.

After a long chase through the winding corridors of the house, Mother Jasoda caught hold of Him, but it was too late, because Krishna, afraid to lose his cheese, put the whole big piece in his mouth, so that his cheeks puffed up the size of a small football. Krishna tightly closed his lips, but the relentless Mother Jasoda, afraid that her Divine immortal Son, Krishna would be choked to death, forcibly pried his jaws open with her fingers in order to pull the cheese out. Baby Krishna laughed and opened his mouth, but behold, there was no cheese there.

To her amazement, Mother Jasoda saw, not the cheese but a Tunnel of Eternity, with the stars and worlds moving there amidst fire, smoke, and thunder!

Mother Jasoda immediately shouted: "Nay, nay, Lord Baby Krishna, close your mouth and have your cheese. I don't want to know you as God, but only as my godly baby. Chrishna closed his mouth and apparently swallowed the cheese and, saluting his mother, went away to play with his neighborhood playmates.

Once an idol of salt tried to measure the ocean by diving into it. It found itself melting away and losing itself, so it came out of the ocean to tell its friends its experience with the ocean. "Dear friends," it said, "I don't want to lose myself in the ocean, and yet I wanted to know the ocean without losing myself. Now I know that the ocean is briny and very deep, and before I melted I pulled myself away." This illustrates the characteristics of some devotees who dive into the ocean of spirit just to discover its depth, but who pull out before they lose their individual identity in God.

Mother Jasoda, as she looked into the Tunnel of Eternity, the space less forest of vastness blazing with unending light, she found herself melting in it, so she pulled away from it and preferred to see God materialized in the definite, tangible form of Krishna. God is Finite and infinite both. God and Creation emphasize the finiteness of God. God with creation dissolved into Him, reflects infinitude.

The devotees like the finite expression of God, whereas others prefer the Infinite aspect of the Divine. Mother Jasoda loved and found God in her son, Krishna. God fulfills all the desires of devotees, as the earthly mother satisfies all the wholesome desires of her children.

HEALTH CULTURE

YOUR HEART (Cont.) (The following is gleaned from the discoveries of prominent Drugless Healers.)

Coffee, tea, and drugs, that either stimulate or suppress heart action, should be shunned as one flees from a plague. As a rule, the too free use of starches is the chief offender, while Nitrogen and Potassium are the heart's special refueling needs. Praeceptum No. 13, page 7, gives a list of potassium foods. Those containing Nitrogen (always to be combined with fruits and non-starchy vegetables) are: Cheese, nuts, legumes, soy beans, dairy products, mushrooms; for non-vegetarians - fish, meat, and eggs also. Watermelon contains a wealth of potassium. Grapefruit and oranges are good; honey vibrates with the heart.

The main causes of heart difficulties may be summed up as follows: Gas pressure, lack of Nitrogen and Potassium in the diet, excess starches, insufficient relaxation, smoking, adhesions caused by prolapsus and operations, intestinal kinks, worry, anxiety, and apprehension neurosis.

Warm packs over the bowels, followed by gentle massage of the whole area, will do much toward breaking up these crusts of old impactions, also light treatments. Inhibiting the left side of the tongue will sometimes aid in a heart attack.

Verily, some seem to enjoy ill health, the fear it puts into the minds of our loved ones, the special attention, care, anxiety, and solicitation it receives from others, and it is a recognized physiological and psychological fact that of all the catalogue of diseases none seem to bear the banners with a sense of recognition almost akin to a defensive pride in possession, as those persons who constantly warn us: "I can't do this or that; I have a weak heart."

"Be thou Whole," commanded the Master. "Take up thy bed and walk. And I am challenging my students in Self-Realization not to resignedly rest upon their haunches of physical incompetency. However, acceptance of these suggestions must necessarily be left entirely to the individual; that is what your WILL is for. God left it to the individual to make his own decisions.

FORTNIGHTLY INSPIRATION

THE ROSE PLAN OF OUR HAPPINESS

To guard our rose plant, we must attend to it properly with much digging, watering, feeding, and guarding it from pests and chill. The rose plant of our happiness can grow only on the abundant fertile soil of our peace. It can never grow on the hard, stony, unfeeling soil of human mentality. We must constantly dig into peace with the spade of our good actions. We must keep our happiness plant well-watered with our spirit of love and service. We can only be happy by making others happy.

The real food for our happiness tree can be supplied only through actual contact with God in daily life. Without our contact with the Infinite Source, from which all our human faculties and inspirations spring, we can never grow perfectly and completely.

FORTNIGHTLY AFFIRMATION

"0, Infinite Truth, forever show Thy flowing face of joy in all my joys and in the flaming light of my love for Thee."

OM! OM! OM! P E A C E !

YOGODA SAT-SANGA FORTNIGHTLY INSTRUCTIONS
BY
PARAMHANSA YOGANANDA
(To Be Confidentially Reserved for MEMBER'S USE ONLY)

THE WAVELET

Someday, when I remove the mystery cork
From this bottle of flesh,
I will slip this long-caged, wistful sigh
Of life back into the Ocean of Breath.
Yet, o Mystery, I will tear aside thy long

Deluding veil which has hidden from me
The liberating knowledge that the all-solacing
Bliss Sea lay just beneath my life's wave.
Long has this little Wavelet been tossed
And buffeted by the storms of rebirth,
Moving from shore to shore, from clod to clod,
Hiding in phosphorescent bosoms of pearls,
Throbbing beneath the subterranean algae,
Or dancing with the amoeba and sea urchins,
Or gliding among the silver-finned flying fish.
Dashing past the bubbles of
Stars in the skiey ocean,
Or dancing on the shores of planetary life.
Many times this Wavelet tarried for a time
In the heart of the Great Life, and yet.
After a short slumber, mischievous and spritely,
It became truant again, and bounded out
Into the rocks of shattering sorrow.
(Continued in next Praeceptum)

PRAYER TO PRECEDE THE PRAECEPTUM STUDY

"0 Spirit, teach us to consider no work greater than Thy
Spiritual work, as no work is possible without the power borrowed from Thee,
Teach us to feel that no duty is more important than our duty to Thee, as
no duty is possible without Thee; and teach us to love Thee best, as we
cannot live or love anything, anybody, without Thy Life, Thy Love."

FURTHER FACTS ON CONCENTRATION

THE DELICATE ART Propaganda by ignorant people has been started **OF BREATH
CONTROL** against all breathing exercises because our great Hindu/Masters
warned students not to practice violent breathing exercises with weak
lungs and because they asked students to practice breathing exercises
under the guidance of a competent teacher, and not after reading about
them in books.

Remember, just as oranges cannot be tabooed for all people because some people with ulcerated stomachs cannot eat them, so also, proper breathing exercises should not be forsaken because some people with extremely weak or infected lungs cannot practice proper breathing [because such] exercises are dangerous. Everybody must properly perform Nature's breathing exercises, no matter whether he has good or bad lungs. Only remember that violent breathing exercises are dangerous, for they may cause trouble even to apparently strong but inwardly weak lungs, cast out all fear when you practice simple, but physically and spiritually extremely beneficial breathing exercises[,] which the Self-Realization Teachings recommend.

WHEN YOU NEED TO BREATHE DEEPLY If you are starving for oxygen because of improper body posture, you need to breathe deeply and to breathe properly. Those people who sit with a bent spine, and walk with a caved-in chest, squeeze the diaphragm and lungs and prevent them from properly opening and receiving the amount of oxygen necessary to clean all the dark blood in the lungs. When the lungs and diaphragm do not open properly, there is a lack of oxygen brought to the blood and the poisonous venous blood in the lower openings of the lungs remains unpurified and is poured back into the system in this condition. If you sit and walk with the chest out and the abdomen in, you will take in the proper quantity of oxygen, and all your dark blood will be changed into red blood, and fresh blood and vitality will be poured into your system. It is better to lie on your back on a hard bed than to sit with a crooked spine and squeezed lungs, moving back and forth in a rocking chair. Use planks on your bed and put a spring mattress on top. This insures a straight and soft bed without being dangerous to your health by bending the spine, as a too soft bed does.

Food is necessary if you are starved; deep breathing is necessary if you are oxygen-starved. But as over-eating is unnecessary when you have food in your system, so is over-breathing unnecessary if your blood contains less carbon due to the right habit of eating fresh fruit and little starch. If you are calm and there is less motion in the body, there will be less decay in the body and you will need to breathe very little, most of the time remaining breathless. That is why calm people breathe less, and the animal type of people, who eat starch and meat all the time, have to breathe like bellows and have to keep their Life Force and mind constantly busy with the physical functions of breathing and with the heaviness and motion of the flesh. Breathlessness and calmed internal organs free the mind, so that it can concentrate upon the soul.

DO NOT HOLD BREATH TOO LONG It is extremely unwise to hold the breath in the lungs to the point of discomfort. Holding the breath forcibly in weak lungs is injurious. Weakness of the lungs must be cured before it is advisable to breathe deeply. People with weak lungs should breathe properly by keeping the body straight. Deep breathing is unnecessary for such persons until their lungs become strong. We must learn to breathe correctly by keeping the spine straight always. The suffocating pain felt when holding the breath in the lungs too long results from the constant pouring of venous blood into the lungs. When the oxygen is used up, the carbon dioxide in the lungs wants to get out and the thick dark blood, unable to be purified, keeps on accumulating and expanding the lungs, which are ready to burst.

Although you cannot kill yourself by holding the breath too long in the lungs, you can injure the lungs and heart. Therefore, you must never listen to any charlatan or ignorant teacher who tries to teach from book knowledge only. Do not follow any teacher telling you to hold your breath in the lungs for a long time, or tells you to practice violent breathing exercises.

When the lungs are filled to capacity with dark venous blood, the blood tries to push back through the pulmonary arteries into the heart. This may result in pains in the heart or leakage of valves, or may injure the over-expanding lungs. Nature made a good provision so that no one can kill himself by holding the breath in the lungs, because when the venous blood strikes back in the heart from the overfilled lungs, the heart palpitates and fitfully shoots its current back to the medulla. The medulla becomes shocked and produces unconsciousness. When unconsciousness comes, breathing automatically starts again.

BE CONSCIOUS OF INHALATION AND EXHALATION 1. in doing the above do not force the breath in and out. Breathe naturally, only watch the course of the incoming and the outgoing breath, mentally chanting Hong and Sau. If the breath naturally stops in the lungs or outside, wait until it flows again of itself.

2. Remember that the purpose of this practice is to increase naturally the intervals when the breath does not flow. If the breath goes in or itself and does not flow out immediately, wait and enjoy the state of breathlessness. When it comes out again, say Sau. If the breath goes out and stays out, wait and enjoy that state of breathlessness, until the breath wants to flow in again.

3. The breath is first thrown out so that you may know when to begin mentally chanting Hong when the breath goes in. In ordinary breathing you are not aware whether the breath is in or out.

4. Do not force the breath in and out in order to chant. Let the mental chant follow the natural desire of the breath to flow in and out.

5. Concentrate upon the intervals when the breath does not flow, without forcing this quiet breathless state.

6. By watching the breath, you metaphysically destroy the identification of the Soul with the breath and the body. By watching the breath, you separate your Ego from it and know that your body exists only partially by breath.

7. By watching the breath, what happens? When you first tense and relax the outer body and throw out the breath, you have removed motion and decay from the outward muscles, but not from the internal organs – heart, lungs, diaphragm, and so on. By watching the breath, breathing becomes rhythmic and calm. Watching of the breath calms and quiets the heart. a restless and worried mind increases heart action, and a quiet mind calms the heart action. A heaving breath also increases heart action and quiet breath calms the heart. By watching the breath calmly, both the breath and the mind become calm. A calm mind and breath slow down and quiet the motion of the heart, diaphragm, and lungs.

When the motion is simultaneously removed (1) from the muscles by relaxation and by casting out the breath, (2) and from the inner organs, heart, lungs, diaphragm, and so on, then the Life Energy, which is used to pump 18 tons of blood through the heart in 24 hours, retires to the spine and becomes distributed in the billions of body cells.

This energy electrifies the cells and prevents their decay, making them self-sustained dry batteries. In such a state the cells do not require oxygen or food chemicals to sustain life. It is in this state that, the vitalized cells do not need to repair decay, because when decay is removed from outer and inner organs the venous blood does not become impure and it does not need to be sent to the heart to be pumped into the lungs to be purified by the incoming oxygen in the breath.

This condition (prevention of the creation and increase of venous flood in the system, by doing away with outer motion and inner motion by watching the breath) does away with two things:

1.   Necessity of living by the human breath.
2.   The necessity of heart action.

When man can live by "the Word of God" (cosmic Energy) and not by bread or breath, and can control the heart, his body battery will be internally charged with Cosmic Energy, and it will not need to depend upon the outer sources of life (Food, liquid, and gases).

a.   This practice teaches the body cells to be bridged over with Cosmic Consciousness.
b.   It destroys the slavery of the body to breath.
c.   It stops decay in outer and inner organs.
d.   It makes the heart action and breathing unnecessary and
insures longevity in the body-house when one wants to remain there longer.

e. The calming of the heart switches off the energy in the five sense-telephones of touch, smell, taste, hearing, and sight, for the heart is the second switchboard of the senses. (The medulla is the main switch). When the Life Force and the consciousness are withdrawn from the five sense-telephones, the sensations of sight, hearing, smell, taste, and touch cannot reach the brain through the nerve-telephone wires, when sensations stop registering in the brain, the conceptions and associated ideas, resulting from them, cease. It is then that the mind or the attention becomes free to contemplate any particular object, or God.

SPECIAL EXERCISES If you are starving for oxygen and have good lungs, first exhale the poisonous breath quickly, then draw fresh air through your nostrils, counting 1 to 12 slowly; hold breath, counting 1 to 12, or 1 to 25. Then slowly exhale, counting 1 to 12. Repeat the above exercise 12 times, 3 times a day in the open air, or more if you find it beneficial.

People breathe like bellows because they have waste material in their systems. The higher you go into the study and practice of Self- Realization Instructions, the more slowly you will breathe. Decay in the cells of muscles and other organs can be partially arrested by getting the body still, but activity and the throwing off of waste matter still goes on in the internal organs, if you breathe quickly, and your heart beat accelerates. Breath is the cord which ties the Soul to the flesh. When you "die daily" and come back to life at will by rising above breath, as is taught in this "Hong-Sau" Technique, you can prolong life indefinitely.

Think of all the restless, searching people there are in the world! They are all seeking the way. O, that only all of them could be told that WHENEVER THEY CAN DO COMPLETELY WITHOUT BREATHING, then, and then only, will they establish a symphony or peace, an altar of Bliss in their hearts, where Cosmic Consciousness will come without coaxing.

THE APOLOGUE
THE LOVE OF GOD AND NATIONS

In a little Kingdom by the sea there lived a queen with her ten sons. The father King had worked himself to death amassing a fortune by fighting hard battles. Before he died, he told his children that he had hidden his fortune, consisting of gold coins, in different places in the bowels of the dark fertile garden of his estate.

He left a strange will indicating that each of his sons would have to search and dig for the treasure with a spade for one whole night, and whatever each one found, he would have to divide equally with the other ten. After ten nights, the entire garden would be dug up, and the fortune left over would be given, half to the Mother and half to the public. The will stated that in all there were about twelve million dollars in gold coin hidden in the royal gardens.

Of the ten brothers, the eldest was saintly and the eighth and ninth brothers were very wicked. The others were fairly good. The most wicked eighth prince was very greedy and ambitious and wanted to dig for the treasure alone on the first night, and as he was digging under the surveillance of the other nine brothers, he suddenly struck a box of gold containing a million dollars.

This eighth wicked brother feigned that he would distribute the money equally on a little mound in the garden. This wicked prince had secretly hired men to dig a 10-foot wide and 20-foot deep moat around the mound and had it covered with thin sticks and loose earth, with only a little solid bridge leading to the middle of the mound.

He asked his brothers to stand just on the brink of the moat while he followed the secret bridge to the middle of the mound. The night was dimly lighted by a waning moon. Then the wicked brother sang a hymn, giving thanks for the finding of the treasure which was soon to be divided into ten equal parts. Then, cunningly, the prince said to his brothers: "Brothers, I want to hold a little competition match in celebration of our found treasure. I want all of you to jump with all your might, and he who jumps the farthest will be awarded ten dollars extra."

Now, the ninth wicked brother became suspicious of this so, unnoticed, he slipped away from the row of princes and hid himself behind a tree. At the given signal, the other eight princes all jumped and crashed through the thinly covered 20- foot deep moat, which was being filled with water from a secret source. Then the eighth wicked brother laughed and hurled taunts at the drowning brothers: "Ah ha, come out and take your share, you fools. Why don't you?"

The ninth brother, wisely waiting behind a tree, then came out, unsheathed his sword, and stealthily came behind the eighth wicked brother, who was going round and round the ditch, watching in merriment his drowning brothers - and slew him at one stroke.

Then the ninth wicked brother, reluctantly however, rescued the other eight princes from the moat, and with his sword dripping with blood, in high glee went to the Queen, and with bravado, exclaimed: "Mother Queen, look here, I slew your eighth son, who plotted to kill all of us."

The mother rejoiced after she heard how her eight sons had been saved from drowning, but with sobs cried out: "Your Excellency, my ninth son, my heart is bursting with grief, for you have killed your brother."

To which the ninth son replied: "What do you mean, mother; would you rather have seen your eighth wicked son alive and the rest killed?" "No, no, " the mother replied, "but I wish you could have saved your eight brothers and your wicked brother too, for he was my son also, and being wicked needed my protecting love."

FORTNIGHTLY INSPIRATION
PERFECT SUCCESS IS YOURS THROUGH CONCENTRATION

Concentration consists in the art of focusing one hundred per cent attention upon one thing at a time. All efficient people possess some power of concentration as the by-product of the vocation or avocation that they follow. People can reason without knowing logic, but its study makes them reason better. Similarly, though they possess the natural power of concentration, still they can greatly improve it by the conscious knowledge of the art of concentration.

The great Spiritual teachers of India found the necessity of discovering psycho-physical methods of concentration, which are extremely important for business, social, moral, or Spiritual success.

A great business man or a colossal social or spiritual reformer is a man of keen concentration. By the concentrated rays of his attention developed unconsciously, he burns away and destroys the roots of every difficulty that comes before him, and thereby makes a success of his undertakings. But he could be a greater success if he knew the conscious art of concentration, which would enable him to focus the burning power of attention upon any difficult problem, just as the sun's rays, concentrated through a magnifying glass, would set fire to objects before it.

FORTNIGHTLY AFFIRMATION

"Today I will worship God in deep silence, and will wait to hear His answer through my increasing peace of meditation."

NOTES

1. The Intermediate Examination which tests your degree of progress and determines your advancement into the Advanced initiate Step (second Step) will be given to you following Praeceptum No. 26, which completes the instructions presented in the Portal Novitiate Step (First Step). Full instructions for the examination will be given at that time. We humbly advise that you begin reviewing all past instructions to be fully prepared to answer the questions satisfactorily and thoroughly.

YOGODA SAT-SANGA FORTNIGHTLY INSTRUCTIONS
BY
PARAMHANSA YOGANANDA

(To Be Confidentially Reserved FOR MEMBER'S USE ONLY)

THE WAVELET, Stanza 2

"Come back, my little prodigal Baby Wavelet,
Return and sleep in my cradle
Of Eternal Calm," said a Voice;
But I replied: "I cannot rest for so long,
And do not want to fall asleep never
To awaken again.
I am Life. I must live and not sleep only.
I must dance, I must throb,
And move o'er the
Ocean of Everywhere.
Then I heard the roaring Wisdom call again,
Bounding over infinity.
"Little Wavelet, you can never be happy
Without Me. Come, Little Wavelet,
You need not sleep all the time,
But may dance with me anon, the dance
Of omniscience on the sea of omnipresence,
Clasping my arms of starry rays,
Or holding my petaled hands of flowers,
Or clasping Me in the bosom of human friends.
Little Wavelet, imprison yourself not
In a little tract of Life,
Or in a portion of fleshly selfishness.
But dance this cosmic Dance
O'er all my Bliss sea of Infinity."

PRAYER TO PRECEDE THE PRAECEPTUM STUDY

"The breeze of Thy Love wafts through me, O Father, and the tree of my life gently trembles its leaves in response to Thy coming. The leaves of my soul are just awakening. Their Rustling murmur, floating through the ether, calls the weary ones to rest in the shade of my peace, which comes from Thee."

HOW TO CURE NERVOUSNESS

DEFINITION: Restless mind vibrating through the nerves is called "Nervousness." Nervousness appears to be a simple ailment but in reality it is very complicated and very uncomfortable. If you are nervous, it is difficult to heal any disease you may have. If you are nervous, you cannot concentrate and work efficiently to attain success, if you are nervous, you cannot meditate deeply and thus acquire peace and wisdom. In fact, nervousness interferes with all the normal functioning of the human body and mind. It upsets the physical, mental, and Spiritual machinery.

The body may be compared to a factory, in which many kinds of products are made by various machines, which are run by electricity conducted through wires from a main dynamo. In the body factory, the brain is the main dynamo which sends energy through a complicated system of special conductors, or nerves, to the different organs and lumbers, which in turn act as the machines to produce vision, touch, hearing, taste, smell, movement, metabolism, circulation, breathing, and thought. You are the manager of your own body factory, and you must see to it that its departments work together in perfect harmony, and produce the highest class of products - physical, mental, and Spiritual.

SPECIAL CAUSES OF NERVOUSNESS Nervousness may be caused by great and continuous excitement, whether it is excessive stimulation of the senses, as in pleasure hunting, drinking, wrong eating, over-eating, faulty elimination, over-activity, over-indulgence physically, or following the modern speed mania, or whether it is mental or emotional over-stimulation, such as long-continued fear, anger, melancholy, remorse, sorrow, hatred, discontent, or worry. Lack of the necessities for normal and happy living, such as proper exercise, fresh air, sunshine, right food, agreeable work, and a purpose in life, aggravate, if they do not actually cause, a condition of nervousness. Nervousness is highly contagious and may also be caused by association with nervous, fault-finding, or otherwise disagreeable people.

Some of the emotions which do most damage are fear, worry, and anger. Fear and worry are very closely connected. Worry is usually fear that something undesirable is going to happen which practically never does happen. Volumes can and have been written on this subject, and it cannot be dealt with at length here. All that can be said now is that a calm analysis of the cause will usually remove worry.

Any violent or continued mental or physical excitement causes a disturbance of the balance in the flow of Life Force through the sensory-motor mechanism and the bulbs of the senses. It is as if you put a two-thousand-volt current through a fifty-watt lamp. It would burn out the lamp. In the same way, too great a stimulation upsets the functioning of the nervous system.

Nervousness may be caused by a restless mind which sends extra energy vibrating along the nerves. There are both physical and mental causes which create a disturbance in the chemical balance of the body and thus cause discomfort which causes a message to be sent through the nerves to the brain. Too much living on the physical plane seriously saps the Life Force and the vitality. Constant fear affects the heart and may result in palpitation and other heart troubles. Worry and anger affect the brain as well as the whole body and lessen your brain power and general efficiency. So, remember that every time you get angry or afraid, you are causing poison to be secreted in the body.

When electric wires in a factory are burnt, they can be replaced by the electrical, but you have been given only one nervous system to carry on the vital functions in the body factory, and if the nerves are burnt up, then you can do nothing to replace them.

OVERCOMING "STAGE FRIGHT" Stage-fright is another form of fear which causes nervousness in many people so that they are never able to do anything naturally. If you are shy and have stage-fright, get your mind quiet and remember that all the power you need is within you, all the power to convince people, all the power to give the direct Truth. The particular kind of Truth that you want to give is in the Infinite Spirit, which functions through you. Overcome stage-fright:

(1) By getting used to talking groups: (2) By imagining whenever you give a talk that you are addressing an empty hall, or that you are talking to children or very simple people.

If you really desire to help and serve people, to make them happy, to give them some Spiritual power that will electrify their Souls, you have nothing to fear. You will be able to do it. Why be afraid of people when you can give enthusiasm, inspiration, and wisdom to them? Let God flow through you, and you will have all the power you need.

THE FEAR OF DEATH Another form of fear is the fear of death. Death should be regarded as a universal experience, a change which everyone passes through. It should be looked upon as a good, as a new opportunity, as a rest from the weary struggle on this earth. When you have made a mess of life, God sends this relief and gives you a fresh trial. Besides, there is nothing to fear, because as long as you are not dead, you are alive, and when you are dead, it is all over and there is nothing then to worry about. This fear is born of the greatest ignorance, and it paralyzes activity, thought, and ambition. Live today well and the next step will take care of itself. Console yourself with the thought that death happens to everybody - saint or sinner - and that therefore it must be some sort of holiday from the troublesome business of life.

CHOOSE THE RIGHT ASSOCIATES   Association with strong, happy, serene, kind, and Spiritual people is of great benefit to the mentally

or emotionally nervous person. Even a few moments' company with a saint can work wonders in producing calmness and quiet. A real Holy man acts as a raft to carry you and suffering. Many persons who know the way to peace and permanent happiness are too slow to follow it. They take lessons and forget. Make use of your Spiritual development. You want to be fed by intellectuality, but your Souls remain dark.

Live a godly life yourself and every one who crosses your path will be helped just by contact with you. Criticize and reform yourself. That is where your greatest problem lies. Affirm Divine calmness and peace, and send out only thoughts of love and good-will if you want to live in peace and harmony.

THE APOLOGUE
THE LOVE OF GOD AND NATIONS (PART 2)

The sons retired. Every night a million dollars were found. The ninth brother began to connive a plot so that he could be the sole owner of all the money which was, according to his advice, being stored in a secret chamber, to be distributed on the eleventh night.

In the dead of the night the ninth wicked son, armed with a vicious dagger and a pistol, entered the dimly-lighted chamber, and after the other eight brothers entered, be securely locked the door, held the key in his hand, and suddenly whipped out his dagger and shouted: "This is your end. Better say your prayers quickly, for I am going to slay you one by one. I am going to own all the treasure, and I am going to be the King by dethroning the Queen. Stand aside and say your last prayers, and if any of you dare resist, I will shoot."

Suddenly there was a hush, and with a firm voice the saintly eldest prince spoke: "Brother, it is wrong for you to kill us all. I dare to tell you that if you kill us your conscience will continually remind you during every minute of your existence that you are the greatest criminal that ever lived, and all this just because you wanted extra luxuries and to be King. I am not afraid of you." He shouted at the seven brothers, who were ready to jump at the wicked brother;

"No one stir; do not use physical force to punish this wicked brother of ours. Let him kill us with our permission, one by one, with our blessing and love. We still love him as our brother, for we know that he is killing us only under the intoxication of evil. But let us all say: "You are wrong; you are wrong. We dare to tell you that you are wrong. You will regret your deeds forever."

The ninth brother shouted: "It doesn't matter what you say. If any of you advance, I will shoot you."

But the eldest brother, unafraid, asked all to stand still and sing: "We welcome you to kill us, while we keep blessing you, now and hereafter, with our love so that you will change your ways." The eldest brother, in spite of the warning, began to advance steadily toward the menacing gun, while the others remained still. A shot rang through the silent chamber and the eldest prince was bleeding, and yet he advanced, saying: "Brother, you may give me death, but I will give you love instead. Kill me first. Shoot again and find out how wrong you are. For my life, spare the others."

At this, the ninth brother threw his gun and dagger away and fell at the feet of the eldest prince. The other brothers jumped on the wicked prince, for a moment losing their imposed self-control, and were choking him to death, but the eldest brother, who was wounded on the left arm, fought with his right hand and rescued the wicked prince, and all of the nine princes returned to the Mother-Queen. The eldest prince spoke: "Mother-Queen, I saved my seven brothers and also my naughty brother who is thy son too, by my blood, and I have made him willingly cast away his wickedness and his weapons."

The Mother-Queen cried out in Joy: "My dear sons, that is the mode of action I love most. Whether you are good or whether you are murderers, you are my children. No matter what you do, you can't take my motherly love away, for I love you all equally and will ever do so. I hope that henceforth you will all live in amity and never rejoice in hurting one another, for remember, naughty or good, you are my children, and ever will be. I cannot take sides with you whether you are wrong or right, you must fight out your own battles. When you fight, I do not rejoice with the victorious son, and my heart bleeds for the vanquished son. I wish you would not fight, but would live in amity. That is the only thing that pleases me."

The above moral story furnishes the nations of the earth with a great lesson in ethics and principle.

In the World War every nation was declaring that God was especially concerned with its success. But remember, the Cosmic Mother God never took sides nor rejoiced or celebrated the victory of the Allies over Germany. Rather, the heart of the Cosmic Mother God broke when one child nation fought against another and rejoiced in doing so.

The Cosmic Mother God, rather, says: "Naughty or good, all of you are my children. It does not please me to see one victorious and the other downtrodden. I hope that all of you, as my children, if you want my cooperation, will live in peace without killing each other.

Make an altar of a united League of National hearts, wherein I shall come to dwell with My Light of Truth and Peace to endlessness."

HEALTH CULTURE

HEALTH VIA CHANGE (PART 2)   Often I am informed by the struggling Soul: "Oh, asthma, (or tuberculosis or diabetes) runs in the family." I do not need to be further told of the self- hypnotic expectant resignation to an identical doom. But this, dear students, is NOT the way to Truth; it is a jellyfish philosophy. What is true, is that if you continue to live as your father did who died of cancer, you, too, may expect to follow in his footsteps. In the study of planetary philosophy, there is a reminder that "the stars incline but do not compel."

I do not maintain that it is easy; like everything else worth attaining, you must WORK for it! But there is a saying that "any old fish can float down-stream, but it takes a live one to swim up-stream." It is the individual's job to free himself from the shackles of undesirable hereditary tendencies, whether habit of thought, or habit of ill-health.

If my words are finding fertile soil in which to germinate, take inventory of your own stock, rearrange your life, CHANGE your habits of living, and keep physical step with your ever-changing Spiritual understanding and developing mental power.

If meat and eggs, coffee, condiments, white flour products, liquor, tobacco, and the rest of the lifeless, devitalized, acid- forming, low-vibrating food imitations still form the coals with which you keep alive the embers of your Blood-stream, then you are still tenaciously clutching yesterday's crude tools of ignorance, afraid to exchange the ox-cart for motor-power.

How to make a start?

To the person in good health, the day's ration should be divided up as follows: 60% fruits and vegetables, 20% protein, and 20% starches and sugar. Let us imagine that it is the maid's day off, and we are precipitated into the kitchen from the parlor, the office, the teacher's desk, the artist's studio, the department store counter, the field, the truck, the minister' s sanctum, anywhere, everywhere, from all walks of life.

We have before us, then, two plates: One, the large dinner (or entree) plate, whose duty heretofore has been to be served chock-full of concentrated, acid-forming "good solid nourishing foods;" the smaller one, by half, is just about able to hold a lonesome leaf of lettuce and a slice of tomato, answering to the name of "salad." Now, let's switch about, building the meal around the salad, the live, high-vibrating, colorful source of minerals and vitamins, such as green lettuce, watercress, parsley, spinach, green and red peppers, celery, tomatoes, cabbage, etc.

FORTNIGHTLY INSPIRATION
ALL HEALING COMES FROM GOD

The Temple of God is within your Soul. Enter into this quietness, and sit there in meditation with the light of intuition burning on the altar. There is no restlessness, no searching, or striving here. Come into this Temple which was not created by man. Come into the silence of solitude, and the vibration there will walk to you with the voice of God, and you will know that the invisible has become visible and the unreal has become real.

Realize that all power to think, to speak, and to act, comes from God, and that He is with you now guiding and inspiring you. As soon as you actually realize that, a flush of illumination will come and fear will leave you. Sometimes the power of God comes like an ocean, and surges through your Being in great boundless waves, sweeping away all obstacles. There is a power which will light your way, which will bring you health, happiness, peace, and success if you will but turn toward the Light.

FORTNIGHTLY AFFIRMATION

"Today I will open the door of my calmness and let the footsteps of silence gently enter the temple of all my activities. I shall perform all dutiful actions serenely, saturated with peace."

"OM"

YOGODA SAT-SANGA FORTNIGHTLY INSTRUCTIONS
BY
PARAMHANSA YOGANANDA
(To Be Confidentially Reserved FOR MEMBER'S USE ONLY.

SHAFTS OF JOY

May the "Niagara Falls" of the joys from my heart
Gush unceasingly over those whom I meet.
May its flooding power sweep away the heavy logs
Of others' difficulties.
Let all wash their melancholia
With the moonbeams of my Bliss.
I will be the tornado of laughter,
Marring the super-structures of sorrow
Spread over miles and miles of mentalities.
I will churn up and blow away all the troubles
Of hearts.
In the lightning-flashes of my mirth,
I will swiftly bring to view the panorama
Of Thy Beauty, hidden beneath
The nocturnal darkness of unseeing minds.
Bless me, that by a single shaft of my light
I will put to flight the standing gloom
Of Ages, nurtured in the dark corners
Of human minds.
Through Thy Grace, a little light of sudden
Wisdom Will dispel the gathered error
Of a million years.

PRAYER TO PRECEDE THE PRAECEPTUM STUDY

"O Silent laughter! Smile Thou through my Soul. Let my Soul smile through my heart, and let heart smile through my eyes.

Prince of smiles! Be enthroned beneath the canopy of my countenance, and I will protect Thy tender self in the castle of my sincerity, that no rebel hypocrisy may lurk to destroy Thee. Make Thou me a Smile-Millionaire, that I may scatter Thy smile in sad hearts freely, everywhere!"

CULTIVATE THE INNER JOYS OF HAPPINESS

INWARDLY HAPPY Although happiness depends to some extent upon external conditions, it depends chiefly upon conditions of the inner mind. In order to be happy, one must have good health, an efficient mind, a prosperous life, the right kind of work, and, above all, an all-round, all-accomplishing wisdom. Without inner happiness, one may find oneself a prisoner of worries in a rich castle. Happiness is not dependent upon success and wealth alone, but real happiness depends upon struggling against the failures, difficulties, and problems of life with an acquired attitude of unshakable inner happiness. To be unhappy in trying to find the hard-to-acquire happiness, defeats its own end. Happiness comes by being inwardly happy first, at all times, while struggling your utmost to uproot the causes of unhappiness.

SUPERIOR LASTING HAPPINESS We can never be happy until we keep progressing seeking satisfaction in doing so, and guarding our happiness from all the influences which destroy it. Happiness comes, not by helplessly thinking, and living it in all the moods and actions of life. No matter what you are doing, keep the under-current of happiness, the secret river of joy, flowing beneath the sands of various thoughts and rocky soils of hard trials. Learn to be secretly happy within your heart in spite of all circumstances, and say to yourself: "Happiness is the greatest Divine birthright -the buried treasure of my Soul. I have found that at last I shall secretly be rich beyond the dream of Kings."

If the Soul becomes completely engrossed in lesser happiness, it fails to be attentive to the investigation of superior lasting happiness. Many persons may reason that renunciation of material pleasures is almost an impossibility in the world of business existence, but every man is not advised to return to the jungle in order to find peace. He must be in the world and yet not of it. He must not be negative, and should not blind himself with material pleasures, and thus fail to enjoy the vision of superior pleasure.

AVOID BAD HABITS Don't make unhappiness a chronic habit, for it is anything but pleasant to be unhappy, and it is blessedness for yourself and others if you are happy. It is easy to wear a silver smile or pour sweet happiness through your voice. Then why be grouchy and scatter unhappiness around you? It is never too late to learn. You are as old as your chronic thoughts, and you are as young as you feel now, in spite of your age.

Ignorant people, like animals, do not heed the lessons which accompany pain and pleasure. Most people live a life checkered with sadness and sorrow. They do not avoid the actions which lead to suffering, and do not follow the ways which lead to happiness. Then where are people who live their lives consciously over-sensitive to sorrow and happiness when they com. Such people are usually extremely crushed by sorrow, and are overwhelmed by joy, thus losing their mental balance. There are very few people who, after burning their fingers in the fire of ignorance, learn to avoid misery-making acts.

Many people wish to be happy, and yet they never make the effort to adopt the course of action which leads to happiness. Most people keep rolling down the hill of life, only mentally wishing to climb the peak of happiness. They sometimes wake up if their enthusiasm for happiness survives the crash to the bottom of unhappiness. Most people lack imagination and ne'er wake up until something terrible happens to arouse them from their nightmare of folly.

Cure yourself of evil habits by cauterizing them with the opposite good habits. If you have a bad habit of telling lies, and by so doing have lost many friends, start the opposite good habits of telling the truth. It takes time to form either a good habit or a bad one.

It is difficult for a bad person to be good, and for a good person to be bad, yet, remember that once you become good, it will be natural and easy for you to be good; likewise, if you cultivate an evil habit, you will be compelled to be evil, in spite of your desire, and you will have to pray: "Father, my Spirit is willing, but my flesh is weak." That is why it is worthwhile to cultivate the habit of being happy.

The man sliding down evil paths finds no resistance, but as soon as he tries to oppose his evil habits by the adoption of Spiritual laws of discipline he finds countless instincts of temptations roused to fight and foil his noble efforts.

DO NOT JUDGE OTHERS Your individual happiness depends to a large extent upon protecting yourself and your family from the evil results of gossiping. See no evil, talk no evil, hear no evil, think no evil, feel no evil. Most people can talk about other people for hours and thrive under the influence of gossip like the temporary influence of intoxicating poisonous wine. Isn't it strange that people can smoothly, joyously, and with caustic criticism talk about the faults of others for hours but cannot endure reference to their own faults at all?

The next time you are tempted to talk about the moral and mental wickedness of other people, immediately begin to talk loudly about your own mental and moral wickedness for just five minutes and see how you like it. If you do not like to talk about your own faults, if it hurts you to do so, you certainly should feel more hurt when saying unkind, harmful things about other people. Train yourself and each member of your family to refrain from talking about others. "Judge not, that ye be not judged."

By giving publicity to a man's weakness, you do not help him. Instead, you either make him wrathful or discouraged and you shame him, perhaps forever, so that he gives up trying to be good. When you take away the sense of dignity from a person by openly maligning him, you make him desperate.

When a man is down, he is too well aware of his own wickedness. By destructive criticism, you push him still farther down into the mire of despondency into which he is already sinking. Instead of gossiping about him, you should pull him out with loving, encouraging words. Only when aid is asked should Spiritual and moral help be offered. To your own children or loved ones you may offer your friendly, humble suggestions at any time and remove their sense or secrecy or delicacy.

SMILE AND BE HAPPY Make your home a valley of smiles instead of a vale of tears. Smile now and never mind how hard it has been for you to do so. Smile now. All the time remember to SMILE NOW, and you will SMILE ALWAYS.

Some people smile most of the time, while beneath the mask of laughter they hide a sorrow-corroded heart. Such people slowly pine away beneath the shadows of meaningless smiles, There are other people who smile once in a while, and they may also be very serious at times, yet beneath the beautiful rocky appearance there may be gurgling a million fountains of laughing peace.

If you enjoy good health for fifty years, then you are sick for three years, unable to get healed by any method, you will probably forget about the length of time that you enjoyed good health and laughed at the idea of sickness, now it is exactly the opposite. Just because you have been sick for three years, you probably think that you will never get well again.

Likewise, if you were happy a long time, and have been unhappy a comparatively short time, you are apt to lose hope of ever being happy again. This is lack of imagination. The memory of a long- continued happiness should be a forceful subconscious habit to influence your conscious mind and ward off the consciousness of your present trouble.

When wealth only is lost, nothing real is lost, for if one has health and skill one can still be happy and can make more money, but if health is lost, then most happiness is also lost, and when the principle of life is lost, all happiness is lost.

Pure love, sacred joy, poetic imagination, kindness, wisdom, peace, Bliss, or meditation, and happiness in serving, are felt inwardly first in the mind or the heart, and are then transmitted through the nervous system to the physical body and outward. Do not camouflage your Soul with the veil of sermons and solemn words. Understand and feel the superior joys of inner life, and you will prefer them to the fleeting pleasures of the outer world.

THE APOLOGUE
SENSE HAPPINESS

A man who lived in the cold tracts of Alaska had tasted some of the luscious, long lady-finger grapes that had been shipped to him by a friend who lived in Fresno, California. The Alaskan was so enamored of the grapes that he secured a job at Fresno, where all kinds of grapes grow so abundantly, and left Alaska for good.

The Alaskan, on his arrival in Fresno, was invited to the house of his friend, and a young lady brought him a bunch of the grapes he so loved. He was almost beside himself with joy, and as he hurriedly munched and gulped down the grapes, he gurgled out: "O thank you, from the bottom of my heart, thank you."

The young lady who owned a grape orchard, finding the Alaskan so overjoyed upon receiving the grapes, said to him: "Good sir, since you love the grapes so much. . ."

"Why, I left Alaska for lady-finger grapes," interrupted the Alaskan.

"Well, sir, you shall have all the grapes you want. I am the owner of a grape ranch and daily I will bring to you all the grapes you want," said the lady.

The next day, very early, the lady arrived at the house of the grape-gorged Alaskan with a large quantity of grapes. The Alaskan, who had not yet digested all the grapes he had swallowed the previous night, came out of the house yawning. He leaped with joy at the prospect of feasting on the large amount of grapes which the lady had brought.

"Oh, how wonderful to have so many grapes. I am very lucky. Thank you, thank you," cried the Alaskan. He tasted a few grapes in the presence of the lady as a matter of politeness, although he could taste undigested grapes of the previous night in his mouth. When the lady left, he gloated over the grapes with admiration and greedy eyes. An
hour elapsed, then he began eating grapes again. All day long he swallowed grapes, grapes, grapes.

Next morning, at the break of dawn, the young lady arrived with a larger quantity of the finest grapes that her vineyard could yield and shouted for the Alaskan. Half sleepy, with a slightly wilted enthusiasm, also a slight touch of vexation at being roused from a deep sleep, but wearing a gentle smile on his face, the Alaskan greeted the grapes and the lady; "Hello, good lady, thank you for the very nice grapes."

On the third morning, as usual, the lady brought a still larger bunch of grapes. The Alaskan, half asleep, and with a half-smile on his face, greeted the lady and said: "Lady, it is very good of you to give me these grapes, but I still have some left from yesterday."

On the fourth morning, the lady called on the Alaskan again with a fairly good quantity of grapes. He reluctantly woke up, and without a smile greeted the lady and said: "0, grapes again. It is very nice of you to bring them, but I have enough. Don't you think so? Besides, I have some left over."

But the lady, disbelieving the story of the Alaskan, and thinking that he was just modest and afraid to impose upon her generosity, brought the biggest quantity of grapes on the fifth morning and knocked at the residence of the Alaskan, who leaped out of his bed as if he had seen a ghost and shouted at the lady: "Horrors, lady, grapes, grapes, grapes, grapes! For Heaven's sake, grapes again!" The lady smiled and said; "Now I am happy to know that you hate grapes. I hope you will never deprive me of my salable grapes again."

The above story subtly shows that "too much of any good thing, or of anything else, for that matter, is bad." No matter how pleasurable a thing is, if you over-indulge in it, it ceases to give pleasure and gives pain instead.

This story was told to me by a sex-slave living constantly on the sex-plane, who ultimately found that his temporary pleasure was changed into physical and mental agony.

So, remember, do not over-indulge in eating, sleeping, working, social activity, or in any activity, no matter how pleasurable it is, for over-indulgence will yield nothing but unhappiness.

HEALTH CULTURE

Self-Realization does not advocate developing the spiritual at the expense of the physical well-being and personal attractiveness, Indeed, throughout our Lessons you will so far have noticed the stress put upon a true understanding and conscientious care that is to be given the body in all its phases.

Contrary to the mental attitude taken by many other teachers, the aesthetic, we believe, is not expected to eschew creature comforts nor to assume a manner of indifference to the beauty that is all about us manifested. Even though you may be a worker for Humanity, in the midst of the crowd, you must make the most of your personal appearance, your physical personality.

Beauty in all its myriad forms must have been originally included in the Divine plan, for we see evidences everywhere: in the flowers and trees, the birds, the sky, the Creative Arts, in the face of a child, a voice, music. Why, then, if God has seen fit to recognize its worth and power, shall we make an effort to eradicate it from our lives in the name of spiritual Attainment?

The old idea of a long-faced missionary sent out to save and redeem lost souls, going among his fellow-creatures clad in ugly, drab costumes of nondescript material and color, is not a true picture of the ideal of spiritual quality we wish to implant in the hearts of students of Self-Realization Fellowship. Beauty and strength of bodily expression should be man and woman's heritage, a gift from the Gods; to cultivate if it has been denied or withdrawn because of lack of knowledge of how to retain it. And so, let me again remind you that it is NEVER too late to make the start. There is but the Eternal NOW, in this as in everything else.

While it is not the intention of this Department to give formulas for the attainment of Beauty, I do admonish my students my students to realize that God manifests upon the physical plane as well us upon the intellectual and Spiritual plane, and no point is gained by disregarding the physical laws or that which will enhance personal appearance, tempered, always with good taste. It is my desire, rather, to arouse your pride in this direction, so that you will devote a reasonable amount of your time daily to the cultivation of your physical, body, WITH WHICH YOU MUST LIVE FOREVER ON THIS EARTH PLANE.

UNFIRED APPLESAUCE DESSERT After removing core, grind apples (with peel) in a nut-butter grinder. Add cinnamon to taste. File it into a dessert gloss; top with whipped cream; over that sprinkle Nutritive Nuggets.

FORTNIGHTLY INSPIRATION

BATHE YOURSELF IN THE OCEAN OF PEACE

After bathing yourself in the Ocean of Peace in the dreamland, as you wake with happiness, say: "In the sleep-land I found myself free from mortal worries. I was a King of peace. Now, as I work in the daytime and carry on my diurnal battles of duties, I shall no longer be defeated by insurgent worries of the kingdom of wakefulness. I am a King of peace in the sleep-land, and I shall continue to be such a King in the land of wakefulness. As I come out of my Kingdom of peace in the sleep-land, I shall spread that same peace in my land of wakeful dreams."

FORTNIGHTLY AFFIRMATION

"Beginning with the early dawn, I will radiate my cheer to everyone I meet today. I will be the mental sunshine for all who cross my path this day."

YOGODA SAT-SANGA FORTNIGHTLY INSTRUCTIONS BY
PARAMHANSA YOGANANDA
PRAECEPTA SUMMARIES

INTRODUCTION The following Praecepta Summaries are presented to you in the form of quick general reviews of the Praecepta, in order to refresh your memory in regard to the most vital points presented, and to fix more firmly in your mind, not only the vital points, but also the relationship between theory and practice of technique, and the importance of one to the other. Reviews are of vast importance, for each time you review a lesson you will discover something that had escaped you in your previous study of the Lesson, or something that had not sufficiently impressed you before. It is through repetition that we learn the most.

Moreover, you will be greatly enlightened by the many new explanatory notes, all of which will be of extreme importance to you in the Intermediate Examination which is to follow the Installments of Praeceptum No. 26.

It has been our sincere purpose to present the authentic "why" of all the principles as expounded by the Masters of India, and, therefore, the summaries which constitute Praeceptum No. 26 will be necessarily continued in a series of installments in order to thoroughly and comprehensively cover the fundamental principles, especially in preparation for the examination. THE FIRST STEP In the First step you, the Portal Novitiate, must bear in mind the importance of the following salient features:

First, the importance of connecting the little Wave of Life (your little body) with the Ocean of Life (the vastness of Nature and God). Nature is nothing but the physical nature of God. Nature is the Body of God and the Life and Consciousness hidden in men, animals, and flowers, and all matter is the Soul or Consciousness of God. As man has a Soul, energy, and body; so also, God is Cosmic Intelligence, Cosmic Life, and the Body of the Cosmos.

If a person constantly looks at a wave, he forgets to concentrate upon the ocean. Likewise, when you concentrate upon, and become attached to, the little Wave of your Life, then you forget the Ocean of Spirit of which your Life is but a Wave. As variously situated electric lamps are lighted by one dynamo, so variously moving and existing human beings are lighted by the one Cosmic Dynamo of Intelligence and Light.

SUMMARY OF PRAECEPTUM NO. 1 In the First Praeceptum you learned that you lead yourself into temptation and trouble, and that you should demand wisdom first and not bread or prosperity only. You must daily use the greatest Universal Prayer: (As in the First Step, Praeceptum 1, Page 3).

In your spare moments, whenever you are lying down or relaxing, you must practice taking your mind out of the small limited bodily tunnel into the Tunnel of Eternity. This would make you realize that you dwell, not only in the body, but everywhere, as a wave exists everywhere with the vast sea.

You are living in the United States of All Races and should cultivate the consciousness of equality. You should give equal treatment to your brown, white, yellow, and dark brothers who are also the descendants of Adam and Eve and who are made in the image of God. Hence, you will work for the prosperity of others as eagerly as for your own prosperity. You exist not only in your own body but with God everywhere in every body. Hence, everybody is your Self.

Ask yourself if you actually fast one a week on fruit juices and other light nutritive food and some suitable laxative. If not, begin to do so right now. This is extremely necessary for a diseaseless, poison-free, healthy, long-lived existence. A healthy, long-lived man can be happy himself and can make others happy as long as he lives.

The best meat substitute is two tablespoonful each of ground nuts and nutritive nuggets, (as sold by Self-Realization Fellowship) the ideal breakfast, lunch, and dinner food. Eat more raw food. Never eat protein without green vegetables. Spinach salad is very good; use often.

From the story of "The Saint Who Chose a King for His Spiritual Master, " you learn to think and feel God (as the ever-new Joy felt in meditation) all the time while you ambitiously do your material duties with utmost concentration. Do not forget Cod while performing material duties because no duties can be performed without borrowing the powers of the body and mind from Him. Always pray the greatest prayer: "I will reason, I will will, I will act, but guide Thou my reason, will, and activity to the right thing which I should do. " (First Step, Praeceptum 1.)

SUMMARY OF PRAECEPTUM NO. 2 "I am the captain of the ship of my judgment, will, and activity."

The title "Swami" refers to a Master, or one who is striving to be a master of his own Self. Swami Shankara, a Master, was founder of the Swami Order of Renunciation and lived in the Seventh Century, A.D. The founder of the Self-Realization Fellowship Movement in America, Swami Yogananda, was inspired by Master Swami Sri Sriyukteswarji, he in turn, by Great Master Lahiri Mahasaya, and he in turn, by Supreme Master Babaji. It is said that Supreme Master Babaji, who is still living in flesh and blood, taught Yoga to Swami Shankara.

Yogoda is the Sanskrit equivalent of Self-Realization - knowing and mastering all Truth within your laboratory of daily meditation. Sat-Sanga stands for Fellowship among all races and Fellowship with God in deep meditation.

This Self-Realization Fellowship (Yogoda Sat-Sanga) is the Second Coming of Christ Consciousness (or Krishna, or Kutastha, or Universal Consciousness) in your own consciousness. This Movement is the fulfillment of the promise of Jesus Christ to send the Holy Ghost, the Great Comforter, which one will be able to realize in actuality, and not merely through theological promises, by the deep regular practice of the Lesson on Meditation, (popularly known as Lesson 5) to be taught in the Second Step.

Every day you must contact God as the ever-new joy of Meditation. Every day you must carry the message of Self-Realization to some Soul. Be a fisher of Souls in order to please God. Develop will power. Will and act until you achieve victory in everything. Through will power yon can energize the body, learn to develop physiological, unthinking, blind, hunting will power into dynamic and Divine Will; what Jesus meant by "Thy Will be done."

Never use will power wrongly, but use your own will guided by wisdom. Will power was given to you for use. It is a metaphysical error not to try to use your will, for you cannot help using your will in every movement and every act. You do not use will power when you are physically dead or mentally dead. Your own true Wisdom-guided will, and your will, guided by the wisdom- inspired will of God, are one and the same thing. Do not isolate your will from God; realize that behind the little motor of your own will there is the Infinite Dynamo of God's endlessly powerful, inexhaustible Will.

Over-eating create[s] poisons and colds. Fasting and elimination heal colds. Eat according to judgment and not according to material habits. You must also be kind in thoughts, actions, and especially in speech.

The lesson you must learn from the story of "The Big Frog and the Little Frog" is that most people are like the big frog. They give up after experiencing a little difficulty in any material or Spiritual pursuit, but you should be unendingly, untiringly persistent in reaching your goal - like the little frog. You must do your best all the time and then if you fail in your endeavor, do your best all over again. In this way you will succeed in any undertaking.

SUMMARY OF PRAECEPTUM NO. 3 This Universe is a pattern of God's dream. Remember, naughty or good, you are His child. Heavenly Father wants to bring the naughty child out of mischief.

Do not lose yourself in the jungle of desires. Find the goal of your life and the shortest route that leads you there. True prosperity lies in possessing the imperishable riches of God-contact, health, wealth, and peace. The surest way to material prosperity is to develop the power of concentration. Learn to develop the power to create at will, wisdom, wealth, health, or whatever you need.

The Power of Concentration and the law of cause and effect determine your acquirements of prosperity. First try to know, as Jesus and the Masters of India knew, that "I and my Father are One." "I am He." You must realize this by daily meditation, and when that conviction ripens into knowledge then, being God's child, you will have everything. Develop unselfish-selfishness. Morning and evening practice the great technique of reinforcing your will with God's will. Affirm, pray, and demand from God until He grants you your wish.

Read thoroughly the technique of making prayers fruitful. (First Step, Praeceptum 3, page5). This is very, very important.

From the apologue of "Two Blind Men Who Sought Riches from God and a King" you must learn that prosperity dependent upon egotism is uncertain and may melt away without notice, but prosperity received from God is unfailing and does not depend upon your egotism for success[;] but upon your God-guided, business man there is no depression, because even in trials he is consciously guided out of difficulty by God.

"Father, bless me so that I may acquire at will what I need."

SUMMARY OF PRAECEPTUM NO. 4 Commit to memory the poem on "Friendship" and apply its truth in all your various human relations. Friendship lies in seeking true pleasure and Soul progress together, and in that way is ever-inspiring.

Consider no one a stranger. First establish perfect friendship in one or two Souls, then offer that Cosmic Friendship to all. Do not poison friendship by demand and compulsion and wrong familiarity, or discourtesy, or harsh speech, or mental cruelty. Practice friendship in your parental, filial, conjugal, or any other relation, as the case may be. Be a true friend.

Friendship consists in becoming increasingly useful in every way (materially and spiritually) to your friends. Therefore, keep unceasingly developing if you want to be a good friend, or inspire friends, or receive others as your friends.

Love your enemies, for they too are your brothers; you are children of the One Heavenly Father. See the image of God in all your friends. Some people from the first meeting prove to be real friends always, while others that we meet daily we never really know.

Behold all races, your brother creatures, assembled beneath the canopy of God's friendship. "Let those who are our own come unto us, until we know everyone is our own."

From the apologue, "The Man Who Refused Heaven," we learn that it would be better to live in Hades under difficulties but with a wise man, for he would make a Paradise of Happiness in a troublesome environment, but it would not be good to live with ten fools in heavenly comfortable surroundings, for eventually the ten fools, by their ignorant modes of living, would convert Paradise into veritable Hades. Beware of the company you keep, for people influence your ideals, habits and all your actions. Move in the best company, or no company at all. Good thoughts and good habits are your best company. Evil thoughts are your worst company. They are devastating enemies.

It is better to have faith in God and obey his dietary laws than to have faith in God and disobey the laws of proper diet and health. Bananas are a very good meat substitute and can be used with milk for increasing weight.

SUMMARY OF PRAECEPTUM NO. 5 Commit to memory "The Divine Gypsy." From India the great spiritual movements of renunciation started, so from India arose Gypsies who broke all conventional laws and went wild, seeking freedom. They roam, and camp, and live by the ignominy of stealing. Minus the stealing, the spirit of gypsying and camping lies concealed in every human being. We get tired of confining artificial existence. It is good to use vacations in camping, singing to the clouds, and roaming into the star-land without paying taxes. Be a mental gypsy with eyes closed. Walk and roam in the endless tracts of mind, free from the limiting boundaries or possessions and lands. Become a Divine Gypsy, roaming through sympathy in all hearts and in all living creatures. Do not make your happiness a slave to anything. Be happy anyway, with or without anything.

REJUVENATE your body by recharging it from the inner source. Theresa Neumann in Germany has been living for eight or nine years absolutely without food. Although you must eat properly in mortal state, you must learn to rise above food-consciousness. When you make up your mind not to be a slave to hunger, you will find that your will power will sustain your body by connecting it with the unexploded electro-protonic energy in your flesh, and the Cosmic Energy which surrounds your body. The wet battery depends upon electricity and distilled water, so the body battery depends upon life Force coming down from the brain — Medulla-battery — as well as from food and oxygen, and sunshine. But as a dry battery only depends upon electricity, and not upon distilled water, so also the body battery, by training can wholly or partly depend upon the Life Force flowing from Cosmic Energy.

The life in the body depends directly upon the Cosmic Energy which comes down the antenna of the medulla, and is stored in the cerebrum and plexuses. Indirectly, the bodily life depends upon food, oxygen, sunshine, and so forth, but the Soul, being identified with the body, thinks that food is the only source of life, so when one learns to live by will power and energy more and more he realizes, as the great Spiritual Masters of the world do, that man's body battery does not depend upon bread (food) alone, but upon every vibrating energy that proceedeth out of the Mouth of God, or medulla, through which the operator-will draws vibrating energy (Word) into the body. When you die, your Soul will live by energy from God. It will not have to live by food or air or sunshine.

The actual proof that the body can be gradually sustained by Cosmic Energy is proven by the following: Whenever you are tired, you can revive some energy by drinking milk or eating food, but the next time you are tired, instead of eating food, try the recharging or tension exercise gently for ten minutes. When you are used to the exercises, you will find that your tired feeling will leave you without eating food. Do this more and more, until you can, in a few years, in an advanced state, (by higher methods) live solely upon Cosmic Energy (without food if you want to). This is an UNFAILING METHOD OF REMOVING FATIGUE BY COSMIC ENERGY, IN PLACE OF FOOD.

(a)   Physically charge your body by rousing Cosmic Energy through will power, as in the tension exercises.

(b)   By feeling the ever-new Bliss-God, felt in meditation, stamp immortality on your changing life and make it changeless. Though waves change, but the ocean does not, so birth, childhood, youth, age, and death will dance in your consciousness like dream-waves without changing the one unforgetful, ever-conscious ocean of your Cosmic Consciousness.

"The Boatman and the Philosopher" story teaches that if you have money, health, theological and intellectual knowledge only, but you do not have Self- Realization, by deep meditation, then you won't be able to cross the tumultuous river of life onto ever-lasting peace-shores of God -con tact.

It is most important to heal the Soul of the disease of ignorance first, then the other two psychological diseases, or physical diseases, will automatically disappear.

SUMMARY OF PRAECEPTUM NO. 6 "Awaken Eternal Energy Within Me," Become a Son of God by enlarging the caliber of your consciousness through concentration and meditation. Receive the Ocean of God by enlarging the boundaries of your consciousness through meditation. The body is externally fed by food, oxygen, and so forth, and internally it is fed by Cosmic Consciousness and Life Force.

Most exercises teach the student to concentrate upon muscles, instruments of exercises, or dumb-bells, bar-bells, and body movements. The tension exercises teach how to energize the body by conscious will. They teach that exercise signifies the exercise of energy first, with the resultant movement of muscles or limbs. Self-Realization technique teaches the student to concentrate principally upon energy.

RELAXATION - (re - again) (laxo - to release). To release the energy employed in a low or high tensed muscle or body part by an act of will. TENSION - Signifies the sending of energy into a muscle, resulting in its unavoidable tension or contraction. Just as you can switch on or switch off energy from an electric bulb, so by operating the switch of will power you can put on or put out the energy from the lamp of the muscles.

IMPORTANT Read very carefully the experiment on Energy and Will in Praeceptum No. 6. Most people think that a human being is composed of only mind and body, but by the tension of any body part you know that there are three principles involved in the act of the tension of a muscle. (1) The will, which sends energy to a body part. (2) The energy, which tenses the bundle of fibers in a muscle into stone hardness. (3) And the muscle, which is tensed by energy and will. Hence, each human being is composed of: (1) Consciousness, (2) Life Energy. (3) Flesh.

When lifting a weight, you don't know what weight it is. You only know from the feeling of how much energy you are spending as to the lightness or heaviness of a weight. Remember, the relation between Will and Energy is: "The greater the will, the greater the amount of energy and tension in any body part." (Commit this important axiom to memory).

In the apologue of "The Mouse Who Became a Tiger" you learn: "Never forget God if you are prosperous, for it is God's power that makes you so, and by intoxicating yourself with the wine of Egotism you might shut off the influx of that power that feeds all the channels of your success in all material and Spiritual paths."

That which satisfies your hunger does not necessarily supply the sixteen elements needed in your diet. Whenever you are hungry, if you eat bread and drink water, you may satisfy your hunger and thirst, but in five months will you die because you stopped supplying the sixteen elements in food necessary for body sustenance. Select your diet in the following way: (1) An abundance of fruit, (2) Less protein, (3) Some fat, such as butter fat, (4) Some carbohydrate. Natural sweets like dates and figs (unsulphured).

Affirm: "I am Thy Child - I am everlastingly youthful."

SUMMARY OF PRAECEPTUM NO. 7 Commit to memory the poem on "God," and whenever you are in trouble repeat this poem mentally or out loud with deep devotion, or just mentally with your whole Soul, say "God, God, God" several times. Each repetition must contain deeper devotion than the preceding utterance. All true Spiritual Scriptures have a three-fold meaning, to suit the physical, mental, and Spiritual needs of man.

IMPORTANT Specially note page 2 of Praeceptum No. 7. Be sure to draw the diagram about the body battery with explanatory notes along with the study of the page. Also, be sure to let someone test your body relaxation as taught in this Praeceptum. Specially study the five stages of physical relaxation described on the same Praeceptum.

Relaxation means releasing energy and consciousness first from the muscles (1) partially, (2) then completely, (3) then you relax into unconsciousness, or withdraw consciousness and energy from the senses, as in sleep, (4) then you consciously withdraw energy and consciousness from the muscles and senses by concentration. (5) In death, energy and consciousness are unconsciously forced out of the muscles, heart, spine, and brain. (6) By higher meditation, you can withdraw the Life Energy from the muscles, senses, heart, spine, brain, and medulla, or from the entire body, and transfer it to the Infinite Dynamo, just like switching off the electricity from a bulb into the dynamo. In death, you can't switch on life into the body lamp, but by learning conscious sensory motor organic relaxation you can switch off life from the body and switch on life back into the today at will, or, in other words, you can die and live again at will, even as great Saints of the world did.

The story of the "Moral Backbone" teaches you not to be spineless, even though you are Spiritual. You must be fiery and resist evil by forceful good without even getting angry or impatient.

While obeying Cod's health laws, keep yourself disinfected by contacting the healing-disinfecting Faith in God. Fast half a day or a full day whenever the body feels weak. Fast on fruit and juices.

Affirm: "I have God; I have everything."

SUMMARY OF PRAECEPTUM No. 8 Review by reading pages two, three, four, five, and six once every week. This is the key to the recharging exercises. Practice this Exercise A, of Praeceptum 8, every day very slowly and with closed eyes in bed, on waking, or whenever you are tired. The more you practice this exercise slowly and with concentration, the more you will realize that, by tension and relaxation of energy from the body, you are not so many pounds of flesh but are the energy and consciousness tied in the nerves, muscles, organs, and bones by the cords of attachment. By realizing yourself as energy in the body and not the flesh, you prepare the way of releasing your caged little life into the Infinite Life. This exercise also awakens deeper consciousness and greater energy in all body cells. All students of Self-Realization do not think of themselves as bundles of flesh, but as the light in the body bulb, ready to be switched off into the Infinite Light, or switched on again in the limiting body bulb.

The story of "Buddha and the Courtesan" teaches you the difference between selfish limiting personal love and unlimited unselfish Divine Love. Quote these stories to your friends.

Acid body leads to sickness. Alkalinity means health and immunity to disease, so eat less of acid-forming food.

Some people know less than others, due to their own self-created limitation somewhere, sometime in the near or distant past, and not due to God's partiality. Break the bonds of your own self-created limitation and let the flood of will power drive away all weakness from your Soul.

THE PLAN OF PRAECEPTUM No. 26 The sectional review of the twenty-five Praecepta constituting the First, or Portal Novitiate, Step, will be continued, for easy and convenient study, in succeeding installments of Praeceptum No. 26, in order to complete the comprehensive program of review. Always remember that conscientious perseverance in review and practice sharpens the perception and understanding.

The Second Installment of PRAECEPTUM No. 26 will follow after a fortnight.

YOGODA SAT-SANGA FORTNIGHTLY INSTRUCTIONS
BY
PARAMHANSA YOGANANDA
(To be Confidentially Reserved FOR MEMBER'S
USE ONLY) FIRST STEP
PRAECEPTA SUMMARIES
SECOND INSTALLMENT

SUMMARY OF PRAECEPTUM NO. 9 Commit to memory "Smile Forever," or portions of it. "Smile newly with the ever-new smile of God every second, every minute. And keep smiling in God forever."

Remember to maintain balance between the one-sided Eastern and the one-sided Western characteristics. Affirm often; "I will be calmly active, actively calm. I am the prince of peace, sitting on the throne of poise, directing the kingdom of activity."

To be too calm is to be lazy; to be too active is to become an automaton. Meditate or fall asleep when you feel overwhelmed with trials. Note the different forms of mental relaxation. Mental relaxation signifies mental rest.

1. Free the mind from haunting worries by imitating the status of drowsiness. Keep the breath calm, the character steady, self-control at your command, and whenever you seek company, commune with God in meditation, or be in the very best Spiritual company you can get.

2 Metaphysical super-relaxation consists in freeing your mind from the body, money, possessions, name, fame, family, country, and the world, and habits of the human race. Every night in sleep you physically become separate from all bodily habits, but these come back from the subconscious mind and emerge into the state of wakefulness. By complete ecstatic communion with God all bodily attachments are destroyed during sleep and wakefulness. Then you become a savior. [Editor's note: "savior" is unclear: the actual spelling is "savious"]

Study page 3, Praeceptum No. 9, the greatest Lesson on Physical Relaxation ever given. Big books on relaxation have failed to give the technique of relaxation.

VERY IMPORTANT PHYSICAL RELAXATION The greatest technique of physical relaxation is: When you tense the whole body and then relax, exhaling the breath, cast away all restless thoughts. Remain without thinking as long as you can, and remain without, breathing as long as you can. This is very important to remember.

Practice the tension and relaxation of each of the 20 body parts in the morning on bed and then out of bed.

Read Praeceptum No. 9, page 4, very carefully and then thoroughly master the art of practicing low, medium, high tension. Remember that low tension signifies the low charging of energy into a body part, medium and high tension signify influx of more energy into a body part.

VERY IMPORTANT When a muscle or body part is fully tensed, remember that you have charged that part with maximum energy. This signifies that you should not tense more, just as you should not send a 2,000 volt of current into a 50-watt bulb. Just as a ship at sea can be run by radio, without the help of any of the crew, so remember that God's Cosmic Energy shooting down the center of the cosmos is vibrating on the antenna of the medulla, or the "Mouth of God." Your will receives the Light of God through the medulla, and stores it up in the brain and the six plexuses. The brain and the plexuses carry on the entire function of the twenty seven thousand billion cells and the bodily organs.

From the story of the "Bandit and the Bull" you learn that, no matter what sin you have committed in the past, once you cultivate Self-Realization by meditation, that may be the portal to the Heaven of Eternal Freedom and Ever-New Bliss.

Read the "Barometer of the Kidneys - Your Skin." Praeceptum NO. 9, page 7.

SUMMARY OF PRAECEPTUM NO. 10 Realize the essence of the Truth in the poem "In the Land of Dreams." Behind the screen of sleep land lies the mystery of the vast formless omnipotent, omnipresent Soul and spirit. Every night God subtracts your consciousness of possession, race, qualities, or disqualifications, and body from your formless, happy, ever-existent Soul.

In sleep you do not remember whether you are a Hindu or an American, or are sick or well, or are rich or poor, or a man or a woman, and yet when you wake up you know that you existed consciously and happily without the consciousness of the body. If you think that you were unconscious during sleep, then, upon waking, you could not possibly remember and say: "Oh, I slept deep, or well," or, "Oh, I had a very light, restless sleep." In sleep land you partially realize that you are space, that you are happiness, that you are formless. This makes you realize the forgotten image of God within you.

You can be a king, or a master, or an archangel in a dream and thus remove all the limitations of space, and human desires, which infest earthly existence. Some dreams have significance when they are filmed by the superconscious, all-seeking mind and played on the screen of your dream movie-house. Some dreams, like comedies which are shown to you by your subconscious mind, are usually meaningless, a result of worries activity.

THE PURPOSE OF DREAMING God shows you by dreams that you can materialize your thoughts into sensations, feelings, am all earthly experiences by the power of your subconscious mind. When you can materialize your thoughts into dreams, you will realize that God materialized His thoughts into the dream of earth and Cosmos. The earth and cosmos are nothing but materialized dream thoughts of God, By knowing this cosmos as God's dream, you can be free from birth and death, sorrow and pleasure, poverty and prosperity, for you will realize that all these dualities are untrue, like dream experiences. Upon waking, you realize the falsity of a good or bad dream experience. Upon waking in cosmic consciousness, you will realize that you were dreaming a body and its sorrows or pleasures.

You learn from the story, "The Man Who Became a Buffalo," that in practicing the art of concentration about anything you must be one with that thing and now keep yourself apart from it. As long as you feel that you are concentrating upon a thing, you are away from it, but when you become very deeply absorbed in it, then you and the object of your concentration become one.

Regarding your health, remember that yellow olive oil is good for smoothness of the skin. Eat potato skins.

SUMMARY OF PRAECEPTUM NO. 11 Memorize "My Devotion." Always believe when you are praying that God is responding to your prayers, even though He does not audibly answer you. Just as unseen water vapor can freeze into an ice-berg, so, by the strength of your devotion, you can freeze the unseen Spirit into the seen form of Krishna, or Guru, or any saint, in a vision with open or closed eyes.

In deep ecstasy worship God as impersonal, formless, omnipresent, ever-new Bliss. In deep devotion and vision worship God as the form of the saint you love, and see Him, talk to Him, and touch Him, and serve Him in the human way. As God has taken the form of all human beings and partially manifested through them, so also he can fully manifest through the body of your Guru (preceptor) or the form of any saint.

Fostering the desire for luxuries is the surest way of losing money and causes unhappiness. Differentiate between your real needs and unnecessary necessities (so-called necessities, which you imagine to be necessities). Happiness can be had by exercising self-control in everything.

Desirelessness is not negative. It signifies that you should be able to forsake the short-lasting desires for bodily and earthly existence, for the superior, ever-lasting happiness of the Soul. It is the vision of wisdom which directs you to seek Soul happiness instead of sense happiness.

WHAT IS GOD AND HOW TO KNOW HIM He is the ever-existing, ever-conscious, ever-increasing, ever-new joy of meditation. Because God is ever-increasing, ever-new joy, there we should seek Him more than temptation and sense happiness. God can be tangibly known and felt as the ever-increasing joy of deep and deeper meditation. Those who meditate only a little while do not know the indescribable happiness which springs forth from, the contact of deep and deeper meditation. To know God you must meditate intensely as well as long, and regularly, and whenever you have spare time. By the incoming of happiness you will know beyond doubt that this ever-increasing happiness will consciously guide you in all things through your intuition. Of course it is better to meditate a little even irregularly than not to meditate at all, for here you may have a chance to work hard to make a deeper contact in spirit.

SPECIAL NOTE You will learn the scientific way of contacting God in the Second Step of the Praecepta.

God is the Invisible Factory of intelligence, from which all things come. Read carefully page 5, the last paragraph. The surest sign that you are in him.

Remember the story, "The Man Who Wouldn't Be a King," and tell it to your children and friends.

Read the DO'S and DON'TS on pages 8 and 9.

Think of God in every action. Affirm daily: "Teach me to feel Thee constantly as the ever-new Joy of Meditation."

SUMMARY OF PRAECEPTUM NO. 12 Commit to memory most of the passages of "Divine Love." "Love is born in [the] garden of Soul progress."

Parental, or conjugal, or friendly love can only be lasting if it is based on mutual soul progress. Divorces result from lack of mutual entertainment. When two people constantly spiritually progress, then they can mutually and perpetually entertain each other. Intellectual entertainment or beauty entertainment do not last long and fail to afford unending happiness, which can only be found by deep meditation. Friends and husbands and wives should deeply meditate together if they want to remain united forever by the cords of Divine Love.

With the love of all tangible, human love, love God as the joy of meditation. Whenever you feel thrilled at the joy of meditation, know that you are with God. It is then that you should love that state of God-Bliss with the love that you might have for the dearest people you love on earth. This is a tangible technique of knowing God.

On pages 2 and 3 especially note the difference between God and the creation of Satan, it is foolish to believe that Satan is not magnetic when Jesus and great Masters already spoke of him. To know how Satan works is to defeat him in his den. If I send my son to create a holy empire and then, when he gets my permission to create, he creates an evil kingdom, I have two ways to use my full power in dealing with my son. (1) I can destroy him by using my supreme power or (2) I can coax him to change his ways and go on counseling him to be good, until he becomes good of his own accord. Thus, God sent an archangel to create the cosmos. He was invested with the full independence to create good things only, a Cosmos without death, disease, or suffering, so that souls, after a perfect human existence, were to go back to God.

But Satan saw that he would lose all his powers if all creation which he created went back and dissolved itself again in God. So Satan created patterns of evil for all patterns of good which he had created after the will of God. So, you see that there is death, disease, suffering, old age, sex, and so forth, as Satan's evil patterns, against life, health, happiness, youth, Divine communion, and Divine ecstasy, as God's pattern.

Now, remember that you are a free agent standing midway between Satan and God. None can influence you except yourself. Whenever you misuse your free choice by doing an evil act, Satan pulls you toward His side. Remember, Satan tempts you by assuring permanent happiness from the senses, and you know Satan loses out because he gives sorrow instead of happiness and breaks all his promises. Because of this, Satan cannot keep an erring soul forever within his sinful fold. God is Almighty and can destroy Satan, but He is choosing a better method of love to coax Satan to change his ways and again create only a beautiful cosmos free from all earthly imperfections. Thus, remember, God created forgiveness, self-control, and Truth speaking, and Satan created revengefulness, extreme sense indulgence, lying, and so on.

Now, the law of cause and effect and Karma cannot tell us that our actions are responsible for the creation of disease, germs, jealousy, hate, sex-temptations. Take away Satan-created selfishness, anger, and greed from human life and the earth would be free from crime, disease, murders, war, and theft instantaneously. We were started with them by Satan. They are not the result of our ignorance or fruits of past actions. Hence, every time you are sexually tempted, remember that it is not your weakness, but that Satan is tempting you to indulge in lesser imitation happiness and that you should forthwith stop identifying yourself with that sex temptation and say: "Get thee behind me, Satan. I prefer lasting God-created Soul pleasures to your illusive promise-breaking momentarily pleasurable, but bitter in the end, sex pleasures."

This is the greatest way to be victorious over evil by not denying it or explaining it away as a psychological error, but by substituting the lesser illusive pleasure of evil by the greater certain joys of good.

If you form good habits, they will keep your Soul magnetized to them, just as a horseshoe magnet does not release a piece of iron bar which it holds, so evil magnetism can keep you enslaved and away from good. Hypnosis robs one of his free will and freedom and deteriorates the brain; hence, it is a spiritual crime. Magnetism expands a soul and should be exchanged among good persons. Do not let anybody hypnotize you. Nobody can hypnotize you in the dark or without suggestion.

A person hypnotized becomes very obvious to all by the peculiarity of his actions.

Failures should not mix with failures, but should mix with successful business men, in attentive hand-shaking and devoted discussion, you exchange magnetism, which is unconsciously exchanged between yourself and your associates; hence, beware of the kind of company you keep. Carefully read and practice the rules of developing magnetism.

Tell the story of the "Himalayan Musk Deer" to those that are spiritually even half-awake - how they are like the foolish musk deer, seeking happiness in every place except within themselves.

You actually begin to live after forty, so live well now that you may more enjoy your life after forty. Eat more alkaline foods, eliminate properly and fast one day a week on orange juice.

Affirm: "I will spurn Satan in all evil thoughts and actions. By thinking, willing, feeling, seeing, hearing, touching only good, I shall be with God constantly."

SUMMARY OF PRAECEPTUM NO. 13 "Make me behold what Thou dost see."

On page 2 I have given you the unfailing law of prosperity. 1. Cut down luxuries; 2. Think and by meditation know yourself as a child of God; 3. Think of all nationalities as your brothers; 4. Lost important of all: Seek prosperity for others and they will seek prosperity for you.

Develop power of concentration by regular practice of technique with great personal zeal. By concentration, you learn to create at will what you need. Develop 100 per cent efficiency by practicing the art of concentration. All prosperity will be measured according to the degree and power of your concentration.

Read carefully and practice daily the meditation on page 4 entitled; "God's Will and Your Will." pray after meditation when the mind is under control and pray unceasingly until you hear God respond to you through vision or your deep intuition.

Conscious or subconscious mind cannot create a new cause of success in anything except in a limited way, but the superconscious mind has unlimited power to create success, as it is not governed by any limitation, but by the boundless prosperity of God.

Tell your children the story of the "Holy squirrel," and develop in them the unflinching Divine determination as displayed by this holy squirrel.

Very carefully read pages 6 and 7 about the value of iron, silicon, iodine, fluorine, sodium, and potassium in your organs. Also study on page 8 about the "Oneness with God." Affirm: "God, I will act, but guide my activity to true success."

SUMMARY OF PRAECEPTUM 14 Memorize the "Candle of Peace." This is a most important prayer. "Take the bowl of my mind and fill it with Thy understanding."

Remember to "Cleanse the altar of your heart with the tears of repentance."

HUMBLENESS VS. EGOTISM Humbleness is a fertile valley of consciousness where the rain of God's wisdom falls fruitfully. Egotism refuses to investigate Truth, whereas humbleness is always ready to learn. Egotism shuts out all knowledge and the desire of the wise to help you for your own good, whereas humbleness will attract all kinds of wisdom unto yourself. Besides, egotism makes one appear big in one's own eyes and very much less in the eyes of others. Humbleness makes one look big in the eyes of others. To have personality requires a conviction of Truth and the courage to utter it, but it does not mean the possession of repulsive egotism.

Egotism slaps wisdom in the face; humbleness entreats the lotus feet of Truth to enter the innermost sanctuary of the Soul. God, the knower of all things and possessor of all things, is not egotistical. Hence, all those that want to be powerful like Him must be free of egotism.

Jesus Christ said: "The least is the greatest in Heaven." An empty vessel makes a loud sound." "A few fish make a lot of noise in a bowl, and the ocean does not make a noise about the whales playing in its bosom." "Little knowledge is a dangerous thing" and makes one display it too much. The wise are so busy and engrossed in their wisdom that they have no time to speak about it to anyone.

Sow hate and you will reap hate, sow love in all hearts and you will reap love everywhere. Every work is selfish. Even when we serve others we do so to relieve ourselves of the pain which we feel when we see others suffer. Resurrect your Soul from the dream of frailties. To acknowledge defeat is greater defeat.

Meditation is the only portal through which you can escape from all your troubles to infinite Freedom. Meditation is the way to forget God's delusive dream of matter and realize and remember the forgotten image of God within you.

Tell the story of the man of India, who was the "World's Most Humble Man," to your children and friends. "Humbleness is the valley of beauty where the waters of Divine Wisdom gather to inundate the dry tracts of the human soul." Avoid an inferiority complex, for it underestimates your powers. Avoid a superiority complex, for it overestimates your powers. Be natural; become great in humbleness and become great by effort and will power.

Alfalfa tea is better than ordinary tea which has tannin. Alfalfa tea is the laundry-man of the body, destroys pus, prevents constipation, and so forth.

Positively read the notes of value on page 8.

SUMMARY OF PRAECEPTUM No. 15 Commit to memory "For Thee I Was Made." o. 15 Especially remember: "My Soul was made to be the channel through which Thy love might flow uninterruptedly into all thirsty Souls."

Do not use your body, mind, and Soul for perishable pleasures, but use them for attaining the unending joys of Spirit. Commit to memory the prayer on page 2. Your Soul must approach nearer to God with each understanding repetition of an affirmation of all the prayers.

Don't often do what you wish to do, but do what your habits compel you to do. Good habits are automatic psychological machines; they help easy performance of specific actions. Bad habits must be destroyed. Though habits are compelling, yet remember that it is you who create them. You can dislodge bad habits by creating good habits. To break a habit, you must remember that it grows from the repetition of an inner thought and yielding to some outward company. Therefore, change your bad company to good company. Remember the temptation of bodily. pleasures - never fed, they are ever satisfied, and ever fed, they are never satisfied.

GENESIS OF HABIT A specific outward company or thought, repeatedly presented to the mind, influences the will, feeling, brain, and muscular mechanism of the body. Record-like grooves are formed in the brain, which awaken certain habits of action through memory or impulse.
Cultivate the spiritual habit of meditating with zeal and you will reach God easily. Relate story of "Strange Musician" to friends.
Remember, you are the sole creator of your good or bad habits.

ORDER IN WHICH HABITS MUST BE PERFORMED Above all, remember: First, form the habit of deep meditation; second, form the habit of doing good to others; Third, form the habit of being moderate in everything and cultivating good character; Fourth, form the habit of eating right, taking good exercise, and planning healthy, wholesome undertakings; Fifth, form the habit of making practical, creative efforts which produce the necessary prosperity. HEALTH Tomatoes vibrate with the liver. Tomato juice diets are very helpful in eliminating body poisons and increasing digestion.

GREATEST LAW OF HABIT Remember the Spiritual law of habit. Let not the material habits crowd out the Spiritual habits, or vice versa. Never neglect the most important habit of meditating for a less important habit of eating or doing unimportant things.
Affirm: "By forming better and better habits I shall build the ladder to climb to Heavenly Bliss."

THE PLAN OF PRAECEPTUM NO. 26 The sectional review of the twenty five Praecepta, constituting the First, or portal Novitiate Step, will be continued, for easy and convenient study, in succeeding installments of Praeceptum No. 26, in order to complete the comprehensive program of review. Always remember that conscientious perseverance in review and practice sharpens the perception and understanding.
The Third Installment of Praeceptum No. 26 will follow after a fortnight.

YOGODA SAT-SANGA FORTNIGHT INSTRUCTIONS
BY
PARAMHANSA YOGANANDA
FIRST STEP
PRAECEPTA SUMMARIES
THIRD INSTALLMENT

SUMMARY OF PRAECEPTUM Commit to memory "In Stillness Dark," or portions of it.
NO. 16

If you can remain half-awake for long, in the land between semi-wakefulness and deep sleep, then through that you will be able to understand the consciously joyous state of superconsciousness. In super-consciousness you combine the wakefulness of the conscious state with the conscious enjoyment of the semi-conscious state of subconsciousness. Affirm: "The dove of my love is winging its way through storms of trials to God." Concentrate and meditate early upon waking and before going to bed, or any time you are free. Fill in the gaps of leisure hours with meditation.

DEFINITION OF CONCENTRATION AND MEDITATION Concentration is the art of disengaging your attention from sensations, sensation-roused thoughts, and thoughts rousing other thoughts, and then placing the freed attention upon anything material spiritual. Meditation is the art of engaging the disturbance free attention upon God, or good things only.

MEDITATE ANY TIME Pretend that you are sleeping and resting and instead meditate in the lying down posture on your bed to avoid detection and criticism of meddlesome and misunderstanding people.

SELECT ENVIRONMENT If you can be quiet anywhere, meditate anywhere, but if noises disturb you, use our "Silence Making Machine" positively every time you meditate. Then you won't have any excuse for saying: "Oh, I can't meditate because of my noise-infected surroundings." Select a quiet place, or the silence of the night, for meditation. Create your own silence by closing your ears when meditating. Act ambitiously, discharging your noble duties with your mind constantly meditating upon God. Select a little room, or a screened off corner with harmonious vibrations, for your meditations. Sit on a woolen blanket spread over an armless chair, facing the East, when meditating.

RELATION OF BREATH, VITAL ESSENCE AND MIND 1. Keep mind busy with good activities and meditation. 2. Keep vital fluid transmuted into muscular and brain energy. Don't waste it in bad company. 3. Keep breath calm by eating less carbonized foods and entirely abstaining from beef, veal, and pork products.

If mind is calm, sex and breath will be under control. If character is good, breath and mind will be calm. If you have breath control by the technique we shall teach, then the mind and sex will be under your control. If you disturb any of the three, you will disturb the others. Disturb sex-control and mind and breath will be restless.

Read page 4 carefully. Do not sleep too much. Practice meditation long and with intensity on Sundays and holidays and any idle days. Meditate in the early morning from 6 to 9 A. M., and at night from 9 to 12 P. M. Regular meditation should be one hour or half an hour in the morning, one or two hours before going to bed, and meditate deeply whenever you can in between.

Study the story of "Monkey Consciousness" for yourself. This is a story which illustrates the restlessness and one-sidedness of the mind. Above all; "To thin own self be true." Affirm: "I feel Him constantly on the altar of peace."

SUMMARY OF PRAECEPTUM NO. 17 Commit to memory: "We are One." Study this over again and again until you actually feel what it says. Positively read again and again pages 2, 3, 4, and 5. When you try to concentrate upon one thing, you usually forget all about it and think about everything else, This is often experienced when you are thinking of a domestic problem at home or a business problem at the office, or a Spiritual problem at home or a business problem at the office, or a spiritual problem in the church. Forget the old method of concentration by diversion, and learn, the scientific method of concentration. Remove the causes of disturbances which affect your concentration and apply the scientifically freed attention on anything material or divine.

Whenever you are talking to people who hold views different from your own; whenever you meet people of different races and note their different habits, remember the story in this Praeceptum and its morals.

Learn to properly combine foods. Read the "Do's and Don'ts" on page 9. Food acts like poison when not combined properly. Harmless, nourishing food by wrong combination becomes poisonous. For example, olive oil is good and nuts are good, but when you fry nuts in olive oil, or any other good oil, they become indigestible, acting as poisons in the body.

Read the weekly inspiration. Concentrate for happiness. Affirm: "Teach me to behold Thy face through the window of meditation reflected in the mirror of my inner silence."

SUMMARY OF PRAECEPTUM No. 18 Commit to memory the following verse from "Where I Found Thee." "I saw myself reflected in everything, and when in concentration I looked at myself, I became transparent, and in my transparency I could not find me, but only Thee, only Thee. Everywhere dumb mutter spoke, Spirit-resurrected by Thy touch."

METHOD OF CONCENTRATION While in church, do not concentrate upon the social conclave, noises around the church, or individuals making a noise, but concentrate upon the inner peace and the sermon being preached. God talks to you through the voice of silence and peace of meditation, if you don't drown His voice by the noise of your passions. With the whip of intuition, drive away the money-changers of material desires and restlessness from the temple of meditation, which is the real house of God.

If you are a business man, or God aspirant, or a house-keeper, or an artist, or anything, you can increase your efficiency 100 per cent by the regular deep practice of meditation. What Jesus meant by: "If thine eye offend thee, pluck it out."

The Life Force in the nerves keeps the Soul entangled with the messages of the sensations in the eyes, ears, hands, and so forth, and when the Life Force is plucked from the eyes and cut off from the hands and the consciousness of the body, then it is reversed on the omnipresent God. Concentration means freeing the attention from sensations, present thoughts, and memory thoughts, by switching off the Life Force from the sensory motor nerves consciously (almost as in sleep) thus preventing the thought-rousing sensations to reach the brain.

Thousands of persons pray in the churches and don't know why they do so, or why they don't get an answer to their prayers. If they knew the law of God-contact, they would easily be able to contact Him.

Whenever you feel the compelling influence of habits, and when you fail to keep your resolution to be good, remember the story of "The Hunter Who Became a Saint."

Lemon is the best antiseptic and contains hydrogen, necessary for the body.

Affirm: "I shall seek Thee in the ever-increasing joy of meditation. Finding Thee first, I shall find things I crave through Thee."

SUMMARY OF PRAECEPTUM NO. 19 Commit to memory: "I Shall Catch Thee in the Net of My Devotion."

God reveals Himself to those who develop their inner powers and use the laws of concentration and meditation. By using the law of thermal-control, heating systems have been discovered. So, by controlling Life Force and the power of concentration, God can be discovered. But remember, though God can the approached through law only, still He, being above law, cannot be compelled to reveal Himself to the true seeker by the force of the law of concentration. Hence, devotion or surrender of the Son-Soul to the Father-Spirit is necessary for demanding the Absolute surrender of God to the devotee. God can escape the small nets of discrimination, pure activity, or concentration, but He cannot escape the net of devotion. When the devotee completely gives Himself to God, then God has to do likewise. God is very exacting when Divine laws are concerned, but He is forgetful and becomes intoxicated and relaxed when He is given the nectar-wine of devotion. God loves to drink devotion from the secret wine-press of the devotee's heart.

Approach God with the mirror of silence. Silence signifies silencing thoughts. That is really possible during sleep. If the silencing of thoughts [is] possible during sleep, then [i]t can be done during wakefulness by the higher methods of concentration. There are threefold disturbances. (1) sensations; (2) thoughts roused by sensations; and (3) past memory thoughts. Read very carefully from page 3 to 5 about sensations.

Whenever you are tempted to bring prosperity by dishonesty, or by evil ways, think of the story of "The Alaskan Sourdough."

Study the Health department earnestly and sincerely. Use "Watermelon Cocktail." Fast 1 to 3 days on watermelon. Very cleansing and healing.

Read "The Mirror of Silence." Affirm: "Let every good thought be an open window to reveal Thy presence."

SUMMARY OF PRAECEPTUM No.20 Reread the poem, "Divine Joy." By all means try to contact God first, then you will know that He is not a God of terror or a Cosmic Detective, read to plunge the javelin of revenge at you, but that He is ever-new Joy. And if you know God as the supreme joy, which will never grow old or stale through Eternity, then you will lose your taste for all other sense-pleasures, no matter how alluring they are.

Ask God, that you by His good will and your own effort, cultivate good habits first, so that bad habits may not have a chance to become first to invade and settle their charm in you. Pray to God that He may not test you by making you forget Him while you roam in the chamber of earthly pleasures. Forgetfulness of God is the highest sin, and the greatest punishment of all miseries spring from God- oblivion.

As you are surrounded by the earth, so your consciousness and Ego [are] surrounded by the dilapidated, decayed walls of evil thoughts, [and] the enemies of temptations will destroy [it]. But if your Ego is surrounded by good thoughts, good feelings, and good sensations, then [it] is protected behind the impregnable castle of Self-Realization, and the soldiers of evil won't be able to destroy [it]. Therefore, always be surrounded by good thoughts, no matter where you go, or what you are thinking.

CONCENTRATION Sleep is the state which proves that by switching off the Life Force and consciousness from the five telephones of touch, smell, taste, sight, and hearing, you can free your attention from all distracting sensations, sensation roused thoughts, and thought-roused memory thoughts. But one does not want to sleep in order to be quiet. Self-Realization teaches you to consciously switch off the Life Force from the five nerve-wires of touch, taste, smell, sight, hearing, and so forth. If you can do this by regularly practicing the technique, then no sensations of touch, smell, and so forth, can disturb your brain, thoughts would not arise, and if thoughts stopped arising in the brain, then memory-thoughts would not be awakened. In sleep, as soon as sensations stop reaching the brain, the thoughts and buried subconscious thoughts stop their activities, so. by the conscious process of this technique, the above can be accomplished. An attention free from disturbances becomes ready for successfully using it in material or Spiritual accomplishment.

Remember, it is not only Yogis of India (Yoga, meaning union) and (Yogi - one who tries to scientifically unite his soul with God), but St. Paul said: (1 Cor. 15:31) "I protest by the rejoicing that I have in Christ (consciousness), I die daily," (withdraw the Life Force from the heart, or die and live again at will).

When the heart stops, one dies or finds his life switched off from the five sense-telephones of touch, smell, sight, and so forth.

In sleep, also due to the slow action of the heart, a state of partial death or sleep, or switching off the energy from the nerve-telephones, is accomplished. Death is the permanent switching of the Life Force from the five sense-telephones by an unconscious method. Sleep is a partial switching of the Life Force from the five sense- telephones by an unconscious method. The Self-Realization technique shows a conscious way of withdrawing Life Force partially from the senses and muscles and heart, or completely from the entire body, as in death, and then installing it back again into the senses, muscles, and heart, or in the entire lifeless body. In sleep, Life Energy retires from the sensory motor nerves and muscles into the heart and spine. In death, the Life Force and consciousness completely go out of the body. By conscious technique, one can switch Life Force on or off at will in any part of the body or in the complete body. The purpose of the technique is to quiet the heart.

Q. What causes the heart to beat and work fast?

A. Restlessness, worry, wrong eating (which is more work for the heart), overwork, strenuous activity, running, violent emotions, sudden shocks and fears, and stimulating chemicals. Therefore, in order to quiet the heart, one must not be restless like children (because of restlessness the heart of a child beats faster.)

WHY CONCENTRATE BY QUIETING THE HEART Calmness, calmness-producing food, and moderate and regular activities, are conducive to making the heart calm. 1. Eat less carbonized food, with an abundance and predominance of fruits and vegetables. 2. Sit calm and practice the concentration lesson, removing all bodily activities. 3. To remove the activity from the diaphragm, circulatory organs, lungs, and so forth, practice the technique of watching the breath.

(a) When motion is removed from the outer and the inner body, (b) decay stops, and (c) venous blood ceases to increase, (d) When venous blood ceases to increase the heart slows down, for it does not any longer have to send dark impure venous blood to be purified in the lungs. When the heart is not given the work of pumping blood, then the energy which makes the heart work slows down and begins to flow back toward the brain instead of toward the senses and the five sense-telephones, (f) When this happens, then, as in sleep, the Life Force automatically withdraws itself from the senses to the muscles and five nerve-telephones toward the brain. Then the Life Force is switched off from the senses of sight, hearing, taste, smell, and touch, (g) Then sensations are unable to bother the attention in the brain. (h) Then this attention is free from the disturbances of the sensations and thoughts, and becomes ready to be used one hundred per cent on material or spiritual objects.

Concentration by quieting the heart you do every day unconsciously in sleep (the only state of real concentration). In addition, I ask you to concentrate by consciously quieting the Heart; as taught in the technique of watching the breath.

Q. How many tons of blood does the heart pump every day A. Eighteen tons every day and 6,570 tons a year. Imagine what terrific work the heart has to do. To quiet the heart is natural. Entertain no fear when the heart slows down. Wellington and Napoleon had fifty heart beats per minute because they always were men of great calmness. Not to give rest to this much-abused slave, your heart, might bring forth an answer: "Sir, I will quit my job."

Do not be frightened about quieting the heart, for by the conscious technique you use the calmness of meditation as a brake to quiet the heart. It is natural to quiet the heart; the hearts of elderly people are quieted by nature after passing through the period of childhood.

Q. Is there a chance to get out of the body when the heart is quiet, and not come back into the body again

A. Not a chance. In the first place, it takes long practice to quiet the heart. As long as food remains, you can't calm the heart. Otherwise, many people who know how to meditate would quiet the heart forever, and would never come into the body again. Meditation is the conscious way of switching on or switching off the Life Force into the body or out of the body. Self-Realization technique teaches concentration, not by diverting the mind from the senses to God, but it scientifically teaches you how to withdraw not only the mind, but also the Life Force, which is the medium of sense disturbances.

Q. What is the Soul? A. Individualized Spirit, spirit is ever-existing, ever-

178

conscious, ever-new Bliss. The Soul is the individualized ever- existing, ever-conscious, ever-new spirit. The one light under the perforated gas burner can be compared to the spirit behind the pores of all human consciousness. The little lights running through the pores can be compared to the human souls which are emanations of the one Spirit.

Protect the mind from the four alternating psychological states of sorrow, false happiness, indifference, and a deceptive passive tiresome peace. Most desires are impostors. Stay away from their alluring talks.

Commit to memory the story of the "Lion Who Became a Sheep," and who was made a lion afterward by another lion. Whenever you become despondent, remember this, and tell this story to people who easily become despondent due to their depressing environment.

HEALTH Do not over-do the drinking or citrus fruits. Prepare the body by taking vegetable juices first. Sip citrus fruit juices to insure insalivation. Cooking destroys the food value of citrus fruits. Eat a little of the peel with the entire orange and some seeds. Study Page Eight* carefully; each paragraph is very important. *[Editor's note: none of the Praecepta has 8 pages; presumably the focus here is on the descriptions of the health properties of fruits listed in Praeceptum 20's Health Culture.]

SUMMARY OF PRAECEPTUM NO. 21 Study the poem: "Rock Me to Sleep On Thy Bosom of Peace." Remember this prayer: "O, Fountain of Love, make us feel that our hearts are all flooded by Thy Omnipresent Love.

Breath is not life; it is one of the conditions in which life exists.
Q. Can life exist without breath?
A. Yes, in suspended animation life can exist without heart action or breath - by brain energy and energy from the medulla.
Q. Why is the body comparative to an automobile battery?
A. As an automobile battery is kept alive by distilled water and electricity, so also Jesus said: "Man (body battery) shall not live by bread (distilled water) alone, but by every word (vital Life Force) which proceedeth out of the mouth of God," (which proceedeth out of the medulla, through which Cosmic Energy enters the body.)

Life Force is the direct power which sustains the body. Oxygen and food are converted into energy by Life Force, and are powers which indirectly support the body. If Life Force fails to digest food and convert it into energy, then the body cannot live. When electricity is missing from your automobile battery, adding more distilled water to it will not help. You must send it to be recharged in the battery shop. So, also, when your vitality is low and your health fails in spite of all health and dietetic precautions, then you must know how to recharge your Life Force by will power and the inner way, instead of simply eating good food and going to health resorts for a cure. Remember, breathlessness is deathlessness. Breath is the cord which ties the Soul to the body. Conquer it and you will be free.

THE TECHNIQUE 1. Face the east, sitting on a straight armless chair on a blanket (meant for Western students). 2. Sit upright, chest out, shoulder blades together, and palms upward at the junction between the thighs and abdomen. 3. Expel breath quickly three times. Then wait for the breath to come in. 4. Watch breath as it flows naturally without drawing it in or out by force or by the act of will. 5. As often as the breath goes in quickly or slowly, all the way, mentally, say, without sound or whisper or use of the lips or tongue, "Hong." 6. If the breath stays in, wait; otherwise, as soon as the breath goes out quickly or slowly, all the way, mentally, say, without sound or whisper or use of the lips or tongue, "Sau." Repeat each sound as instructed with each corresponding incoming and outgoing breath.

THE MEANING OF HONG SAU "Hong" is the vibration of the incoming breath; "Sau" is the vibration of the outgoing breath. Conscious chanting of the words together quiets the breath, as that is the breath's astral vibration. Continued practice of the technique enables the yogi to experience himself as separate from the body and breathing. He then is able to behold himself as the soul.

WHAT IS SLEEP In sleep, we experience voluntary, unconscious sensory relaxation. In death, complete relaxation involuntarily takes place, due to the stopping of the heart's action. If one can learn to control the heartbeat, he can experience the conscious death, leaving and re-entering the body at will; many Yogis of India, who have practiced "Hong-Sau" have, through it, achieved mastery over the action of the heart. Such Yogis have learned to leave the body voluntarily, honorably, and gladly, and are not thrown out roughly, or taken by surprise by death, when their lease on their body-temples expires.

BEST TIMES TO MEDITATE The four times of change in the body during the day correspond to the four seasons. The purpose of this Lesson is to realize the changeless in the four changing periods of the body, by vitalizing and magnetizing it with Life Currents and Cosmic Consciousness. These Currents arrest change and suspend the decay in the cells. Therefore, it is best to practice the changeless-producing Lessons four times a day for sure scientific results. Meditate between 5 and 6 A.M.; 11 and 12 A.M.; 5 and 6 P.M.; 10 and 12 P.M.; or 11 and 12 P.M.

The Fourth Installment of Praeceptum No. 26 will follow after a fortnight.

YOGODA SAT-SANGA FORTNIGHTLY INSTRUCTIONS BY
PARAMHANSA YOGANANDA
(To Be Confidentially Reserved FOR MEMBER'S USE ONLY) FIRST STEP PRAECEPTA
SUMMARIES FOURTH
INSTALLMENT

FOUR STATES OF CONSCIOUSNESS

CONTINUATION OF SUMMARY OF
PRAECEPTUM NO. 21
1. Through bad habits and never practicing self-control or concentration, you are all the time restless and unable to concentrate even when you sit still in a quiet place. 2. By willing practice of the technique, even though you may not like to do so for a while, once in a while you will be calm, while remaining most of the time restless. 3. By meditating and concentrating with greater intensity and for a long time, you will most of the time be calm and once in a while restless. 4. By meditating and concentrating very deeply, long, and continuously, as taught, you will always be able to be calm and joyous, and never restless.

Affirm: "Teach me to feel that Thou art the power throbbing just behind the engine of the heart."

SUMMARY OF PRAECEPTUM NO. 22 Commit to memory this great vision of all things studded in the Cosmic Consciousness. This is from the poem of this Praeceptum, "Thy Home-Coming." This poem describes how, in Cosmic Consciousness, you will find the fugitive God coming back to you amidst the festivity of all Nature. Memorize also the prayer preceding the lesson on page 2, "Teach me to behold myself in others."

(a) To have good character and control over your sex life is extremely important in contacting the Supreme Being. God created Divine Ecstasy of Meditation. Satanic Ignorance created pseudo substitutes for them -sex temptation and wine. Sex is for creative purposes, while wine is the greatest tool of the Evil Force to obliterate wisdom and discrimination. Hence, wire and all doping drugs must be complete forsaken. You must have moderation first and then renunciation if you are gripped by the sex habit, or the dope or wine habit.

"When wealth is lost, little is lost; when health is lost, something is lost; when character is lost, all is lost."

(b) Control your mind. Don't do anything against the dictates of your conscience and discrimination. Learn to resist evil by will power. Don't do anything because you wish to do it. Do everything that it is your duty to do. Calm the breath and creative force by the power of your mind. Mind is the operator of all your powers.

The person who tries to concentrate by harmonizing breath, Life Force, and vital essence, gets quicker results than the person who meditates without disciplining breath by technique, or controlling character and sex life by strong will power and reason.

Please remember that without an erect spine and a proper posture during concentration and meditation you will lose half the good result in attaining control and peace. This is very important.

Read page 3 again and again. It is very important to follow the instructions. Remember, if the breath comes in slowly or quickly during a natural inhalation all the way with the breath, mentally (without whisper or tremor of tongue, or sound from the lips) chant "Hong." If the breath does not come out, wait, and when it comes out of itself, quickly or slowly, mentally chant "Sau." If the breath does not go in, wait until it goes in of itself. Keep on repeating this.

POSITION OF THE EYES Positively practice the concentration technique with eyes half open, gently concentrated at the point between the eyebrows. When you sleep (subconscious), you keep your eyes closed. When you are awake (conscious), you keep your eyes open. When you are in the superconscious state (consciously enjoying an ever-increasing joyous state, as in sleep), your eyes should be half open, fixed at the point between the eyebrows. This is the Center of Christ Consciousness.

The eyes of sleeping children (who are pure) and those of dying people, usually turn up to the point between the eyebrows. This Center is connected with the medulla at the back of the head. The entire energy of the body during death goes out through the spine, from the point between the eyebrows to the medulla, and then out of the body.

In sleep, the energy flows reversed, from the muscles and senses to the point between the eyebrows, then to the medulla and brain. That is why the nerves of the eyes and eyeballs are switched on to the point between the eyebrows and the medulla. That is why, since meditation and concentration consist in switching the consciousness and nerve force toward God through the medulla (the Mouth of God), one should learn to gently concentrate the eyes at the point between the eyebrows (Christ Center) during all meditation.

As you like to close your eyes in order to be in the subconscious, or to open your eyes in order to be consciously working through the eyes, you will love infinitely more to look up into the spiritual Eye, situated at the point between the eye-brows, when you get used to it. Practice without straining the eyes, but practice you must, always concentrating at the point between the eyebrows.

Study pages 4 and 5 carefully. The story of the "Woman Who Loved God as Her Son" (concluded in Praeceptum No. 22) teaches the various ways that one can love God. Learn to love Him as a Father, a Mother, a Friend, a Beloved, or a Master, or even as a dear Child.

Use the soup often for pepping up your health. Affirm: "Father, manifest Thyself through all my joys."

SUMMARY OF PRAECEPTUM NO. 23 Commit to memory, "The Wavelet." Feel yourself as the ocean of God Consciousness, as well as the tiny wavelet of this present life, dashing on the shores of the senses and flesh.

PRAYER "Teach me to consider no work greater than Thy spiritual work."

Study about the delicate art of breathing and breath-control. Our purpose is to teach you proper breathing, as long as you have to breathe some way. Read all of pages 2, 3, 4, and 5. Note (a) the purpose of watching the breath is to increase naturally the intervals when the breath does not flow. Watch the breath in order to do away with it. (b) Mentally chant "Hong" and "Sau" with the ingoing and outgoing breath as it naturally flows, without using will power. (c) concentrate, enjoy, and identify yourself with [the] state when the breath does not naturally flow as a result of practicing the technique of watching the breath, (d) The more you watch the breath, as taught in the technique, with deep attention for a long time, the less you will breathe, remaining breathless most of the time. This will calm the heart and consequently increase longevity. (e) By watching the breath, you metaphysically learn how to separate your watching Soul from the body, breath, and the conscious processes.

Learn to live directly by Cosmic Energy coming though the medulla and not by breath only or food only. Prevent oxygen starvation by practicing the technique on page 5.

Always tell this story (related on page 5) to others whenever you find that they excite you to war. Include all nations in your love for your own country. Patriotism should be used to make your own nation happy and not to excite hatred and attract terrible, death-dealing wars.

Remember to worship God in deep silence.

SUMMARY OF PRAECEPTUM NO. 24 Let your life throb in the stars, flowers, birds, beasts, in the glittering beauty of gems, and, above all, in the most dazzling love of all hearts.

Nervousness implies tampering with all the nerve wires and the electricity of life, which runs the entire body factory. Hence, you cannot afford to be nervous. Avoid the psychological and physical causes of nervousness, as told on pages 2 and 3. Calm company, inner calmness through meditation, and eating plenty of fruit are the best antidotes for nervousness.

HEALTH Live on 20% protein, 60% fruits, and 20% sugars and starches, if you would be healthy. Eat fruits most of the time, avoid eggs and meat. Eat large servings of raw vegetable salads and small servings of cooked food and protein. Read and follow the sample meal described on page 7.

Feel the Temple of God within your Soul as the joy of meditation. Affirm: "I will let silence and peace walk into me through the portals of my calmness."

SUMMARY OF PRAECEPTUM NO. 25 Let your joy be like the Niagara Falls, powerful and plenty, to inundate other Souls with happiness. Become a smile millionaire, scattering your Divine smiles freely everywhere. Be a Prince of Smiles. Let Prince Smile remain enthroned on the throne of your happiness.

Be inwardly happy always, retaining and remembering the happiness born of meditation. This will make you outwardly happy too.

Guard your happiness from the robbers of cranky, crabby, sorrow loving nervous souls. Remember, no one can make you unhappy if you refuse to allow them to do so. Happiness can be achieved by meditating long and regularly above all else, and by adopting the actions which generate happiness. Ignorant people, like animals, do not quickly remove the causes which make unhappiness. Avoid gossiping as you would avoid poison. Never gossip with your husband or wife, or children, or friends. Cultivate the habit of discussing the good in people with those that you love. Good thoughts attract the good in people. Evil thoughts attract evil.

"Judge ye not others, except yourself." Remember, it is easy to gossip long about others, but try gossiping about yourself for a while and see how you like it. Whenever you feel like talking about others, try talking loudly about your own secret weaknesses and faults before your enemies and friends. You won't like this. Correct yourself first. Make your home a valley of smiles, blossoming with happiness. The breeze of your constant Divine Smile is going to keep the li[f]e of those you love throbbing with joy and immortality and blessing.

Remember the story of "Sense Happiness" whenever you feel tempted in any way. Tell it to others who want your advice when they are tempted by evil.

Develop spirituality, intellectuality, prosperity, and health culture, with equal emphasis. Learn to lead a balanced life.

Commit to memory: "Bathe Yourself in the Ocean of Peace."

Affirm: "I will share my joy, prosperity, and wisdom with those who specially and really need them."

FINIS OF SUMMARIES

This concludes the Summaries of the Praecepta, constituting the First Step in the study of Self-Realization. It is our earnest, sincere, and humble request that you devote yourself through conscientious concentration and attention to the complete and harmonious assimilation of these summaries. These vital, comprehensive facts will be most advantageous to you in answering the questions which are to be given in the Intermediate Examination. By testing, the intellectual progress and understanding through a group of general questions and answers, we can determine the status of spiritual perception, or Self-Realization, which is directly affected by the mental comprehension, and thus, ascertain the most effective method to be used in each Member's case. The examination papers and particulars will be mailed to you and sufficient time will be allowed to permit you to receive the examination, answer the questions, and return your answers to us. This all precedes the beginning of the Praecepta in the Second Step.

FIRST INTERMEDIATE EXAMINATION

INTRODUCTION The Fortnightly Praecepta can be made very valuable to you if you read and study their contents faithfully and seriously. You can refer to the subject-matter over and over again. The Praecepta are always at hand, like the Dictionary and the Sacred Scripture, ever ready to be consulted, but the education and enlightenment that you receive from studying these Lessons will be entirely governed by the amount of time and close application that you put upon the work.

The thing that is the easiest to obtain in this life is seldom valuable. We know from reading the lives of great men and women that they became great in their particular vocations and in the building of their character only through the most rigid study and sacrifice, but the result obtained was worth far more than the efforts that were put forth, and that is usually the case.

Perhaps you will think that you have little time to give to the Lessons, but all of us have 24 hours a day to give to something. You will find upon reflection that you really waste much time upon trifling duties and entertainment, time which you could use to much better advantage in the study of the life principles contained in the Fortnightly Praecepta. Indeed, there is no comparison between the two methods — one leads to nothing but a temporary peace, and artificial satisfaction. The other leads to Self-Realization, permanent peace and happiness. We implore you to use your tine to the very best advantage. The study and practice of these lessons will not only help you in this life but will also prepare you for the life that is to come.

PURPOSE In order to further help you in your development resulting from the study of these Lessons, we have decided to give you between Steps a thorough examination on the Lessons, in order to determine just how much benefit you are receiving from your study of these valuable principle. We wish you to obtain full value from every standpoint.

This examination will indicate your degree of progress and your readiness for the Second Step which is to follow. It will also indicate your present needs, whereby we shall learn the most effective way to help you. We shall be able to discover your weak points and your strong points, and in that way be able to guide you correctly in your future studies.

EXAMINATION INSTRUCTIONS Please answer the questions briefly, clearly, and concisely. Answer each question in as few words as possible; (5 to not more than 20 words). Read the summaries of the First Step as given in the 4 parts of Praeceptum No. 26 for a concise review before answering the questions. Then do not refer to the Fortnightly Praecepta unless absolutely necessary.

The more you answer from memory, the more it will show what you really have learned and assimilated. Also, draw on your personal experiences in describing and answering many of the questions. Write only your answers down and send to us. Give the Praeceptum number and the number of the answer. For instance, Praeceptum 1, Answer 1. Do not send to us the questions that we have sent to you.

We have set a time-limit of two weeks for you to answer the questions and return them to us, and to allow us time for making corrections. The Second Step will follow after two weeks devoted to the examination. (If you are a very busy man or woman and have limited time to write, answer these questions to yourself and refer to the Praecepta to ascertain the correctness of your answers. Then let us know of your

185

approximate examination percentage. On your true, conscientious testimony we shall give you credit, but positively write the answers if you have sufficient time). All Members will be started in the Second Step and their answers will serve as a guide to the successful analysis of each Member's progress in Self-Realization.

QUESTIONS

PRAECEPTUM NO. 1 1. Why should the ideals of India and America be combined?

2.   Write down in a very few words the Universal Prayer on the "Tunnel To Eternity."

3.   Write vividly what you feel during the above meditation: Peace, Joy, Increased Bliss in the body or in the mind, or in both, a Sense of Expansion, Assurance, Feeling that you know all, Calmness, or Going beyond the body.

4.   Why should you fast once a week? Why should you eat meat substitutes?

5.   Outline the moral of the story: "The Saint Who Chose a King for His Spiritual Master."

PRAECEPTUM NO. 2 1. Who are the Supreme Master, Great Master, Master, and Guru of this Movement?

2.   What is the true meaning of Self-Realization Fellowship and Yogoda Sat-Sanga?

3.   How can God be contacted in meditation?

4.   Should you use your will or let God use your will mechanically?

5.   What are the ills caused by over-eating?

6.   When should you apply the moral you learned from the story of the "Big Frog and the Little Frog?"

PRAECEPTUM NO.3

1.In what lies true prosperity?

2.Why should you first realize: "I and my Father are One?"

3.What do you understand by trying to create at will what you need?

4.What is the difference between necessary "necessities" and unnecessary "necessities?"

5.What is the technique of reinforcing your will with God's will?

6.What is the moral in "Two Blind Men Who Sought Riches from God and a King?

PRAECEPTUM NO. 4

1. What are the two most important lines in the poem "Friendship"?

2.   In what does true friendship consist?

3.   Why should you love your enemies?

4.   What is your worst company?

5.   Why is it necessary to obey dietary laws as well as have faith in God?

2. **PRAECEPTUM 5** 1. Compare an ordinary battery with the body battery.

2. What are the direct and indirect sources which feed the body battery?

3. How can energy be roused in the body?

4. Illustrate how all possessions are useless without Self-Realization.

PRAECEPTUM NO. 6

1.   How can you hold the Infinite Spirit in the little cup of human consciousness?
2.   What is the difference, between exercising with dumbbells, etc, and tension exercises?
3.   Define relaxation and tension.
4.   How would you show the difference between will power and energy?
5.   Illustrate how you might fall down from the pinnacle of success if you forget God.
6.   How should you select your food?

PRAECEPTUM NO. 7

1.   What are the five stages of relaxation? Define each stage.
2.   What lesson did you learn from this affirmation: "I have God; I have everything."
3.   What lesson did you learn from the story of "That Moral Backbone?"

PRAECEPTUM NO. 8

1.   Describe in detail how you practice Exercise "A".
2.   a. How long and how many times do you practice the tension (rejuvenation) exercises?
b.   What do you feel immediately after exercising?
c.   Does the vitality gained by the exercises last through the day?
3. What causes acidity or alkalinity in the body?

PRAECEPTUM NO. 9

1.   How long and how many times do you meditate every day?
2.   Have you become a fisher of Souls? Do you do your highest duty to God to convert your loved ones and friends to this Teaching?
3.   How do you relax the whole body, or any part?
4.   How many kinds of tension are there?
5.   What is the "Mouth of God" and why?
6.   What is the moral of "The Bandit and the Bull? "

PRAECEPTUM NO. 10

1.   Write in 15 words the meaning of the poem "In the Land of Dreams."
2.   a. Write the classification of the significance of dreams. b. What is the main significance of dreams?
3.   Write the moral of "The Man Who Became a Buffalo."
4.   How would you prepare "Skin-Beauty Tea? "

PRAECEPTUM NO. 11

1.   Do you put into practice plain living and God thinking?
2.   Is desirelessness negation?
3.   What is God?
4.   Analyze "The Man Who Wouldn't Be King."

PRAECEPTUM NO. 12

1.   Define "Divine Love."
2.   Who is Satan? b. What does Satan want?
3.   What is the difference between hypnosis and magnetism?
4.   Explain how to develop magnetism.
5.   If you are a free agent with free will, how can God or Satan influence you?

PRAECEPTUM NO. 13

1.   What is the thorns of "Thy Magic Power? "
2.   What are the five rules of prosperity?
3.   What does a man of concentration ask God?
4.   How would you harmonize your will with God's Will?
5.   Write the moral in the Apologue, "The Holy Squirrel."

PRAECEPTUM NO. 14   1.   Write your idea of humbleness and egotism in 20 words.

                         2.   What purpose does Alfalfa Tea serve?

PRAECEPTUM NO. 15   1.   Write what you learned from the poem, "For thee I Was Made?"
                         2.   What is the Genesis of Habit?
                         3.   What is the moral of the story of "The Strange Musician?"
                         4.   Who is the creator of your good and your bad habits?
                         5.   What are tomatoes good for?

PRAECEPTUM NO. 16   1.   What is the theme of "In Stillness Dark? "
                         2.   Refine meditation and concentration.
                         3.   When should you meditate?
                         4.   What is the relation between breath, vital essence, and mind, and how to discipline them?
                         5.   What does the story of Monkey Consciousness" illustrate?

PRAECEPTUM NO. 17   1.   What is the purpose of the poem, "We are One?"
                         2.   What is the moral of the story in this PRAECEPTUM?
                         3.   Read the "Do's and Dont's" right now and let us know if you have followed them.

PRAECEPTUM NO. 18 1.   Write the substance of the poem, "Where I found Thee. "
                         2.   What is the inner meaning of the saying of Jesus: "If thy hand [offend] thee, cut if off; if thine eye offend thee, pluck it out. "
                         3.   What is the specific use of lemons?

PRAECEPTUM NO. 19   1.   What is the difference between the sleep state and the state produced by concentration?
                         2.   To whom does God reveal Himself?
                         3.   What are the threefold disturbances to the mind?
                         4.   What is watermelon cocktail, and of what value is a watermelon fast?

PRAECEPTUM NO. 20   1.   What distinguishes a Yogi?
                         2.   What is the meaning of: "I die daily? " (1 Corinthians 15: 31).
                         3.   What makes the heart restless?
                         4.   What quiets the heart? (Be as concise as possible.)
                         5.   Describe the various stages of body and mind when decay is consciously removed from the outer and inner body.
                         6.   What is the Soul?
                         7.   Outline the moral of the story, "The Lion Who Became a Sheep. "

PRAECEPTUM NO. 21   1.   Describe the technique of concentration and watching the breath.
                         2.   Why does watching the breath produce concentration?
                         3.   When are the best times to meditate?
                         4.   What are the four states of consciousness?

PRAECEPTUM NO. 22   1.   Why did Satan create sex temptation and wine?
                         2.   Why should you have an erect spine and posture during concentration?
                         3.   What happens when you consciously watch the breath?

4.   How does the attention become free?

5.   Write the story of "The Woman Who Loved God as Her Son."

PRAECEPTUM NO. 23. 1. What is the metaphysical effect of watching the breath?

PRAECEPTUM NO. 24   1.   Define nervousness.

2.   What causes nervousness?

3.   What is the best meat substitute?

PRAECEPTUM NO. 25.   1.   Do you carry the joy felt in meditation all the time or part of the time?

2.   Fill in the blank: "Judge ye not others except. . ."

3.   Why shouldn't you gossip about others?

4.   Can you write what you learned from "Bathe Yourself in the Ocean of Peace?"

Finis

189

The editor has attempted to follow the paging of the original manuscripts available to him. As a result some pages end mid-sentence, only to resume on the next page.

Some Praecepta pages apparently were longer than others and therefore smaller font size is utilized in my book.

Where wording was at times difficult to translate, I appealed to other articles. For instance, the line that reads in my manuscript "Truancy of fleas" [actually published in one MS Word document I found online] is found correctly articulated in a poem as "truant flesh." (Praeceptum 16, p. 1, "In Stillness Dark") Here is a picture of some of that poem's typing:

IN STILLNESS DARK

Hark!
In stillness dark,
When noisy dreams have slept,
The house is gone to rest,
And busy life
Doth cease from strife, --
The Soul in pity soft doth kiss
The Truant fless to soothe, and speak
With mind-transcending grace
Its soundless voice of peace.

I have noted in context one impossible line having to do with putting "felons in lemon." I assume Yogananda was saying to add a lemon peel to a lemon drink, but I do not presume to correct the copy thus. (Praeceptum 19, p. 6)

There is one interesting line that current SRF, Inc. Lessons reads to this day as "Approach God with a Song of Smiles." (Praeceptum 26/3, page 3). The context (i.e., Praeceptum 19) however has everything to do with approaching God in the mirror of silence that we put up as we meditate. Since enough words and letters are available to justify a different reading, I have presumed to read the line as "Approach God with the Mirror of Silence."

Although anecdotes abound of mimeographing and changing the individual Praecepta at Mother Center, the reality I find in the original surviving manuscript I used confirmed the anecdotes in the breach! The over-typing of letters, dyslexic and haplographic errors and spellings, along with India-British spelling intermixed with American-English spelling, overuse of commas, and unpredictable capitalization of words — what a messy set of pages some students received as their lessons. Here is a sample:

S-I * P.6

YOGODA SAT.SANGA FORTNIGHTLY INSTRUCTIONS

BY

PARAMHANSA YOGANANDA

-oo-

(To be confidentially Reserved FOR MEMBER'S USE ONLY)

Editor's Notes

Anecdotally speaking I understand that the Praecepta came about from hand-recording Master's talks. He said on several occasions that he had written nothing in the Praecepta. The transmission of the text from the listening recorder to transcription, to typing and retyping, sending manuscripts to Dakshineswar and/or Ranchi for editing and printing before the years in which Mother Center personnel became involved — all these are precious 'grit' to the textual critic's amanuensis mill!

I am aware of the role assigned by Master to Louise Royston to take excerpts from lectures he had given and articles he had written, and make a course of lessons out of them. Later on, of course, other lay disciples (such as Kamala Silva) edited and submitted talks they had heard and transcribed, preparing them for inclusion in the Praecepta. However the Praecepta folios all demonstrate a publishing location in India with editing there. The textual material supports these observations. In addition Master consistently told students to write the Indian headquarters in Dakshineswar and/or Ranchi if guidance were necessary. They were to submit their exam answers there as well.

Note that on the final page (p. 14) of Praeceptum 181, he identifies Ranchi as the headquarters of Self-Realization Fellowship and urges students to "Resolve to make a pilgrimage to the Self-Realization Headquarters at Ranchi, and Yogoda Math at Dakshineswar."

Editing this material has been a wonderful experience. I do it out of love for original material (witness the other public domain works which I have republished).

It is most wonderful for me because it gives me a closer sense of Master's presence, like the aroma of the Easter lilies which permeates our home this Easter Vigil evening, March 26, 2016.

May Master's blessings be upon all readers.

As always I welcome suggestions; I especially would love to obtain a complete copy of page 7, Praeceptum 26/3.

Donald Castellano-Hoyt, San Antonio, Texas
dcastellano.hoyt@gmail.com.

Other Books Authored or Edited by Castellano-Hoyt

Books Written By Donald Castellano-Hoyt

1.   The Eternal Religion on; Glimpses of Divine Glory
2.   Enhancing Police Response to Persons in Mental Health Crisis

Books Edited and Republished by Donald Castellano-Hoyt

1.   The Holy Science, the 1894 Serialized Version, Swami Sriyukteswar
2.   Descriptive Outline of YOGODA, Swami Yogananda, Sri Nerode
3.   Phineas F. Bresee; A Prince in Israel, Rev. E.A. Girvin
4.   The Heather Invasion, Mabel Potter Daggett
5.   Yogoda or Tissue-Will System of Physical Perfection, Swami Yogananda
6.   Bud Robinson Stories and Sketch, Rev. C. T. Corbett
7.   My Hospital Experience, Bud Robinson
8.   It Can Be Done, Ranendra Kumar Das
9.   Yogiraj Shri Shri Lahiri Mahasaya, Jogesh Battacharya
10.   Reincarnation, Ranendra Kumar Das
11.   Saint Theresa, René Fülöp-Miller
12.   Scientific Healing Affirmations, Swami Yogananda
13.   Stories of Mukunda, Brother Kriyananda

Made in United States
Troutdale, OR
11/04/2023